FV

JAPANESE ART, WITH
ON KOREA AND VIETNAM
1.95

THDRAWN

CHINESE AND JAPANESE ART

JEAN BUHOT was born in Paris in 1885. At first he devoted himself to an artistic career, but his early interest in Oriental languages and culture gradually became predominant. In 1924, when he was made Secretary-General of a new organization called The Friends of the Orient, Buhot had already mastered Sanskrit, Chinese, and Japanese. Soon afterward he became associated with the Musée Guimet and in 1931 began intensive study of Japanese history, religion, literature, and art. In 1936, having published numerous critical essays in *La Revue des Arts Asiatiques*, Buhot commenced his long affiliation with L'École du Louvre, where he gave courses in the history of Chinese and Japanese art. In 1940 he was appointed Professor of Japanese, a position he held until his death in 1952.

Chinese and Japanese Art

WITH SECTIONS ON KOREA AND VIETNAM

by Jean Buhot

TRANSLATED FROM THE FRENCH BY REMY INGLIS HALL
EDITED BY CHARLES McCURDY

Maps by Henri Jacquinet and Pierre Simonet
Drawings by Claude Abeille

FREDERICK A. PRAEGER, *Publishers*
New York • Washington

BOOKS THAT MATTER
Published in the United States of America in 1967
by Frederick A. Praeger, Inc., Publishers
111 Fourth Avenue, New York, N.Y. 10003

Translation Copyright © 1967 by
Doubleday & Company, Inc.

Library of Congress Catalog Card Number: 67-10368

CHINESE AND JAPANESE ART was originally published as
"Extrême Orient" in Encyclopédie de la Pléiade
HISTOIRE DE L'ART I: LE MONDE NON-CHRETIEN
by Librairie Gallimard in 1961. This edition is published
by arrangement with Doubleday & Company, Inc.

CONTENTS

PLATES FOLLOW PAGE 322.

CHINESE ART

A history of Chinese art, even today, cannot be approached positively. Of course, the great works of art are represented in many European collections, and more numerously in American ones. However, we find ourselves looking at objects that have survived by chance, objects that only rarely can be given exact dates, and that are not easily distinguishable from recent production. This has come about because in China several factors are intertwined in a manner that is particularly irritating to the archaeologist. China creates works of art indefatigably, but has, so far, been unable to conserve anything but ideas. She has neither preserved her wooden architecture nor protected her rock sanctuaries. She has melted down her bronze statues, permitted her wooden and lacquer objects to become dust. Since ancient times, her innumerable temples have been pillaged, and indeed are still being pillaged today. Scientific excavations have never really been possible. Those undertaken by Chinese experts just prior to the Japanese aggression in 1937 added a great deal to our knowledge, but the objects we know about are, practically without exception, the result of chance finds or clandestine digs, the sites of which have been revealed to the public. Far from resolving the problem posed, these digs constantly unearth fresh enigmas. As for recent periods of Chinese art, it is obvious that private collections possess many fine pictures that have been neither exhibited nor reproduced.

In these pages, our main object will be to characterize the expressions of the Chinese genius during the different periods, point out its astonishingly large production, its variety over the years, and its ability to reappear continually during the course of three thou-

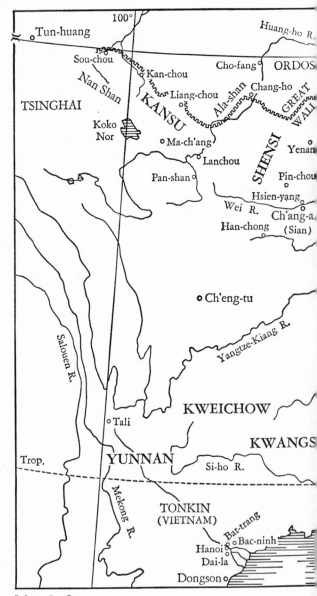

MAP I. CHINA

sand years. We will apply ourselves to pointing out not only the serious gaps in our knowledge, but also those rare occasions when we are positive of our facts. In the same way as China's history underwent alternate phases of contraction and expansion—these phases sometimes lasting as long as several centuries—so did her art achieve peaks and depressions, with cyclical comebacks, as it were, that apparently have no connection with historical events. However, in addition to these rhythmic variations, changes in social structure caused constant shifts in the popularity of one technique over another. Buddhist sculpture was born the moment the tradition of the minor arts appeared to have exhausted itself; painting triumphed when sculpture became moribund; ceramics attained their height when the art of bronze casting ceased to exist. This is why our study of Chinese art will not be a continuous history which, especially without extensive illustration, would risk being dull, confused, and inadequate. We will also omit a great many proper names, since the characters will be sufficient. Taking only the most characteristic phases, we will attempt to discuss them in sufficient detail, so that nothing remains obscure in the periods we are obliged to leave out.

THE ORIGINS

Many Europeans, whether or not they have read the *Edifying and Curious Letters* by eighteenth-century Jesuits, imagine China to be a country that did not evolve for five or six thousand years. Her history cannot be traced before the second millennium, and dates can be verified only after the ninth century B.C. Therefore, less is known about China's earliest period than that of Egypt or of Mesopotamia. Taking a view contrary to that of the first Sinophiles, the experts of the last century sought to look outside China for the origins of Chinese civilizations, of ideographic writing, and of the Chinese race itself. This error has been condemned by the discoveries of such prehistory scholars as Father Licent and Father Teilhard de Chardin, etc. It now appears certain that the Chinese have always inhabited China and that during the ten or so millennia of the Neolithic age, theirs was an agrarian society (at least in northern China) much as it is today. Our archaeological knowledge of other regions is less sophisticated; we know nothing, for example, about the coastal regions whose culture may have extended into the Pacific during an earlier period. Scholarly attention has naturally been primarily centered around sites mentioned in the oldest texts; however, illiterate people were not necessarily primitive.

Therefore, the cradle of Chinese civilization would appear to be the central valley of the Huang-ho (Yellow River), that is to say the region covering one or two hundred miles that extends from the sudden bend toward the east, where the river is joined by the Wei, an important tributary, to the point where it flows in a straight line toward the northeast and the Gulf of Pei-Chih-Li. At the dawn of the prehistoric era, the whole of China was wooded, and considerably hotter and more humid than it is today. Tigers, rhinoceros, crocodiles, and elephants abounded in the valley of the Yang-chou-kiang. The Chinese of the Huang-ho were also acquainted with these animals. It now seems likely that the Siberian forest was separated from China by a less arid zone, much smaller in area than what we call today the Mongolian Desert.

THE THREE DYNASTIES

When the Chinese refer to the Three Dynasties they mean the Hsia (1989?–1523? B.C.), the Shang or Yin (1523?–1028 B.C.), and the Chou (1027–256 B.C.). It is possible that metal was unknown to the Hsia dynasty, since all that remains of this period is pottery, of which we will speak later. The astonishing bronze vases, which for the past sixty years have fascinated Europeans, were formerly rather vaguely attributed to the Chou dynasty. Like the Chinese, one did not dare believe in the existence of objects dating prior to 1000 B.C., or thereabouts. The excavations that were made between 1928–1937 at Anyang have proved that we have at least a few specimens of late Shang art. This art is sumptuous, rich. It inspires our admiration, and yet, because we ignore its antecedents, it remains mysterious in its form. Because we know nothing about the religious beliefs of that period, its spirit remains equally mysterious. The ideas and rites of the Chou dynasty have been explained to us in studies by Henri Maspero and Marcel Granet, but these Shang objects attest to a mentality of which all trace disappeared with the rise of the Chou dynasty. So sudden was this rise that it is even doubtful that the prehistoric religion was still alive when it inspired masterpieces! Anyang (about sixty miles northwest of Kaifeng) was the site of the Shang capital from approximately 1400 B.C. onward, and was abandoned after the decline of the dynasty in 1028 B.C. It is therefore reasonable to attribute the objects found in these excavations to the eleventh or twelfth century B.C., though it is not impossible that some of them might have been earlier.

THE ANYANG EXCAVATIONS

Using European methods, Chinese archaeologists discovered the site of the ancient town and that of the royal workshops, where artisans cut jade and cast bronze. Silks of extraordinarily fine quality already existed, for their imprint can be seen on oxidizations (of bronze). In what had been an archive room they found piles of bones with inscriptions, thin slivers of deer bone, and fragments of tortoise shell that were prepared by gouging out little gourdlike hollows. The king's soothsayer would place a red-hot rod into one of these hollows, causing sparks to fly out. Then he would read the oracle's reply. The question posed to the oracle, and the oracle's reply, were then inscribed on the same fragment. These inscriptions are not in ancient Chinese. The paleographers have almost completed the deciphering of these inscriptions, and have discovered names of princes previously mentioned in the *Bamboo Annals*.

The peasants of the region had noticed that the soil did not have the same quality in some places as in others. They investigated, and dug up antiques whose provenance was rarely known to the collectors. The experts were able to locate the great sepulchers, though nothing remained of them above the ground. They were great square ditches, sometimes sixty-five feet square, approximately forty feet deep, and could be entered, before being sealed, by a ramp on the southern elevation—which in China is always the receiving side—and by steps on the other three sides. At the bottom was a bench upon which had been deposited the funerary objects in bronze or baked clay. The bench surrounded an excavation that formed a funerary chamber, a sort of subterranean tunnel, the dividing walls and ceiling of which were decorated with pictures in austere colors of black, green, and red that the excavators were able to copy before they disintegrated into dust. The dead person was often found sleeping face downward, and on occasion, just above him, was a little cave containing the skeleton of a dog charged with guiding him, like the blind, toward the Yellow Sources, the realm of the dead.

Other ditches around the royal tomb contained skeletons of many decapitated human beings. Their skulls had been buried separately, ten at a time. The tomb also enclosed the remains of different animals: horses harnessed to chariots, even an elephant. After the burial, the ditches had been carefully filled in.

Most of the objects found at the time were identified, though they were inaccurately dated. They were, in fact, earlier. The major discovery of the Anyang excavation was Shang statuary. Statues of white marble, depicting tigers, birds, and buffalo never higher than a little over three feet were discovered in some of the tombs. Not one of these specimens found its way to Europe, and few photographs have been published, but the bronze elephant in the Guimet Museum, Paris (formerly in the Camondo Collection), gives a fairly good idea of what they were like. These statues are not realistic, and yet the characteristics of each animal depicted were powerfully and concisely executed. They also have a particular spatial quality that was to grow increasingly rare in late Chinese art. Ornamental, almost fanciful likenesses of hair and scales adorn the bodies of these animals in a checkered pattern, and rather characterless little seated human figurines are packed between the feet of the pillars supporting the funeral chamber.

H. G. Creel has assembled all the data concerning the Anyang excavations that might be of help in reconstructing the Shang civilization, a civilization that was highly evolved from a material standpoint; that is to say, from what we have been able to decipher so far. As with other antique civilizations, the power was in the hands of the warriors, but in fact these were led by the priests, representing a small intellectual elite. There was no sacerdotal caste. Nor is there any evidence of an ethic; the purity rites and the taboos were sufficient, the mores cruel. Humanity's most powerful deities were ancestors. It was to them that one turned for advice and favors. Through an extrapolation of Chou mysticism, we think we understand the symbolism behind the ritual objects, but their ornamentation belongs, as we have said before, to a much earlier religious spirit.

THE RITUAL VASES

The superb bronze vases (Cernuschi Museum, Guimet Museum, etc.) were used in sacrificial offerings to heaven, to the earth by the sovereign, to the *genius loci* by the vassals (perhaps), to ancestors by the heads of families. They can be classed in various types, the list of which would not be quite the same during the Chou period. Chinese nomenclature is confusing on account of homophonic characters: for example, you have the *yi* in the shape of a tall box with a pyramid-like lid, and the *yi* in the shape of a saucer. Then, there is the word *tsun*. Strictly translated, it means a vase that contains liquids, but it can also refer to a specific type of vase and to fancifully shaped receptacles. We will not attempt to describe the various types, since they are always labeled in museums. The best example of a ritual vase is the *ting* (Fig. 1). It is a small caldron standing on three cylindrical legs and furnished with two rectangular handles. It symbolizes the privilege of the sacrifice and consequently the power of the ancestors. To carry off an enemy's *ting* vases meant the destruction of his house. From the Shang dynasty onward, the vases occasionally bore inscriptions of two or three words, the meaning of which remains ambiguous. "Made (by, for whom?) for so

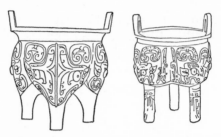

Fig. 1. Li-Ting and Ting. Tripod Vases. Shang Style.

and so"; "(To) such and such an ancestor, son, grandson"; "(For the perpetual use of) the descendants," etc. The bronze vases were kept in the family for several generations. Vases found in one tomb might not all be of the same period. Here we run into a problem; it was not unusual to place the deceased's most precious possessions at his disposal (that is to say, to bury them with him). However, we have difficulty in understanding this, because objects necessary to the living were also entombed. Were not the vases enclosed in the tombs replicas of talisman vases? It is unlikely that the bronzes were molded by the "lost wax" method. Piece molds discovered at Anyang do not confirm this hypothesis; they must have not only served as a mold for the bronze, but also made a new positive in wax, designed in such a way as to allow for slight alterations, or, on the other hand, to remove an inscription. The Cernuschi Museum in Paris has a *tsun* (Fig. 2) in the shape of a crouching monster which is different in only one or two insignificant details from that in the Sumitomo Collection. Indeed, it is hard to believe that they did not come out of the same piece mold. Thus, replicas destined for the comfort of the dead could have been quite easily made.

THE STYLES OF THE SHANG PERIOD
Plate 1

We will forget all typological scruples and state that the vases we now know to belong to the Shang period show a large diversity in style. We tend not to ques-

Fig. 2. Squatting Monster. Zoomorphic Vase. Bronze. Shang Epoch.

tion their being contemporary or whether one came before the other. None of the attempts made so far at placing them in a chronological order seems convincing. In citing the most famous pieces, going from the plain to the ornate (which might well be the wrong chronological order), we will place in the first category the vases that have little ornamentation, or none at all. In the second category we will place those whose ornamentation is for the most part confined to a fragmented frieze and does not alter the general shape of the vase (occasionally combined with this style there is a geometrical pattern which we will not mention again). In the third category are those vases in which the ornamentation is vigorous and covers the whole surface of the vase. The celebrated Swedish philologist Bernhard Karlgren calls group III "style A," group II "style B." Inscriptions are rarely found in style "A," and were less developed in style "B." Max Loehr suggests that style II B borrowed its occasional geometrical ornamentation from the painted pottery that we will discuss later. But even the hypothesis that there might be a connection between the two is subject to very different interpretations. It is hard to believe that the bronze art of the Shang period could have been derived from ceramic art. Other experts have said that style III A could have been the prototype of wooden sculptured vases, but it is obvious that at least a third of the vases were made to stand in hallways.

Certain bronzes that were simple in shape and easy to make might certainly be older than we imagine. In the meantime, as far as we can make out, none of them leads us into the highly evolved designs of the Anyang culture. A primitive art form usually turns to natural shapes, that is to say, simplifies, in order to accentuate the character or to adopt them to a particular material, to a given technique. A decadent art schematizes these shapes, virtually transforms them, through intelligent copying of previous art forms. The achievement of Chinese art lies neither in stylization nor in such schematization. Apart from the geometric motifs that steal into style II B, animals are the only subject matter. However, great liberties were taken, and they were executed with an almost pious precision, implying a perfectly lucid thought which, however, we find hard to penetrate. The motifs behind this style are certainly of a religious nature, and blend with ease into a world where our "logic," our so-called sense of reality, seems to make no sense at all. This is why all our attempts to identify the symbolism of such and such an animal, to "see" such and such a mythical beast, are doomed to failure before we start. However, a sort of sacred terror emanates from these unintelligible and rigorously controlled compositions, and it is striking to us even today. The composition of the focal point in a sculpture of this period is often inspired by this notion of sacred terror. It takes the shape of a masked mythical beast placed in the axial position of the ornamentation, and is often repeated several times. The great eyes of the beast are in higher relief than any other part of the decoration. Fascinated by these two eyes, it is only later that we distinguish something that resembles a nose, then eyelashes, horns, and yet another design in the place of ears. These masks never have lower jaws. They are called *t'ao t'ieh* "the glutton" (Fig. 3), the name

Fig. 3. T'ao T'ieh Mask. Motif of the Shang Style.

given by the Chinese to this mythical figure during the third century, when they no longer understood its import. Certain of the *t'ao t'ieh*'s features are to be found in the Polynesian tiki, giving us reason to think that the beast might symbolize the presence of ancestors, the continuation of the race on a transcendental plane. Occasionally they remind us of a bull's head, or that of a ram or tiger. The totemic explanations that have been suggested cannot be checked. Several centuries after the disappearance of the *t'ao t'ieh*, not only in Chinese art, but also in Indian, and more particularly in Indonesian art, we come across the *kirtimukha* (grotesque mask), which from close up bears a remarkable resemblance to the *t'ao t'ieh*. Their similarities might be accidental, though they are curious nevertheless.

If we were to take a closer look at the face of the *t'ao t'ieh* on a Chinese bronze, we would observe that each section has its own individual significance. For example, the nose is like a shrimp or an insect. Two animals in profile constitute the central pivot of the composition. They might have been birds or elephants. Their eyes would form the eyes of the *t'ao t'ieh* and so on and so forth, throughout each section of the mask. We know that primitive peoples often thought that the organs of the body could function independently, as separate units. The wooden and bone carvings in a recent epoch executed by the natives of the Marquesas Islands attest to a complete belief in this idea. The persistent ambiguity of motif and shape in sculpture are not indigenous to the Shang dynasty alone. At the beginning of our own era we saw in India a "garland" that was the combination of a serpent and a lotus, with the head of a crocodile. Reptiles and lotus, both aquatic symbols, are thus molded into one by the primitive mentality.

This elusive creature is not only to be found in the *t'ao t'ieh*; it is intertwined throughout all Shang decoration. It is rather like those dreams we have when objects we believe we can see quite clearly escape us the moment we attempt to analyze them—what we took for a quadruped could just as well have been a bird or a fish. These animals are constantly on the move, contorting themselves, attacking with beak and claw. As in all periods of Chinese art, animals take on human characteristics; a heavy crest balances a beak; feathers coming down to the feet give the bird a supplementary foothold. This style abhors vacuum. Reptile shapes seem to predominate, and we have got into the habit of calling all these monsters *k'uei* (one-horned dragons). One of the chief characteristics of the authentic Shang style is that these motifs are tightly packed into the latticework of an invisible net. The throwing of this invisible net causes a tension in the work, giving the ensemble a particular cohesion.

There is a hierarchy in the patterns of style III A. The base is carpeted with a tiling of little spirals called *lei-wen* (thunder pattern). They are molded like the others, but executed with such minute detail one would think they were engraved with an etcher's needle. Other patterns rise from the base, like the *k'uei* for example, in slight relief. The horns, nose, and eyes, particularly of the *t'ao t'ieh*, rise in relief from the rest of the face and catch the light. Thus the composition, however complicated it may be, is always perfectly clear-cut and lucid. The vertical crests that divide the belly of the vase into three, four, six, or eight panels contribute to the imposing order, to the solid and proud appearance, of the III A style. The title of generatrix suits them perfectly. Pinched at equal intervals, they look rather like the seams on medieval European leather vases. Their origin is unknown; they were not made to disguise the joints of the piece mold, since the latter can be seen along the side of crests on badly made specimens.

THE ZOOMORPHIC VASES

Along with vases made to contain either solid foods, liquids, or to be used for cooking, for preserves, or to consummate sacrifices, the Shang epoch has left us the zoomorphic vase, the use of which is uncertain, though it appears to be the pure expression of a rather primitive form of mysticism. The Cernuschi Museum monster, the one we have already mentioned, can be called a crouching tiger, if we wish it to be a crouching tiger; however, its tail and backbone are those of an elephant. Reptiles are crawling up its thighs; a fairly realistic little ox is standing on its head; finally, in its mouth it holds a perfectly realistic human being. The

Fig. 4. Elephant. Zoomorphic Vase. Bronze. Shang Epoch.

latter is calmly wrapping his arms around the beast's enormous snout. The monster is not about to devour the man; rather, he is giving birth to him. Carl Hentze proved this by comparing the animal to other figurations borrowed from countries situated at a great distance from China.

The bronze elephant in the Guimet Museum is also a vase; his lid has disappeared. He belongs to style II B, whereas the elephant belonging to the Freer Gallery in Washington belongs to style III A (Fig. 4). More numerous are the urns in the shape of birds; however, it would be futile to determine whether they were blackbirds, owls, or pigeons. Owls placed back to back decorate the common urn, but the rows of rams placed back to back (British Museum, formerly in the George Eumorfopoulos Collection) make a rather strange composition, though it has, nonetheless, a beautiful rhythm. Among the tripod vases there is one type called the *chüeh* (Fig. 5) which, though not at all fig-

Fig. 5. Chia and Chüeh. Tripod Vases. Shang Style.

urative, suggests an "abstracted" bird. The vase has handles as large as those on coffee cups, and rests on three
spread and curved legs fashioned like feathers. It is
probable that this vase was made to resemble a bird,
though for what reason we cannot determine. (The
word *chüeh* means sparrow.) Two little ' ᴸaps rise
from the lip of the vase, the use of whic we do not
know. They also appear on the *chia* (Fig. 5) where
they are larger than on the *chüeh*, though they are the
same shape, except that their edges are not drawn out.
The *li* seems to be composed of three conical-shaped
vases that have been joined together into one at the
top. This tripod-shaped pot, best suited for the fire,
is specifically Chinese, and is also to be found during
the high period of "gray pottery."

The Shang style—haughty, ferocious, and rare—was
not reserved solely for ritual objects. It also produced
arms, riding and carriage equipage, bells, stone statuary, and painted decorations. There also exist a large
number of jade objects whose use we do not know.
They consist of little plaques cut out in the shape of
animals: fish, birds, imaginary reptiles that are lively
and powerfully executed. A few rather sober incisions
complete the design. Also remarkable are the blades of
jade, which are always very thin and, on occasion, extraordinarily long, with bronze handles encrusted with
turquoises. The neolithic art of polisheᵈ stonework
was still being practiced; it copied the already sophisticated bronze patterns to make knives and daggers for
ritual use. However, we know nothing about the transition period.

A development in bronze art toward the end of the
second millennium leads us to believe that the Chinese
had discovered the use of metal quite independently
of European centers, not even through Siberia, as was
thought for quite some time. S. V. Kisseliev's theory,

discussed by René Grousset in the *Revue des Arts,*
1951, No. 2, goes even further. He suggests that the
Anyang civilization taught the art of bronze casting to
Siberian metalworkers, the first examples of which, dating back to the year 1000 B.C., are rather crude. The
article also mentions that the artists were not interested in imitating the "Shang style," but rather the
"Eurasiatic animal style," which is radically different.
What is even more disturbing is the fact that the Anyang excavations revealed "animal" bronzes—ferrules,
spear shafts, knife handles, etc., of very fine quality
(there are numerous references to these objects in
Grousset's article). The turquoise incrustations on
these specimens would seem to point to their being of
Chinese making: indeed, so much so that the "animal
style" originating in China turned out to be a sort of
twin brother—though somewhat disguised—of the
"Shang style." This theory has many pitfalls, and it
would be impossible to make a closer study of the period without further data.

NEOLITHIC AND PREHISTORIC POTTERY
Plate 2

Shang art objects are not the oldest discovered in
northern China. During the past thirty years, excavations have revealed pieces of pottery that go back to
the third millennium. What we call "gray pottery" is of
little artistic interest and would be hardly distinguishable from primitive ceramics of other countries during
the same period if it had not been for the presence of
the *li*.

On the other hand, there is no *li* in "painted pottery," of which the "red period" offers the most variety.
Everything about this style of pottery seems to point
to a foreign heritage. It looks like the neolithic pottery
of the Near East, from the Danube to India. The

Swedish geologist J. G. Andersson recognized the style as soon as he discovered fragments in the village of Yang-shao at Honan. This lucky strike also revealed numerous other neolithic and preneolithic strata that were spread over a large area of Honan, Shansi, Shensi, and Kansu provinces. Andersson discovered fragments on sites of ancient homesteads and, in cemeteries, vases that were intact. The chronological classification of innumerable minor varieties of pottery is a long way from being positively established. The oldest seem to turn up to the west of the Huang-ho loop, at Kansu. This period of pottery (very different from the "gray period," and much more sophisticated) spread into the lower valley. The only date we are certain of is the point where this style came in contact with Anyang art. This style was to survive the fall of the Shang dynasty by four or five centuries, and was to last, therefore, for almost two thousand years (2500–500) without blending with Chinese ceramic art, despite the two often existing side by side. No less extraordinary than this long symbiosis is, at least at the beginning of its evolution, the resemblance between this painted pottery and neolithic Bessarabian ceramic art. A "convergence" of the two is not sufficient explanation, and, if it is a question of one influencing the other, we still have no idea of the route that it might have traveled from the Danube to the Yellow River.

The most beautiful style of this period can be seen in a jar with a spiral design that always runs in the same direction. The potter used two tones of color, apart from the natural variety in baked clay. These colors were a wine red and a warm black. Later on, he superimposed little specks of a mat white. The spirals were serrated at the edges. The commonest type is the urn that is as wide as it is high, consisting of a truncated area below its widest point, almost hemi-

spherical above this area, with a slightly elevated cylindrical neck. There are also two small handles at its
widest point (Fig. 6). The lines are very beautiful, the

Fig. 6. Neolithic Pottery with Spiral Design. Style of
Pan-Chan (Kansu).

material fine, the surface slightly overglazed, and, despite the limited use of color, the effect is sumptuous
(the Far East Collection in Stockholm); representative but inferior examples are found in the Cernuschi
and Guimet Museums.

We know that, for primitive people, red pigments
held magic properties, and were particularly important
for funeral uses. They represented blood, and therefore life. The fringes bordering the red band have been
compared by Andersson to the lips of the cowrie, one
of the rare "beasts" that figure in painted pottery, with
the familiar thousand feet. One also comes across,
though rarely, rather childish drawings of human beings. The cowrie, *Cypraea moneta,* is the shell found
in the Indian Ocean that was used as money throughout the continent. Its ideogram is used to this day as
the key to all Chinese characters to do with riches. Its

shape evoked that of a woman; its white and glowing surface, a human eye. The cowrie was therefore full of multivalent symbolism to do with wealth, fecundity, and life.

During a later stage of painted pottery, the spiral was replaced by circles or oval-shaped loops. Then, following the usual pattern of a decadent art, the curves were replaced by straight lines, the spirals became a Greek key pattern. Very simple, rectilinear patterns, which, on occasion, one thinks might have something to do with ideograms of water, rice fields, or rice itself fill the background in black and white. Zigzags or a single or double line depicting water are the sole decoration found from the middle of the vase downward, for the bottom half was never painted; the urn was obviously made to be placed on the ground.

Tall urns are quite different in design. They were sometimes composed of two powerful diverging curves, like the tusks of a mammoth. (It would appear that this prehistoric animal was known in China.) Two large black dots or two little circles remind us of bronze *t'ao t'ieh*. "The God with the raised arms," as Grousset calls him, seems to have been a very schematic character.

Painted pottery has not yet been discovered in the lower valley of the Huang-ho. However, its final development occurred more toward the northeast, on the gulf, near the Korean frontier. The urns were still globe-shaped, though the curves had become rather vulgar. They were decorated with pictures in white, black, red, and canary yellow, unbaked. The patterns were entirely rectilinear (Greek crosses framed by disconnected concentric squares; horizontal and slanting lines making a sort of checkerboard, etc.). The Japanese archaeologists who discovered this degenerate pottery at Pi-tzu-wo attributed it to the last centuries of the former epoch.

Although the "black" period of pottery turned up in the Shang kingdom, and during a period prior to the Bronze era, it originally came from the east; to be more precise, from Shantung. This pottery is very fine, extraordinarily slender (sometimes less than an eighth of an inch thick), and in design has the rather stiff appearance of copperware.

Finally, the "famille blanche" pottery is a contemporary of the bronzes that we have been talking about. French museums have fragments of this period, and the Freer Gallery has a vase in mint condition. This vase has a rosy hue to it, with an off-white and glowing surface glaze. In comparison with the communal pottery, which was made of gray or brownish clay, the "famille blanche" pottery was a luxury object, a substitute for a bronze vase. It copied a number of the characteristics of style II B, but there is only one in the Guimet Museum. It is a small *hu* (long-necked vase). Its decoration is essentially composed of a zigzag pattern that is smooth, and checkered alternatively with *lei-wen* (squared or rounded spirals) around the neck, interspersed with geometric suggestions of *k'uei* (dragon) grasshoppers that could just as well be *t'ao t'ieh*. More often than not, the zigzag pattern forms *t'ao t'ieh* human limbs, with a head composed of the *t'ao t'ieh*; the torso is in the shape of a triangle, and the hands have three fingers. This is the "god with the raised arms" that figures on the bronze drum in the Sumitomo Collection. It might be either a storm god or possibly a rain god.

THE CHOU PERIOD

The Chou deposed the Shang dynasty in 1027 B.C., and ruled nominally until 256 B.C. over the same empire, which now stretched throughout most of northern China. But during these eight centuries (if we include the brief Ch'in dynasty, from 256 B.C. to 221 B.C.) there were diverse political, religious, and cultural events, and, for the sake of art history, it is a good idea to divide the years into three periods:

1. The first period is usually known as the Yin-Chou, and during this period the Shang graphic formulas survived (their successors called them the Yin after a former capital). This period lasted for approximately two centuries, the tenth and the ninth B.C.

2. The latter part of the Chou era, where nothing was left of the Shang ideology, its tradition exhausted; and art appeared to be desperately searching for a revival in all directions (eighth, seventh, and sixth centuries B.C.).

3. The era of Warring Kingdoms (fifth, fourth, and third centuries B.C.) when the Chou dynasty had lost all political power and its vassals were perpetually at war with each other. This troubled period also marked the era of the philosophers, and gave birth to a coarse, more human, art form, in complete contrast to that of previous centuries.

THE YIN-CHOU PERIOD

We know quite a lot about the Chou religion through books such as the *Li-Chi* and the *Chou-Li*. Despite their late appearance, we attach a considerable amount of importance to them. How was it that China managed to progress from a primitive mentality, whose vestiges we have seen in Shang ornamentation, to this cold and abstract religion? There is an abyss between the two schools of thought. At the dawn of the new dynasty, we find the same ritual vases as those of the Shang or Yin dynasties. However, it was not long before the more extraordinary ones disappeared, among them the *li*, the *chia*, and the *chüeh*. The zoomorphic vases also disappeared, except for the *kuang*, a sort of saucer with a lid. The Yin-Chou epoch left us some specimens of *kuang* that are extravagantly baroque in design. They had reversible lids, surmounted by little cups that could also serve as feet. The bronze caster is no longer a master magician, but rather a simple decorator who does not appear to be guided by religious orders. He covers part of the surface of the vase with vertical or horizontal grooves, or small ugly dots, or nipples. These dots were already *de rigueur* for bells, and were to ·remain so (Fig. 7). Rolf Stein has sug-

Fig. 7. Bell. Style of the Warring States.

gested that they represent stalactites feeding on the nutritious sap of the earth. It is significant that the *k'uei* were no longer powerfully executed, that their line was to become soft and indecisive. This indecisiveness is even reflected in the same vase, where one *k'uei* is handled with relative realism, and the other tends toward a schematization, causing a certain amount of confusion. The *t'ao t'ieh* still has the place of honor in the axial position, and all the designs around him join together to make a banal mask. In several tenth-century vases, the *t'ao t'ieh* is reduced to a single eye enclosed in a rectangular frame, whose corners are decorated with crescents. Karlgren calls this unexpected conglomeration of styles, which had not been present in either style A or style B, or in a combination of the two, style C. For our part, we are struck by the extremes between the tradition of style II B and the tradition of style III A; the first remains faithful to exterior form and to discrete ornamentation, the second evolving toward explosive reliefs that tear through space in all directions. The vertical crests jut out even farther, shaped like hooks and harpoons; the seams of the vase are perforated with small notches in the shape of musical notes. The persistent emphasis on ferocity makes these vases really beautiful; one has the impression that one would hurt oneself if one were to touch them. On the other hand, the bronzes belonging to tradition II B become soft and lifeless. Ludwig Bachhofer has tried to draw up a chronological table of all the Shang and Yin-Chou styles. It is probable that the various styles, perhaps on account of regional differences or workshop traditions, always existed side by side.

THE MID-CHOU ERA

In a study of Chinese art history, one should be wary of chronological tables. The Chou style continued to progress in a rather confused manner toward short cuts, makeshift ornamentation, and shoddy work. Even the quality of the bronze they used seems inferior to that used by the Shang foundries. Instead of burnished patinas of a beautiful apple green or artichoke heart that made the first Shang bronzes look valuable, we have brown or gray-green oxidizations and rough surfaces that make those of the Chou period look like scrap metal. Furthermore, the dull and rather vulgar relief often looks almost commercial.

The completely schematized *k'uei* are now nothing more than concave or convex ribbons—which the artist has almost haphazardly folded this way and that. One has the feeling that the artist was trying to avoid the spot where the *t'ao t'ieh* used to be. One of the uglier solutions to this problem was to cover the entire surface of the vase with vermiculate strips of uniform strapwork (George Eumorfopulos Collection, first half of the sixth century B.C.). The vertical Yin-Chou fluting was abandoned; horizontal fluting became the fashion. Osvald Sirén reminds us of the possibility that the Achaeminians introduced a fairly realistic treatment of the feline-shaped handles.

New types of vases came into being; for example there was the *hu*, shaped like a rectangular plateau with a reversible lid, the globular *tou* standing on a tall stem. However, the most common vase proved to be the round or square-shaped *hu* with a rounded belly gently rising to a tall neck (Fig. 8). The top is sur-

Fig. 8. Hu. Vase in the Chou Style.

mounted by a sort of coronet. An extraordinarily large *hu* about twenty-eight inches tall is in the Guimet Museum (formerly in the Vignier Collection). It is typical of Middle Chou art, for it creates grandeur out of viciousness and brutality.

The ritual jades

It is to the Chou period that we attribute a quantity of jade objects that are of little artistic interest but have, according to the books, considerable symbolic significance. The first is the *pi*, a disk with a cylindrical border, pierced in the center by a hole whose diameter is not larger than a third of the total size of the object. Preferably fashioned out of a cold gray or greenish jade, it represented the sky or the eye of the sky, namely, the sun. There is a very ancient *pi* in the Gieseler Collection at the Guimet Museum which was fashioned into four pieces, proving that the *pi* was always a symbol of some kind, and never a weapon. The *ts'ung*, a symbol of the earth, is a square prism of brown or yellowish jade (for the earth is square and its color is yellow). It is pierced from top to bottom with a cylindrical hole that is extended at either end into a small lip. The idea of the two principles yin and yang (feminine and masculine), whose combinations engender nature, evolved toward the middle of the Chou epoch. However, it is certain that the *ts'ung* and the *pi* had no sexual significance. Around the edges of some *ts'ung*, though not the oldest ones, one can often find divinatory figures formed of three lines. We should also mention the notched disks, upon which are engraved two straight lines at an angle to the central hole. It is possible that they were used for looking at the stars during the various seasons. Trapezoidal rectangular jade plaques, rounded at one end or pointed, large jade rings, notching rings, etc., were marks of imperial pleasure or displeasure (Fig. 9). The ritual significance of jade objects was obviously forgotten when, under the Han dynasty, they were made into worthless objects by decorating the surfaces with the "rice pattern" and "reed pattern" of *lei-wen*, etc.

Reputed to have the property of storing the sun's rays, to be filled with yang, to be everlasting, jade was used to fashion phials, grasshoppers, and other small objects with which one stopped up the orifices of a

Fig. 9. Jade Appliqué in the Form of a Dragon. Style of the Warring States.

corpse. It would appear that a *pi* was often placed over the solar plexus, at least during the Han epoch. Also among the jade funerary objects were short swineherd's sticks and the "sleeve weights" of a former period.

Analogies with American Indian folk art

Before leaving this magic-oriented period, we should say a word about the resemblances between this art and one that is a long way away in both time and space, namely American Indian folk art. However, let us point out that these resemblances do not pertain to the whole of American Indian art—far from it—and that the objects in question were to appear later in Central America, in the wilds of Alaska, and in Peru. In China they were being made from the Shang period until the era of Warring States. Most scholars have not bothered to examine this question because of the difficulty of making sense of the available data. Also, few people have a sound enough knowledge of both civilizations. The obvious comparisons that everyone has been able to comment upon have to do with patterns, style, and expression, in spite of differences in technique. These comparisons become even more fascinating when an extensive inquiry is made into the subject, like that made by the Dutch art historian Carl Hentze. It is generally thought that America was first inhabited by people who arrived by way of the Bering Strait some fifteen thousand years ago. The people who migrated from northern Asia to America might well have left some of their traditions in Siberia; it is also undeniable that the Shang style has more in common with that region than with southern Asia. By examining symbols that are still to be found in present-day art among the Chukchi, Goldi, Giliak, etc., Hentze was able to explain many of the enigmatic details to be found in Shang painted pottery and bronze work. He also found the same symbols among the Indians of the northwest coast of America (British Columbia and Alaska) as well as in pre-Columbian Central America. The highly developed art of the latter goes back to the

equivalent of our Middle Ages. That this was a purely
fortuitous "meeting point" is not a satisfactory answer
to the question. Beyond that, our imagination has difficulty in coping with the idea of a heritage that might
well go back so many thousands of years.

THE ERA OF WARRING STATES

Toward the middle of the last millennium, just before
our own era began, the magic-oriented mentality
gradually ceded to the philosophical spirit. This shift
in temperament is attributed to Lao-tzu, or rather to
the *Tao-teh-king,* for he may have been a mythical
person. This is the era of Confucius and his positivist
ethic. And it is in honor of Confucius that we often
call this important development in Chinese civilization
the "era of the Annals." This intellectual distinction
was immediately reflected in the arts, and was to continue to develop until the Han era (220 B.C.–209 B.C.).
Our knowledge of the art executed between the sixth
and the third centuries B.C. has been available only
since approximately 1920. This period has been named
the "era of the Warring States," in allusion to the
usurpers who fought one another for supremacy—the
Chou dynasty had been reduced to functioning as the
high priests of the empire. In the year 230 B.C., power
fell into the hands of Prince Ch'in of the west country, which was more belligerent than civilized. He pro-
claimed himself emperor, with the title of Shih
Huang-ti, the first Yellow Emperor (Huang-ti had
been the first mythical sovereign), as if he were attempting to write the history of his own dynasty. His
empire stretched over a large part of China. It included Szechwan (which despite its isolation had already assimilated the Yin-Chou culture), and pushed
out toward the south, beyond the great lakes. One
of Shih Huang-ti's generals went as far as Indo-China.

The only countries to remain independent were Yunnan, and Ye (the southeastern region, just off Formosa). The Han historians seem to have exaggerated the Neroesque qualities of the great Emperor Ch'in; art continued with its natural development.

We have mentioned that despite the slow decline of Chou art, there was always someone faithful to its principles. From this art form sprang the new tradition. In the ritual vases free from ornamentation that came from Siun-hien, the artist was concerned with the silhouette and the proportions. The belly of the *ting* is subtly designed, suggesting a complex balance. However, it is so natural, a mathematician could probably give us its equation. Its curve comes to a halt beneath an overlapping lid, and its feet, formerly straight, now curve outward, as do the handles, like an S in profile. These contrary designs suggest something of the style of Louis XV.

The treasure of Hsin-cheng (near Lung-men) was discovered in 1920. It is thought that it was buried in 575 B.C. at the latest. Among the treasures are bronze vases of various styles, some old-fashioned, others in the new style. The *p'an long* (undulating dragon) is in this new style. These so-called reptiles no longer have heads, and one cannot tell male from female. They are both intertwined so closely together that they could be placed in a small rectangle. Their bodies are striped, scaled, and finely granulated. The base of the vase is free of decoration. The innovation lies in the juxtaposition of these identical *p'an long* in areas of "flat relief." It was originally thought that their effect was achieved by making an impression in soft wax with a piece of carved wood, like a butter pat. However, we have slowly discovered that there are minute differences in each of them, proving that they were made individually. The pattern changes slightly

from one area to another. The base of the vase is free
of ornamentation.

The Li-yu style

The new *p'an long* pattern is seen to even better advantage in the treasure of Li-yu. This treasure came
from Shansi Province, near the northern frontier
(1920), but in this excavation they were found with
bronzes that seem to have been made after the Han
period. Also, there were no experts on hand when the
discovery was made. Some of these bronzes can be examined at the Guimet Museum. The round *ting* is an
exceptional piece; its proportions refined (Fig. 10). In

Fig. 10. Round Ting of Li-yu. Bronze. Epoch of the
Warring States.

these baroque Chou bronzes we can already see animals with realistic silhouettes on the exterior of vases

and bells. On the lid of this particular vase (Fig. 10), there are perched three ducks and three humped oxen. The ducks are placed high in order to clear the vase, and make lovelocks in the shape of an S that give the whole vase a light and pleasant air. The crouching oxen remain enveloped in the mass of the base, and seem somehow to form a meeting point between the salient ducks and the uniformity of the flat *p'an long*. The whole vase is modeled with great sensitivity. Even the twisted coil of the ring on the lid is superb.

The artist who designed the oblong four-footed *ting* vase apparently felt that it needed feet that were less curved, indeed, almost straight. There are small buffalo on its lid. The *yi*, a vase in the same series, gives us a perfect example of the strapwork and braiding characteristic of the Li-yu style. Five to seven centuries later, the Chinese were to make excellent pastiches of these vases, but they lacked the exquisite sensitivity of the Li-yu period. (A splendid mirror in this style is at the Metropolitan Museum in New York.) Other characteristics of this new ornamentation are that the bodies of the *p'an long* go alternatively over and under each other (Shang art avoided all superimposition), and each dragon has a small tongue that sweeps sharply backward; it was later to come to a point with a little salient tip.

One might well say that the arts have no patience with tentative efforts; there are masterpieces and there are unfortunate attempts made to improve on them. The sudden perfection of the Li-yu style gives us an opportunity to observe the various stages of its gradual decline. For example, we have the *ting* in the Karlbeck Collection with its low-slung belly. From this we can conclude that *ting* no longer stood in hallways. The old ritual vase has turned into an *objet d'art*, though it might still have a certain amount of symbolic signifi-

cance. The *p'an long* on a four-ringed *ting* vase in the
Metropolitan Museum are almost realistic. Deeply
carved and perhaps at one time encrusted with semiprecious stones, they reflect the art of Li-yu, with inlaid enamel ornamentation very much like that of the
third century. Friezes of lozenges divided horizontally
appear to be derived from the cowrie shell, the prehistoric pattern that the bronze caster sometimes borrowed from painted pottery. However, by inverting the
design, what was the background has now become the
important part of the design—triangles facing each
other on the top and bottom of the vase.

Just prior to the Han epoch, the *hu* took on a geometrical shape in the form of a swollen belly, sometimes with a rectangular area, and a cylindrical neck.
A literal translation of the word *hu* is "gourd." According to a study by Rolf Stein in the *Bulletin de l'École
française d'extrême Orient* (Vol. XLI, 1941, pp. 394–
406) it was during this period that the idea came into
being that the *hu*, square like the earth and round
like the sky, had the property of imprisoning evil spirits. The style of the period dictated that the surface
of the vase be imprinted with small triangles of the
same size and backgrounds of a continuous pattern.

Another manifestation of the Li-yu style can be seen
in the fine bell (fourth century?) in the Stoclet Collection. The handles of this bell consist of two magnificently arched dragons standing side by side. The
artist has rather ingeniously made their bodies square,
not cylindrical, thus harmonizing these lively figures
with the geometrical quality of the bell. The fine
stripes and granulations, the favorite decoration of the
period, have been adapted exquisitely to the patterns
the Chinese borrowed from the northwestern nomads.

Mirrors prior to the Han dynasty
Plate 3

The bronze mirrors constitute a separate art form that evolved over a period of fifteen centuries with the organic continuity and the variety that one usually notices in a progressive society. It is easy to understand why they are popular with collectors. Of course, the reverse side of the mirrors was always decorated, though the mirror side was not even framed. They were polished so often that some of them are slightly convex.

It is possible that the oldest known Chinese mirrors date from the seventh or sixth century B.C. They were sometimes called *chien*, a word that means metallic bowl. Even though the old texts mention *chien* at a much earlier date, one cannot assume that China, from that moment on, had real mirrors (*ching*). The early mirrors were mostly square, and the ornamentation on the reverse side was usually cast separately. The pattern (Middle Chou, with a marked "animal art" influence) is repeated around the center in three, four, or six sections, with a plain band around the whole design. It would appear that the transition to circular mirrors was a rapid one. A small hole was pierced through the back of the mirror, through which a piece of wire was threaded for hanging purposes. Until the Han period, this hole remained very small and jagged around the edges.

During the era of the Annals, the background is carpeted with *lei-wen*, or free-floating lozenges, taken from fabric designs (a pattern that can also be seen on a *ting* vase in the Berlin Museum), or again, tongues that sweep back in an arc. However, these repeated patterns were soon to be superimposed with a few animal motifs in flat relief. These animal motifs

haphazardly wander over floral and geometric backgrounds. Three, four, or five of these homogeneous
though not identical silhouettes seem to be dancing,
devillike, around the central hole. One could almost call
it a scherzo in drawing, one of the most magical creations of the Chinese genius (Fig. 11).

Fig. 11. Mirror. Style of the Warring States.

The small circle in the middle that forms a ring
around the central hole became larger in later epochs,
and took on a starlike shape. The design ripples outward like a stone thrown into water. A concave poly-
gon prevents the ripples from going any farther, thus
causing eight, twelve, or sixteen small, half-moon-
shaped tufts to appear in the design. This pattern is
typical of the common Han mirror. The slight con-
cavity of these smooth ripples causes a play of light. On
occasion they spell out large E's facing away from the
hole in the center, varying from three to seven in
number.

Many mirrors decorated in this manner were discovered thirty years ago by Orvar Karlbeck in the en-

virons of the Huai River. Thus they were immediately
dubbed the Huai mirrors. They date back to either
the fourth or the second century B.C.

A large variety of styles followed the Huai style of
mirror, whose chronology we are still uncertain of,
though Karlbeck did try to classify them. The mirrors
were still just as tenderly executed, discrete, and precious as those made at Li-yu. The animal patterns—
now altered almost beyond recognition and reverting
more and more to foliage patterns—are depicted in
single, double, or triple relief, executed with astonishing delicacy and neatly divided into three, four, or five
sections. One should mention that the ornamentation
of mirrors of this period is typical of the contemporary
decorative style and has no ideological import at all.
After the middle of the Han era, things were to
change. However, only scientific excavation will enable
us to date the beginning of this extraordinary evolution, for pre-Han mirrors have neither inscription nor
date.

Eurasian animal art

We have mentioned barbarian animal art, incorrectly
called "Scythian art" or "the art of the Steppes." The
influence of this art form on Chinese art was of unsurpassed importance during the era of the Warring
States but we are becoming increasingly aware that it
was also influential before this. Kisseliev, in his recent
thesis, even goes so far as to suggest that the source of
this art lay in the Anyang region. Prior to this theory,
the origins of this barbarian animal art were thought
to spring from the Caucasians. For a short time this
art intermingled with Assyrian cultures, and its spirit
dominates that of Luristan. It is possible that it was
brought to southern Russia by the Scythians during
the sixth century B.C., and transmitted to the Sarma-

tians who came after them, during the third century
B.C. Throughout the thousand years of the Chou dynasty, it was certainly always present in oriental Siberia,
and also in the area, now desert, that lies between Siberia and China. The barbarians, somewhat degenerate by this time, then migrated toward Europe, and
reappeared in southern Russia and in Hungary. They
then made their way toward northern Europe, reaching as far as Ireland, where their influence can be seen
in seventh- and eighth-century primitive Christian art.
Finally, they influenced the Scandinavian art, particularly that of the Vikings (ca. 1000 A.D.). Their influence on artistic endeavors in primitive areas of the Eurasian continent extended over a period of twenty-five
centuries. Their monuments, and especially their small
metal objects, have been known for a long time. "Classical" civilizations have always been contemptuous of
the barbarian influence, and it is only during the past
fifty years that we have begun to pay attention to this
phenomenal artistic influence that spread from the
banks of the Yellow River to Saint George's Channel.

The main characteristic of this art form was its sole
use of animal forms, to the total exclusion, save in its
ultimate phase, of the human figure, vegetation, or geometrical patterns. One can almost say the same thing
for Shang art. However, the latter bears no resemblance to "animal art," an art in which the features
are hardly discernible, executed with considerable li-
cense, and sometimes fantastic. The ornamentation of
our own Renaissance, which came to us from Italy via
Iran, has made us familiar with tuber plants and flowers with leafy stems. We are caught unawares, almost
shocked, by the way these artists quite unself-
consciously use animal shapes in designing a chain bit
using two horse legs placed in opposite directions, by
putting a hare in place of a crest on a vulture, or deco-

rating the thigh or shoulder of a griffin with the head
of a bird of prey, etc.

The only animals depicted in Shang art were sacred
animals. On the other hand, the oldest of the small
Caucasian bronzes are highly stylized; they consisted
of oversimplified dogs more "real" than nature itself.
During the latter half of the second millennium, we
have, in Luristan, among the famous small bronzes
shaped like lyres which were used as figureheads on
top of scepters, the hindquarters of two horses serving
as support for two cats being strangled by Gilgamesh.
However, the hero's anthropomorphic features are, as
usual, indistinct. The Kourganes, inhabitants of the
Kuban region, which lies between the Black Sea and
the Sea of Azov, produced the purest of animal-art
objects that are attributed to the sixth century. One
of the most typical examples of this art is the famous
deer of Kostromokaia-Stanitza (Fig. 12). The gallop-

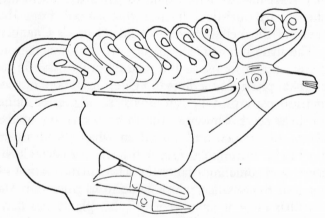

Fig. 12. The Deer of Kostromokaia-Stanitza. Gold.
(Animal Art.)

ing motion is highly realistic, with the legs tucked
under the body, the head looking straight ahead, and

antlers forming a frieze along the whole length of the body. We also have a *gorytus,* a sheath that carried the Scythian's bow. It is decorated with the same deer, repeated several times and embossed in gold leaf. A rampant panther has claws composed of tiny panthers in the same pose as the large one. Objects executed in the same style were found in the Crimea, in the lower valley of the Dnieper, on the site of the ancient ports of the Black Sea. It is easy to recognize the objects made by Greek goldsmiths for their Scythian clientele; the style is too realistic, the chasing too expert to be mistaken for the superimpositions, juxtapositions, and other liberties that pleased the barbarians.

The longevity of this barbarian tradition is astonishing. For example, a ferrule in the shape of a wild ass's head is tentatively attributed to the sixth century B.C. The British Museum has a Roman medal commemorating the victory over the Dacians in 250 B.C., and on the trophies we can see quite clearly, imprinted on a standard, a wild ass's head. A close examination of all discoveries would have to be made in order to be able to sketch a history of "animal art."

The figures fashioned by Greek goldsmiths in minute detail on the celebrated Tchertomlyk vase (Lower Dnieper) are probably Sarmatians. Discovered during the eighteenth century, all that remains to us of this vase are some excellent engravings and other objects that came from Central Russia. These barbarians, with their short tunics, high cheekbones, aquiline noses, small chins, their long, fine hair parted down the middle with a chignon over the forehead, were to be found at Minusinsk on the upper stretches of the Yenisei River. They can also be seen, along with many other ethnic groups, in the stucco heads of Hadda (Afghanistan).

Animal art has been called the "art of the Steppes."

However, it existed in such diverse places as the Caucasians, the Ukraine, the Urals, the Siberian hills and the Mongolian Desert. If we were able to make excavations beneath the sands of the corridor of Central Asia we should probably find traces of this art. It was the art of not only the Scythians, but also the nomadic and hunting tribes. Its monuments were always portable and easy to assemble without permanent installations. Small wooden sculptures and leather cut-outs have been discovered at Pazirik, the western section of Siberia. Thirty-seven miles south of Urga, in Mongolia, appliquéd fabrics belonging to the same period were discovered at a place called Noin Ula.

We lack the space to give further details of the splendor and power of this art work. According to Kisseliev, Minusinsk learned the bronze technique from the Chinese. At a later date, corresponding approximately to the Han era, belt buckles were the special craft of the region. They were made of two symmetrical plaques, horizontal underneath, rounded on top, and projecting into a rectangle on the free edge. Over the whole surface of this distinctive shape were inscribed compositions full of complex movement: eagles attacking chickens, a long-haired tiger devouring a horse. Later, human figures began to appear on the buckle. They were neatly executed against backgrounds of hunting scenes, the first models of which were certainly "Hellenistic." At the same time, concave leaves, shaped like small spoons, crept into the intricate patterns, all of which were ultimately absorbed into Chinese art. Later still (fifth century?), cows were depicted, their outlines schematized, their treatment vulgar, and the leatherwork of rather poor quality, thus heralding the end of this art movement in Asia.

The northern reaches at the mouth of the Yellow River are known as Ordos country, the name given to

a race of people who inhabited the region. The site
was difficult to defend against the nomads, who on
more than one occasion occupied the territory. It is
thought that most of the small barbaric bronzes that
local merchants sold to collectors in Europe came from
this region. They do not belong to the Siberian tradition and are in the pure "animal style" that came into
being during the twelfth century B.C.

The influences of animal art on Chinese art
Plate 4

The Anyang artists were aware of and appreciated nomadic art; however, they do not seem to have modified
the Chinese tradition. One might compare the turquoise encrusting of barbaric objects with the gilt-
bronze settings that Europe admired in the *k'ang-hi*
porcelain vases. Not before the gradual decline of the
Chou dynasty did Chinese art, by that time somewhat
exhausted, adopt some of the eccentricities of this exotic nomadic art; see the contortions and superimpositions of the *k'uei*, the embellishing of empty spaces,
the processions of animals around the exterior of vases,
the dynamic and realistic quality of the feline forms
that served as handles to these vases, their highly articulate execution, and finally the certain taste for
drama that was never really Chinese.

The Chinese harnessed horses but never rode
them. They, like the heroes of Homer, mounted chariots attended by a driver and an archer concealed behind branches. We can see scenes such as this engraved
on a large bronze bowl at the Freer Gallery (about
third century B.C.). The enemy cavalry, therefore, was
more mobile than the charioteer, and later when the
Chinese did form a cavalry of their own, they adopted
the Hun cloak and secured it with a metal clasp. The
Chinese acquired a taste for barbaric jewelry, for many

specimens have been discovered near the same frontier. Indeed, it is often difficult to differentiate between the German object and its Chinese imitation.

Stylistically quite different from the Siberian buckle, the clasp was more or less covered with ornamentation of some kind, and had a button underneath. A hook was attached to the other section. The Chinese clasps generally held to be the oldest might well date from the fourth century B.C. They were relatively small—one to two inches in size. The button was large, and the main part depicted either an animal or the head of an animal. However, if one examines these clasps carefully, one will find that a bird with its wings open, for example, could also be an elephant's head—something never found in nomadic art. The surface of the clasp was embellished with stripes and granulations in the Li-yu style. Then there are the clasps that look as if they were carved from a plaque, which remind us of the animated abstract silhouettes of the Huai style. Later still come more different types of clasp—long ones with grooved, rectangular plaques, and a design depicting an animal mask, others with the outstretched neck of a bird acting as the hook, and the "spoon-handle" clasps that came in three sections three to six inches or more in length. On occasion, they were enameled and encrusted with semiprecious stones. Clasps with decorative designs of musicians, monkeys, etc., realistic animals such as fish and panthers, or imaginary beasts inextricably entwined in intricate patterns, obviously belong to the late Han period (Fig. 13). Clasps of exceptional size (seven to twelve inches) encrusted with pieces of jade were probably used to hook a weapon rather than hold a belt together. After the Han era, these clasps became ornamental rather than functional. Only further scientific excavation and

Fig. 13. Clasp. Han Style.

research could establish the precise dates and chronological order of these clasps.

Of all the foreign influences to which China responded, that of Eurasian animal art was probably the richest and the longest lasting. It made the Chinese aware of the beauty of animate objects, of nature, and at the same time taught them to treat natural forms with a freedom that has always been missing in Mediterranean cultures.

Needless to say, animal art did not cause the Chinese to take an interest in the human figure. The persistent refusal to get involved with the human body is perhaps what most surprises Europeans about Chinese art. And yet, might one not say that Greek anthropocentricity is abnormal, almost distasteful? There are a certain number of statuettes dating from before the Han era, though whether their use was funerary or ritual is not known. They depict people offering sacrifice, guards, etc. They are as realistic as the little man coming out of the Shang monster's mouth. The Chinese have always been perfectly capable of modeling the likeness of a man, but the idea did not particularly interest them. One must recognize that Chinese clothes always presented a problem to the primitive sculptor. By attempting to get the proportions correct, he might fail to make clear the fine quality of the fabric worn by his model. Throughout the history of Chinese art, even after the Han era—the only moment when they forgot their fears and were closest to European influence—this inhibition persisted.

THE HAN EPOCH

As one approaches the Han era, one has the feeling of entering a world we know already, an era that is vaguely reminiscent of, though by no means similar to, Ancient Greece or Rome. However, during Christ's lifetime, China had little to do with the Roman Empire, even though it would not have been difficult for the two countries to know each other and to exchange customs and cultures.

During the last two centuries of the ancient era, from about 209 (or 206) B.C. to 9 A.D., the early or western Han had their capital at Chang-an. (Actually it was Hsi-an in Shansi.) Somewhere between 9 B.C. and 22 A.D. came the reign of the usurper, Wang Mang. For two more centuries, from 22 to 220, the late or eastern Han resided at Loyang in Honan. The young and powerful dynasties always established themselves in the west of ancient China. Weakened and menaced by the barbarians, they moved to the east, to the Huang-ho Basin. In the event of major disaster, they went south of the Yangtze, into the Nanking region. This happened many times during the history of China, and will doubtless happen again.

During the Han era, China became aware of the outside world and of her position on the Asian continent. This was because of an unexpected war between the primitive inhabitants of the region. The Huns had

chased the Yueh-chih, Scythians who had been neigh-
bors of the Chinese, toward the west. In order to defend themselves from the increasing power of the
Huns, the Chinese proposed an alliance with the Yueh-
chih, whom they thought inhabited a region not far
from Central Asia. However, the Yueh-chih had fled as
far as the Indian border. Chang Ch'ien, sent out as
ambassador to sign a concordat, reached Sogdiana,
where he was imprisoned for twelve years. He returned
to Chang-an via Tibet in the year 126 B.C., having lost
his escort. But he was now well informed on Central
and western Asia. Thus it was that China came into
direct contact with Iran, and learned secondhand
about the Roman Empire. She was already selling silks
to Rome and purchasing glass and other merchandise
from her. In the meanwhile, Parthia, situated between
the two countries, and determined to continue playing
the lucrative role of intermediary, prevented all direct
communication.

The Hans annexed the independent kingdom south
of the empire that had been founded by one of Shih
Huang's generals, who had already begun to instill Chinese culture into the Indochinese area. In the northeast, in 108 B.C. the Chinese occupied the Korean
peninsula between the fortieth and thirty-eighth parallels. From the Koreans, the Chinese learned about the
Japanese—who were still savages—and even something
about their mores. China began to make contact with
allogeneous peoples within and without her boundaries, and, like India at the time, began to open up
her frontiers.

The nightmare of the mythical era was over. Ancient
beliefs were thought of as superstitions that still caused
amusement, but no longer instilled fear. The Chinese
finally faced reality and acquired a taste for it. The
whole of Han art exalts effort, movement, physical ex-

ercise, and distant travel. Deer hunters and stalkers
and acrobats were favorite subject matter. The landscape incorporated cautiously into designs, and patterns of foliage, became almost more important than
the animals depicted, as we can see in Figure 14,

Fig. 14. Brick with Stamped Design. Hunting Scene
in a Landscape. Han Style.

where we have schematized mountains with animals
and hunters. Even funerary art promised the deceased
the joys of being a landowner. No single epoch has
been so exclusively concerned, nor done so well, with
depicting the simple pleasures of being alive.

VASES AND SMALL BRONZES

The authentic ritual vases were no longer made. The
vases for daily use, whether they were made of bronze
or baked clay, were identical. Their forms were functional, almost modern, and executed with the style
and elegance of great art. The bronzes were slim to
the point of being almost pliable and were encircled
with rings like those in pots made on a potter's wheel.
Rings replaced fixed handles. The *t'ao t'ieh*, having
lost its former splendor, became just a mask to hold the
rings. The community-made, sandstone vases were often covered with a sad-looking, olive-colored glaze. The

most common shape was that of the traveling flask. The straps by which it was carried were studded with bronze and constituted the main ornamentation.

One would have to include among the most refined objects of this period the inlaid and enameled vases (sometimes with a lacquered base) with quite smooth surfaces. This technique seems to have reached its height during the third and second centuries B.C. (Fig. 15). The abstract decoration is probably older than

Fig. 15. Inlaid Design. Han Style.

the figurative decoration. It consists of thick and thin lines, as if the block had been scraped in one direction, and ends in scratches of fine spirals. Equidistant animals stand among foliage and geometrical patterns. The same drawings are to be found on silks discovered in the Leou-lan sands. Objects of all kinds—*bibelots*, sword handles, axle pins, pyxides, snaps, mirrors, etc. —treated with this technique have a visual and tactile quality that is unsurpassed. These objects also retain something of the rather inhuman pride found in great art. Later, vases were decorated with hunting scenes popular at the time, and also legendary or traditional motifs. André Leroi-Gourhan made the rather curious remark that the subject matter of these decorations is very much like that on proto-Corinthian vases, namely birds and serpents above and below, quadrupeds in the middle. Furthermore, Leroi-Gourhan's idea has given us to some extent a key for the deciphering of Chinese decoration.

FUNERARY ART

Along with this passion for life, the Han epoch suddenly developed a funerary art. It did away with the human sacrifices that accompanied the funerals of the Shih Huang Ti period. Instead, it placed on the tomb, for use in heaven, all of the deceased's favorite objects and amenities that he had most enjoyed in life. His concubines, servants, livestock, horses, dogs, etc., were all represented in the shape of clay figurines (*ming-ch'i*). Clay models represented his manor house, his well, his armor, his kitchen stove, even down to the fish in a pan ready for the oven. These inanimate objects have considerable documentary value, but even more important is that they are aesthetically perfect. The artist was more concerned with movement and *élan* than with portraying a realistic man or beast (Fig. 16). During the T'ang epoch these objects were depicted realistically, and were banal in comparison to the figurines of the Han era.

The funerary chamber was still underground, but if it was the tomb of a prince it was marked by a barrow

above the ground. The barrow is now surrounded by
small buildings; and two lions guard the entrance to
the south side. At the tomb of Ho ch'u-ping, a young
general who defeated the Huns (he died *ca.* 117 B.C.),

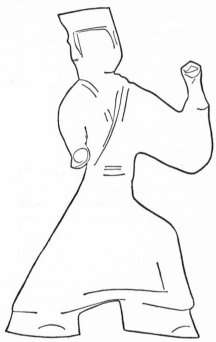

Fig. 16. Dancer. Funerary Terra Cotta. Han Epoch.

there used to stand statues of horses, one of which,
still there, has long been looked upon as the first and
almost sole Chinese pre-Buddhist statue. It is, however, poor work, and inferior to the half-buried objects
surrounding it. Also, it is suspected of being a seventh-
century copy.

We will be discussing the fairly complex Han sepulchers found in Tonkin in northern Indo-China. In Korea they consisted of a single square room entered

through a vestibule and were constructed with either thick planks of wood or bricks. Occasionally the brick tombs were in the shape of a convex cube, with parabolic arches. Scientific excavations conducted by the Japanese in 1922 on the site of the ancient Chinese commandery at Lolang unearthed objects signed by artisans of the imperial workshops dated between *ca.* 102 and 85 B.C. They were mostly bowls and cups lacquered in black and vermilion, with or without rims of gilt bronze. Friezes consisting of straight and curved lines were about the only ornamental innovation of the Han era. At Changsha, on the southern shore of Lake Tungting, lacquered objects have been recently discovered whose coloring varies from brown to salmon pink (Fig. 17).

Fig. 17. Decoration on a Lacquered Object of Changsha (Hunan). Han Epoch.

The more modest sepulchers were tall sarcophaguses made of enormous hollow bricks (about 27 by 19 by 30 inches) decorated on the outside with repetitive ornamental or figurative drawings. The Toronto Museum has a varied collection of these sarcophaguses. The funerary chamber contained quite ordinary pottery.

CARVED STONES

During the late Han dynasty, and particularly in the northeast, small houses were constructed around the tombs. They were "offering houses" with an opening in the façade and rich decorations on the inside (Fig. 18). The Museum of Fine Arts in Boston and a few

Fig. 18. Juggling Scene. A Type of Decoration Found on the Han Offering Houses.

other collections have baked flagstone that came from these buildings; mythical or real people were painted on these stones in color and with tremendous spirit. In Shantung there are several ruins of these small offering houses where the stones are similarly decorated. Some of them are simple in shape, others in "hollow relief"; some have a flat silhouette on rugged background, or silhouettes on smooth, shiny surfaces. The carved stones around the tomb of Chu Wei, a study of which has been conducted by Otto Fischer, demonstrate the maturity of Han painting. The people are depicted with great spifit and considerable foreshortening. One scene of a banquet taking place in a large hall has a perspective that is quite European. The floor, ceiling, and side walls all converge toward the vanishing point, something that was not to be seen in the Far East until the seventeenth century A.D.

Conserved in great number, stones from several small offering houses of the Wou family have been studied by experts, including Édouard Chavannes. The figures form smooth silhouettes with rugged backgrounds, complemented by several incisions. The arrangement in the houses is always the same: on the walls with tympanums to the right and left are depicted mythological subjects; on the far wall, a little higher up, are Confucius' "seventy disciples," all of them alike and static; and below these, the legendary kings: Fu Hsi, the Builder, and his wife Nü Kua; Shên Nung, the first Farmer, with his two-pronged spade. There are also scenes of several excited people: the famous regicides, who are honored here because they performed the will of God by destroying a dynasty unworthy of its mandate, the virtuous wives, and pious sons. Below these scenes we have two charts describing the deceased's career: the official visits he made, the banquets he gave at his *yamen*. All these drawings are decorative and very lively, the silhouettes giving us an accurate idea of the events in his life. Over the centuries the Chinese have made prints from these stones which can be found in shops and are reproduced in books. These prints have been used to make forgeries, some of which have managed to get into our museums and cannot be distinguished from the genuine. Chavannes reproduces only one of them, and another can be seen in the National Museum in Stockholm. The drawing on these blocks has a sharpness and sensitivity that is found only in great works. They are even more remarkable when one realizes that these decorations were really commonplace.

THE HAN MIRRORS

Primitive man quite happily accepted the most common phenomena in physics as supernatural and transcendental. Thus, the *chien* was used to gather dew, the most potent of all magic liqueurs, and also perhaps to light fires. The *chiao*, the real mirror, was thought to be a source of light, a window onto another world, a means of exorcising the devil; in short, an object infinitely precious to the living and even more so to the dead. As we have seen, the mirror had already been in use for several centuries. Under the Han, they were decorated with magical and cosmological symbols which for a long time isolated them from the contemporary art of the time. They were also dotted with inscriptions; during the early Han era, these inscriptions were banal, four-word wishes. Then these wishes became longer and more flowery; they were also dated and signed. The hole in the back of the mirrors was surrounded by a square disk, put there to suggest the earth in the same way as the circle around the hole had previously signified the sky. It is possible that varying numbers of "nailheads" represented the stars; experts have attempted to decipher the Chinese notions of astronomy in these decorations, such as the twelve months and the twenty-eight houses, etc. The quadratic plan was soon enriched by the addition of the four *Ssu Shên*, the genies who ruled over the four corners of the earth. A pair of birds—the Winds?— sometimes realistically executed, but more often appearing each as two schematized feathers, was placed at each angle of the square. On each side of the square stands a mysterious T-shaped figure; opposite, flush to the edge of the mirror, another L-shaped ribbon, and standing flush to the edge and equidistant from each other are people on horseback called V's. The TLV mirrors have been described as a kind of astronomical chart which, in fact, forms a sundial. These mirrors have a marked resemblance to the Indian *yantras* that depict a schematized globe and its four doors.

An area of ornamental foliage, which is either of Iranian influence or the final manifestation of the old reptile pattern, appeared at the very beginning of our own era. It consisted of spoon-shaped leaflets borrowed from Siberian art, a belated introduction of the vegetation motif in Chinese art. The four *Ssu Shên* and the figures surrounding them are modeled with considerable sharpness but, at the same time, almost with a fear, a need to keep them mysterious and indecipherable. The mirrors in which the figures are in flat relief, seeming to imitate contemporary carved stones of the same era (second century), are rare, and, unlike the others, are quite easily decipherable. It should be mentioned that the central hole in the back of these mirrors became much larger after the middle of the Han epoch.

Many factors contribute to the belief that the southern barbarians from Kwangsi and Tonkin, products of the Dong-Son culture, were first-rate magicians. The Chinese borrowed from these barbarians their serrated combs, the teeth of which were either straight or oblique. These teeth also became mandatory on mirrors. Far from becoming schematized, the decoration was increasingly cluttered, overcharged, and confused. According to some experts, toward the end of the Six Dynasties Buddhist figures were combined with traditional myths. Half-moon-shaped bastions and cubes alternated around the exterior of each rim, containing four characters which represented long inscriptions. Toward the beginning of the seventh century, vine leaves were introduced into the pattern, along with sea horses and other motifs that came from the Near East. The central square disappeared. And the tradition of mirror decorations joined the general trend toward profane art.

GENERAL CHARACTERISTICS OF HAN ART

There was no such thing as art for art's sake during the Shang epoch. Under the Chou, however, the idea was beginning to come into its own, because of the establishment of religious laws. One can say that it was during the Li-yu period and the era of Warring States that this change occurred. It is the pervasive air of triumph throughout the Han epoch that makes it feel so close to our own. It is impossible to assign any magical, funerary, or other purpose to the encrusted vases of which we have spoken. The same pertains to the statues of sheep, bulls, bears, dogs, etc., made of bronze, silver, stone, clay, etc. They are full of character, rivaling Indian and Egyptian animal sculpture. There is a power, style, and dynamism embodied in this sculpture that sets the era apart from others in the history of Chinese art. Decorative invention, on the other hand, seems to have come to a halt during the early Han era. After the original and refined style of the inlaid vases, there was no new ornamentation until the T'ang epoch. From that time onward, the artists borrowed from exotic arts, such as that of the Dongsonians, the Huns, and the Parthians. They also made rather austere copies of ancient motifs, which lacked sensitivity.

The old texts mention edifying murals that decorated the palaces. If we admit that the painted bricks and carved stones were the work of minor artists, what heights could great masters of the period have attained? Chinese painting had not yet achieved the same quality as the Greeks had, for example. The picture was painted by an artisan charged with repeating the same composition over and over again.

The greatest pieces of sculpture are best represented by the funerary lions. The lion has a curious history in Chinese art. It was considered a legendary animal, despite the fact that several live lions were sent by distant monarchs as gifts to the Chinese court. There is an almost life-size Chinese lion sculpted in black marble with yellow streaks. This statue, which now belongs to Italy, expressed the suppleness, strength, and ferocity of the animal with far more accuracy than a purely formal resemblance might have achieved. By the second century the lion is almost abstract in composition, like those surrounding the tombs of the Wou family.

SECULAR ART OF THE THREE KINGDOMS (Third Century) AND OF THE SIX DYNASTIES (Fourth, Fifth, Sixth Centuries)

During the third century the empire was divided into three parts, comprising Wei, in the north; Shu, in Szechwan, which had always been a sort of China within China; and Wu, in the southeast and Tonkin. They were known as the Three Kingdoms (220–265). From the fourth century to the end of the sixth century, the division was approximately the same, though in each region a large number of lesser dynasties were founded, many more than six in number, despite the period being known as that of the Six Dynasties. The North fell into the hands of a barbarian tribe known as the T'o-pa (or Toba), fervent Buddhists whose religious art, which we will discuss in a separate chapter, is splendid.

But the secular arts appear to have suffered a decline. The carved stonework took an unfortunate swing toward bas-relief. The *ming-ch'i* are uneven in quality. Quite large statues of horses (ten inches) were now being placed in tombs. Their legs were of wood, their bodies of baked clay, carelessly made, the head being the only section of the body the sculptor had taken care to define. The one in the Osvald Sirén collection is sublime, as good as, or even better than, the best Greek horses (Fig. 19). We can say, once and for all,

Fig. 19. Horse's Head. Terra Cotta of the Han Epoch.

in reproach of China, that this division of work spoiled many works of art for Western taste. The desire to be generous, though not overly so, toward the dead, a desire that was to manifest itself more and more as the years went by, could therefore be one of the reasons for this half-baked and raw, polychromed funerary pottery. Pastel blue, pink, and pale yellow blend with a very delicate gray, and are really quite delightful, but the gilt bronze objects, such as incense burners, boxes, supports, etc., forsook the beautiful Han style, and were turned into a baroque of extreme ugliness. Gilt and jeweled bronzes were popular during the fifth and sixth centuries.

The Szechwan antiques are even less well known. The cultural capital was probably in the Nanking region. The notable monuments in this area are the large animals standing guard over princely sepulchers. There were two types, the "lion" and the "chimera." They stood perpendicular to the center of the avenue and were made to be seen in profile. They are a pure combination of form expressing a sovereign and almighty power. The largest of these statues are still *in situ* in farmyards, or standing next to a peasant cart.

No list of the monuments that have survived the centuries could give us any real idea of the artistic activity during the Six Dynasties. The paintings, no longer in existence, had been developed to such a high level that they had their critics and their theoreticians. Buddhism, quite different from any philosophy or religion that China had known until that time, was already showing the way to new art forms.

BUDDHIST ART IN CENTRAL ASIA

In Central Asia, in the desert corridor that stretches from Pamir to the Gobi Desert, there still exist many monuments belonging to a civilization that lasted until the Arab invasion, namely, until the ninth century in the West and until the eleventh century in the East. The region's climate changed during this historic epoch. Even in the Tarim Basin, which has an intolerable climate today, traces of neolithic sites have been discovered. People were already retreating toward the edge of the basin by the beginning of our era. There were many towns situated at the intersections of the rivers coming down from the mountains and hills that linked China with the rest of Asia and Europe. Mountains of sand now cover the oldest vestiges of these prosperous cities. Objects found on the surface of the ground rarely date before the fifth century. Gaps in our knowledge and the fearful complication of the ethnic, linguistic, and religious elements that make up this hybrid civilization seem, so far, to have discouraged all study of the period. The only data available to us come from copious documentation gathered during scientific expeditions. Among these data, we have the survey made by Sven Hedin in 1896, which is practically a geological one; the German archaeological expeditions conducted by Grünwedel and von Le Coq (1902–1904); the British expedition led by Sir Aurel Stein; the French expeditions led by Paul Pelliot; the Japanese ones led by Count Otani; and many articles based on these documents by such people as J. Hackin, R. Grousset, E. Waldschmidt, and E. Matsumoto.

The Iranian merchant entering China had the choice, after traveling around Pamir in the north, between two roads that bordered on the desert. The northern one went through Kutcha, Kizil, and Turfan; and the southern one, which might have been accessible by climbing the steep valley that rises from the Indus—as Hackin did on the Citroën expedition—went through Khotan, Yotkan, Miran, and Lop Nor Lake. After a distance of approximately 497 miles, both roads met at Tunhuang Oasis, which lies almost 625 miles from the nearest Chinese city.

A large number of archaeological sites have been recognized around the towns and cities we have just mentioned, most of them lying to the west and on the same meridian as the northern hills. The religious communities were prosperous, as has often been mentioned, and were on the commercial routes. The merchants would ensure themselves against mishap on the road by being generous to the monks. That the region, whose prosperity depended on transients and was therefore unstable, had no ethnic unity or tradition, gave its culture a flavor of its own. From one stage of civilization to another, from one century to another,

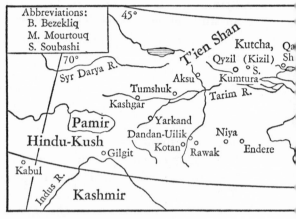

MAP II. THE SILK ROUTE

its change of inspiration and style is very marked. We must abandon the usual method of establishing continuity in style, and instead divide the monuments into regional groups. The first will be Kizil and the area east of Kutcha; the second will be Turfan, the center of the north route; and the third will be Miran, situated at the beginning of the southern route; while the fourth will be Tunhuang, where we come in contact with Chinese art.

THE KIZIL GROUP

Plate 5

Kutcha is actually the capital of the region, but the archaeological sites are Kizil, Qumtura, Aqsu, Kirish, Sorcuq, Tumsuq, Subasi, etc. Albert von Le Coq mentions funerary barrows left by the Sarmatians, and traces of Sarmatian animal art can occasionally be found in the small stucco heads from Tumsuq. The majority of incoming people were obviously Iranian. The domination of the Chinese during the Han period

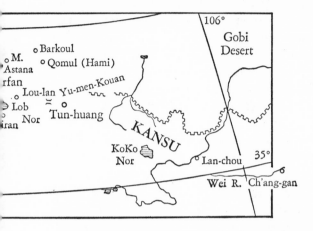

soon became nominal. Indian influence was strong in the Buddhist monasteries. One might say that, on the whole, sculpture was more Indian, painting more Iranian. The latter is most interesting.

Fifth-century compositions were still more or less static, their grouping juxtaposed rather than composed, and the colors flat. This style is Iranian. To begin with, the medieval appearance of lay clothes is astonishing. The king and queen look like those depicted on our playing cards. The king wears a sort of chasuble that falls down the back and front in large rectangular folds, while the queen wears a tight-fitting jacket, taken in at the sides, and a wide skirt. Over her veil, she wears a sort of beret. The Buddhist priest accompanying her wears a small pair of boots. The fragment of a painting entitled "The Painter," which is often reproduced, could almost come out of a Gothic tapestry.

The "War of the Relics" is an excellent panel with fine mural qualities, the balance of black masses playing with tones of brown, ivory, and apple green. A gray-blue covers the dark interior of the archway in the Kucinagara ramparts. All the people in the picture wear halos, like those in archaic Persian miniatures. Their proportions are determined by the needs of the composition, not by any law of perspective.

It is obvious that the inhabitants of the country (the Tocharians, according to German archaeologists) enjoyed a good story, for their paintings are, above all, narrative. They illustrate a number of Buddhist legends not mentioned elsewhere. The paintings were often placed in a frame of lacy, almost triangular leaves; the colors were of contrasting stripes of ultramarine and bright red, or of brown and Veronese green, the two color schemes overlapping each other, like artichoke leaves. The grottoes that contain these murals were more often than not triangular in shape with barrel vaulting. At one end of the grotto there was usually a stupa, which one could walk around.

In the later murals (seventh century), painted with great freedom of movement, one can see the prototype of superimposed painting that does not depend upon natural lighting. This superimposing was not unknown in India. The salient areas of the face are systematically planned as the light areas, with gray tones forming the shadowed areas such as the cheeks and the side of the nose. A Bodhisattva looks like a rather gauche imitation of the "Handsome Bodhisattva" from Ajanta, small copies of which were probably circulated. Certain large panels are surmounted by trompe l'oeil architectural drawings, also to be seen at Ajanta. We are still a long way from China! The monks depicted are Persians with bluish beards. They wear patchwork cloaks, following the rule of their order. One of the curious features of this art is the frequent presence of shaved heads, obligatory accessory of Christian asceticism and symbol of impermanence to the European. The Chinese, so in love with life, had no need for these somewhat repugnant pictures to remind them of life's transient nature. They also were fond of depicting Sakyamuni before his enlightenment, hideously emaciated from his extreme austerities and reduced to a skeleton. This is a subject that the Far East has never really accepted.

Most of the other sculpture consists of fragile figurines with unfinished glazes. Pelliot brought back fragments which had been baked hard in a monastery fire. Among them are several small stucco heads that are similar to the Hadda heads though less distinguished and less serious in intent. The Buddhas, like those from Hadda, are Greco-Buddhist of the most conventional, the most unreal, and the dullest variety. However, the faces of the Bodhisattvas, the angels, and the other companions seem to have been taken from life— from young country girls. The grotesque heads have a Mediterranean luminosity. The wooden sculptures have survived well in the extreme dryness; one of the little seated Buddhas (about ten inches high) is simple, human, and full of warmth.

THE TURFAN REGION
Plate 6

Kao-ch'ang (the Chinese name of Turfan and the ancient capital of this country) is equally rich in archaeological sites, such as Idiqutsahri, Sangim, Murtuq, Bazaklik, etc. The heights of this culture were attained during the three centuries of the T'ang epoch (seventh through ninth centuries). To begin with, it was similar in style to that of the Kizil. The arrival of the Uigur Turks from the north, and their settling in the region, brought a sort of dry purity to the art, which seems to be characteristic of Turkish art in every country. Besides, the population belonged to very different races. Among the "praying" and the "charity givers" are found redheaded and blond men with blue eyes, who were probably real Tocharians; also Persians with long black beards, thick eyelashes, and long well-shaped noses. The Uigur can be recognized by their oval-shaped, hairless faces and remarkably fine features. Were they of a higher mental caliber than the Kucheans? Their narrative painting is doctrinal and hierarchical; great standing Buddhas, full of majesty and with elliptical halos around their heads, are surrounded by small praying men. The color harmonies are splendid and unexpected: reddish browns and oranges next to gray-mauve blues. However, these *pranidhis* are monotonous. Buddha's face is often quite conventional and expressionless. The proportions are good. The execution is neat and incisive, almost to the point of being harsh and rather cold. Apart from the murals, many banners have been discovered in the region of Turfan, along with paintings on paper and leaves of manuscripts, most of which have nothing to do with the Buddhist religion. There are Nestorian paintings, whose style probably goes back to Iranian prototypes that we know nothing about. Some Manichaean miniatures have survived. Their style is emphatic in colors of green, black, and vermilion. The faithful of Manes wear surplices of a pure white that plays with the whiteness of the paper upon which they are painted. Pleasing foliage decorates the margins. These illuminated manuscripts are very much like those of Carolingian Europe. Purely Chinese fragments have been discovered that certainly do not come from the provinces; for example, "People under the Trees," brought back by the Otani mission. It should be pointed out that the mixture of styles in Central Asia is quantitative, not qualitative. They existed side by side quite independently, and did not influence each other.

In Turfan art, nature is represented by backgrounds of identical, schematized mountains, and well-drawn animals such as deer and ducks. In front of a statue of Buddha, or his stupa, the floor was painted; German writers assure us that these paintings were genuine frescoes in the Italian style, in which the pigments blend and solidify from the reaction of lime with sand. As far as we know, there are no other examples of mural art in Asia that use various types of glue paint.

Ruins of various stupas are still standing in some places. Often, all that remains of them is the square foundation consisting of one or two floors and decorated with false doors. These edifices must have been quite dull in appearance, and yet the Chinese patterned their elegant and lively pagodas on these buildings.

THE SOUTHERN ROUTE

This route went through Khotan, Yotkan, Dandan-Oiluq, Rawak, Niya, Maralbashi, Endere, and Miran, etc. Once again the characteristics of the art of this region vary a great deal. It had more in common with Mediterranean art than with Iranian. Paul Pelliot used to say: "I do not believe in the Pretender Titus." This Titus is mentioned in a fragment that describes how he was paid thirty thousand *bhammaka* for his paintings. And yet everything here has an atmosphere of Greco-Roman boredom. At Niya, Aurel Stein discovered a perfect cameo depicting Athena Promakhos. At Miran, "Buddhist angels" with bird's wings stare at us with their large black eyes from a background of

Pompeian red; they are merely poorly drawn cupids. Even Alexandrian features are to be found among the majority of the other figures. Only the Buddha has a halo. At Dandan-Oiluq, a four-armed Bodhisattva has a Persian head. Local Buddhists honored unknown deities from elsewhere. One is seated on a piebald horse, the other on a camel. A rather badly drawn, sinuous lotus garland, like those that encircle the architraves of fences around Indian stupas, winds its way through a mural. People with great dark eyes and only half their bodies visible, thread their way over and under the garland alternately. The Visvantara-Jataka, Buddha's final afterlife, during which he practices unending charity, is naïvely portrayed. When the Prince wanted to be alone, trees appeared behind his elephant, though the landscape is not brought up to the presence of this animal. This phobia of the inanimate is very Greco-Roman.

The works of art we have just mentioned are gauche and simple. However, we cannot say the same of a famous fragment reproduced by René Grousset in his *History of the Far East,* in which one can see a small, naked woman, decidedly Indian—judging by her shape and appearance—drawn with considerable grace and confidence. Next to her, and larger in scale, are two monks of extraordinary beauty, meditating. It is unlikely that the two were done by the same artist, particularly the second, which is the work of a master. A piece of tapestry discovered at Leou-lan depicts a head whose features, coloration, and shape are very much like the Ravenna mosaics.

TUNHUANG

Tunhuang Oasis (approximately 40 degrees north latitude and 95 degrees east longitude) was occupied by the Chinese from about 147 B.C. onward, and was lost only when their political history reached its lowest ebb. The Tibetans made several sorties during the T'ang epoch. Later it was threatened by the Si-Hia, who inhabited the northeastern section of the high plateau. The oasis was an important strategic and commercial center between China and Turkestan, and between Tibet and Mongolia. Nowadays, the modern routes bypass the city, and the Buddhist sanctuaries are constantly being rebuilt.

There are some five hundred grottoes, more than two hundred of which date from the fifth to the eleventh centuries. The interiors of the older grottoes were decorated with a number of murals. In the later grottoes, which contained more sculptures than paintings, and not very interesting sculpture at that, a trompe l'oeil was sometimes combined with a polychromed relief. In 1035, the monks, fearing an attack from the Si-Hia, hid rolls of paintings, banners, and manuscripts. When Aurel Stein was passing through Tunhuang in 1906, a monk, desirous of restoring the sanctuaries, sold him some of the rolls of paintings. A few months later, Paul Pelliot managed to gain the confidence of the monk, who showed the young scholar the whereabouts of the hiding place, and sold him several thousand rolls of paintings—about a third of what remained of the collection. Others were sold at Peking and dispersed among museums and private collections. Aurel Stein carried off the rest in 1914 (five large casefuls). These antiquities were shared among the British Museum and the Delhi Museum. Pelliot's manuscripts went to the Bibliothèque Nationale. The paintings, which at the time were considered more valuable, went to the Louvre. Those that seemed to be only of religious or historical interest went to the Guimet Collection. In 1945 all the paintings were placed under one roof at the Guimet Museum. Our increased knowledge no longer gives preference to the large monochrome pictures of Bodhisattva that the Louvre had decided were the great flowering of Chinese art.

The press has never written a great deal about this discovery at Tunhuang. And yet it was one of the great archaeological finds. It gave us hieratic paintings, banners, votive and pious pictures, all sorts of letters and documents, sketches, studies, paper cutouts, xylographs and even the wood blocks of woodcuts, all in an excellent state of preservation. The recognizable blocks are dated 868, 947, and 980. The invention of wood blocks was not a recent one but Japan has preserved some *dharani* that were engraved during the eighth century. The manuscripts, multilingual and in different handwritings, revealed a language with two dialects known as Tocharian, belonging to a branch of the Indo-European family whose existence we had no idea of at all.

Nothing at Tunhuang, unfortunately, seems to date prior to the oldest Buddhist monument standing in China itself. It would be interesting to know something about the Buddhist art that had served as its model. Nothing can be found, for example, of fourth- or fifth-century art. On the other hand, most of the Buddhist art found at Tunhuang is purely Chinese Buddhist art and is already highly sophisticated.

Buddhism in China had become a religion that the Indian Buddhists of the first century, for example, would have had great difficulty in recognizing. Some of its tenets even went so far as to contradict completely the primitive doctrine. Through contact with the Persian religions, Chinese Buddhists believed in a Buddha of "Infinite Light," Amitabha, or of "Eternal Life," Amitayus, enthroned in a paradise situated to the west. In this paradise the faithful were delighted to serve Buddha in perpetuity, each seated in the Divine Presence upon a lotus which had germinated the moment his heart opened to the faith. The pools painted on the floor at Turfan are prefigurations of the lotus pool at Sukhavati.

The Chinese need for symmetry that so enlarged the pantheon of Far Eastern Buddhism and was perhaps also the cause for the survival of the ancient concept of qualitative space (the four *chen,* etc.) had attributed a paradise to each of the four large Buddhas surrounding the Supreme Buddha, the Bestower of Light. The attribution of the four paradises varied with the different sects, but the Western one always remained Amitabha's. The monk Ch'an-tao (seventh century) is supposed to have done some three hundred paintings of these lesser Buddhas. The fundamental concept seems to have sprung from the Heavenly City, Jerusalem, but all the interpretations we have are purely Chinese, as the architecture proves. Behind the Buddha, surrounded by a divine court, extend the terraces, galleries, and pavilions of a fantastic palace which continues indefinitely in space. On each side of the palace stands a tree covered with a net sparkling with jewels. In the foreground is the rectangular pond filled with lotuses upon which the blessed sit. Below this grand composition there is usually a predella consisting of small tableaux relating to the legend of Amitabha; to the left and to the right are other anecdotal tableaux, one below the other. By a clever trick of perspective, the vanishing point is such that all the subjects incorporated in the whole seem to make one— a sort of birds-eye view seen from a considerable distance. The convention was used to describe the life of Buddha on banners.

Other large panels depict the Buddha seated between two Bodhisattvas. There is no decoration in these pictures save for a dais with pendants that acts as counterbalance for the upper part of the composition. This formula comes from the T'ang bas-reliefs, and also from the Horyuji murals.

Of more interest to us are the walls of the sanctuary, which are liberally covered with religious pictures (Grotto 70 for example). Kucinagara is depicted as a Chinese stronghold, isolated in a mountainous countryside that people liked to explore. Beneath the high ramparts of the city two armies face each other, each consisting of no fewer than four men and a corporal. The two armies are in perfect alignment. It is almost as if the Chinese artist thought a melee would be inconvenient, might even cause confusion during the course of such an event as a war of religious relics. The naïveté does not detract from the great beauty of the composition. The variety of murals at Tunhuang is as great as that of easel painting—no small feat.

The *Sutra of Cause and Effect* appears to have been popular during the T'ang epoch. Illustrations of the sutra are depicted above the texts describing the life of Sakyamuni. The Grand Departure is painted with considerable vitality. The future Buddha is penetrating deeper into the forest on horseback. He looks rather like a learned Chinese gentleman only too delighted to be out communing with nature. There is the same familiarity in the Four Meetings, depicted as scenes that might be seen daily in the street.

All the Mahayana deities are fully developed hieratic pictures. The large Bodhisattva, Avalokiteshvara, is more masculine in some pictures, as he usually was in Indian Buddhism; in others, he is more feminine, as was more often depicted in both Chinese and Japanese Buddhism from the Middle Ages onward. Certain of the pictures are painted in a style similar in color and technique to the Tibetan miniatures of recent years, and their artists were probably pupils of the Indian religious painters rather than the Chinese. The arabesque is usually symmetrical, the colors warm and sumptuous, like a particularly fine stained-glass window.

The somewhat harsh precision and coloring so typical of Turfan art can be seen in another group of hieratic paintings in the Guimet Museum. The compassionate Bodhisattva, Ksitigarbha (Ti-tsang), is depicted in the midst of ten judges from Hell, who look like Chinese magistrates. At the bottom of the picture is a full-length portrait of the donor who is being led by the Bodhisattva (Yin-lo), the guide of souls to the after world (Fig. 20). This painting is a fine example of the naïve and calmly confident era of faith. The

Fig. 20. Donor. Detail of a Tunhuang Banner. Tenth Century.

artist was probably a monk, a native of eastern Turkestan, brought up by Chinese priests.

A fragment of one of these paintings can be seen at the Guimet. It depicts the head of an old monk (the great disciple Kashyapa) and bears the oldest inscribed date of 729. The monk is seen in both profile and full face, as if the two views had been superimposed, with the right eye of the head in profile becoming the left eye of the full portrait. This was not done by mistake. It is believed that the head was an intentional and successful tour de force with which the Ciceronian monk could amuse the pilgrims before passing the collection plate.

In the Aurel Stein Collection there is a painting of a "planet god," a deity forgotten by modern Buddhism, descending from his celestial carriage. It is a fine example, a picturesque composition, full of movement. The execution is sophisticated, free, and full of variety. The famous pilgrim Hsüan Tsang, who returned to China in 644 after a long stay in India, is shown with a staff in his hand, wearing a large hat and carrying a heavy load of sutras on his back. This portrait displays the rather brutal vivacity of modern Chinese imagery.

The Tunhuang hoard included authentic Chinese prototypes of statues and paintings that were later to turn up in Japan. However, there is no question that the history of Buddhism and its art could be considerably clarified if, by some luck, a major site were discovered in southern China.

THE BEGINNINGS OF CHINESE BUDDHIST ART AND THE WEI AND SUI EPOCHS (Fourth to Sixth Centuries)

The arrival of two mysterious strangers at Chang-an during the fifty-sixth year of the Christian era marks the traditional appearance of Buddhism in China. Henri Maspéro has suggested that the "Good Law" must have started during the early Han era. Whether or not this is strictly accurate, it is recognized that the progress of Buddhism was slow in the beginning. The activities of the missionaries and translators during the third century are well documented. However, there is no trace of a high art dating prior to 338. Grousset quite justifiably points out that the barbarians, who did not share the Confucianist ideals of the older generations of Chinese, were the first to be won over by the idea of predication, and contributed considerably to its success in China. Hence the reason for nearly all early Buddhist art being confined to the north. This early art had a strong inclination toward Indo-Hellenistic styles that were prominent in Central Asia. In the meantime, intellectual activity was probably stronger in the south, where many foreign priests arrived by boat.

Once again, it is the barbarians, during the fourth century, who intervene in history, with more important implications than were previously suspected. From 316 on they occupied the north; by 335 their subjects, even the Chinese, were free to embrace monastic life. Buddhists had no secular clergy, and the monasteries were indispensable for the survival of the church. Indeed, it was at this time that Chinese Buddhism came into its own, with small bronze statuettes that were hardly works of art, yet were portable and easily dismantled—exactly the sort of object that was convenient for the believer in a pagan country. These bronzes were rather awkward copies of statues the missionaries and travelers brought with them from the "western regions." The Indian monastic gown, until that time unknown in the Far East, was poorly executed, almost a caricature; the Chinese gave it a sym-

metry not to be seen in the original Indian work, for
asymmetry was alien to them. One of the small bronzes
is dated 338, only three years after the first official or-
dinations of Chinese monks (Fig. 21).

Fig. 21. Bronze Buddha (338).

Grousset mentions the names of several strangers
who disseminated translations of Buddhist texts
throughout China. There was nothing systematic
about the spreading of the "word." Converts acquired
a scattered knowledge of texts belonging to various
sects and persuasions that were not, incidentally, isolated from each other, nor inclined to bicker over
dogma. However, it was through trips made by
Chinese pilgrims to India that more immediate repercussions were felt in the art world. The most famous
artist of the period, though by no means the only one,

was the monk Fa-Hsien (379), who left Tunhuang by the northern trail, crossed Gandhara, spent six years in Magadha, and returned via Ceylon and Java, where he stayed at least five months, finally landing at a port in the Shantung area in 414. The story of his travels, a copy of which we have today, encouraged other student pilgrims, and it was thus that good statues of Marutha, whose characteristic drapery was copied faithfully, but with a certain naïveté, in 444 (Stoclet Collection) and with elegance in 486 (Metropolitan Museum).

Charming votive steles also began to appear at about this time. They were shaped like pointed leaves, thought to be the bo leaf from the tree of enlightenment. Inscribed on these steles are Buddhas, sometimes flanked by Bodhisattvas and sometimes not. An inscription is engraved on the pedestal. The other side of the stele is often decorated with *Jatakas,* or scenes in the life of Buddha, executed in the same style as the "sculptured stones." During the second half of the fifth century the Chinese quietly accepted Indian leadership in design and style, using, for example, the cobra (Naga), a mythical god and symbol of water. It is particularly remarkable that the Chinese departed from the Greco-Buddhist style which Central Asia had long regarded as the only valid way of depicting the Master's face. Instead, they gave him a face that is lively and pleasing.

YÜN-KANG
Plate 7

The Tabghatch, a race of Turkic Tartars whom the Chinese called the T'o-pa, and who originally came from eastern Mongolia, took over from the Huns and occupied the extreme northern tip of China. During the fifth century, they spread out as far as the Han

River, halfway between Huang-ho and the Yangtze, and forged an empire that extended from Tunhuang to the Korean frontier, a distance of 1,553 miles. The Tabghatch appear to have played a significant role in the history of Chinese art, and also to have channeled some of the characteristics of Central Asian art to Korea and Japan. Like all barbarians who occupied areas of China, they rapidly Sinicized themselves, and founded a dynasty under the name of Wei. In 453, their Emperor Siun was converted to Buddhism, and the best of the Yün-kang statues date from his reign.

The Yün-kang grottoes are situated nine miles or so to the west of the Wei capital of P'ing-ch'êng (or Tatung). Nearly all the sculpture from these grottoes belongs to the second half of the fifth century and to the sixth. Many of them have been disfigured with whitewash. However, during the last war, the Japanese cleaned some of them, and photographs taken at the time once again reveal their extraordinary beauty. The original must have been crowded with figures, for the entire surface of the walls was usually covered with paintings. In fact, Buddhism recommended that its proselytes gain spiritual advancement by painting as many Buddhas as they could, thus increasing the number of images of the Master; and hence we have the "Thousand Buddhas" which can be found all over Central Asia, China, and Japan. It was not required that each figure be different. (One should mention that this avoided the danger of overloading the composition. These rows of identical Buddhas, each standing in his own niche, are, above all, soothing.) The donors commissioned larger bas-reliefs, and had themselves depicted in corners or on pedestals. At Gandhara, the niches were either rectilinear, in broken spandrels, or were contained in trefoiled arches, the latter consisting of a nave with cradle vaults, flanked by side aisles with half cradle vaults. However, the last-mentioned design was incomprehensible to the Chinese, who never copied it. On the other hand, the broken-spandrel type of niche was copied highly successfully. They were even improved by the addition of gathered curtains, often made from Central Asian tents, which softened the austere quality of the motif. There was also another type of niche in the shape of a broken arch, which was built when a natural location was found for the grotto. Whatever the shape or the structure of the niche, the front was usually decorated with Buddhist angels that look as if they had just come down from the sky. An incense burner hung from the middle of the plinth. These burners look as if they were copied from Indian or Mesopotamian vases. They are to be found all over Central Asia, though the Chinese did not understand them.

Were it possible to recognize the dominant influence of one particular sect, then it would be the Dharma-lakshana (Fa-hsiang). This sect was dedicated to a special cult of Maitreya, Buddha's future life. Most of the Buddhas at Yün-kang are Maitreyas. They are often seated, European style, with their legs crossed, like the Christ of Vezelay (Fig. 22). This Buddha commemorates the Grand Departure, when Prince Siddhartha, seated on the conjugal bed, is preparing to leave his sleeping wife—the Bodhisattva pose par excellence. These are not legendary characters but Maitreyas, with the chin lightly supported by the hand. This is the posture of the compassionate Buddha, and of the Maitreya Bodhisattvas. Their faces, full of tenderness and devoid of carnal grossness, are on the same high plane as the masterpieces of Christian art. They bring something quite new to Chinese art, and even the art of Central Asia. One is immediately struck

Fig. 22. Two Bodhisattvas Seated in European Fashion, in the Styles of Yün-kang and Lung-men.

by the similarities between this art and that of Rome,
for the root of both these art forms is their ability to
assimilate other styles, and their clear expression of
faith, despite the very different ideologies behind both
of them. However, this comparison is only superficial;
our Roman sculptors were the greater craftsmen. We
get a far greater feeling of volume and movement in a
Roman bas-relief than we do in any embossed Chinese
statue.

About 480 to 485, in the sixth grotto and in other
sanctuaries as well, small bas-reliefs (easily deciphered
in those excellent Japanese photographs) were conse-
crated to the life of Sakyamuni. However, all the scenes
depicted were adapted to the Chinese way of life. For
example, in "The Women's Sleep," the unfortunate
women are seated bolt upright, looking very proper,
strapped into their long dresses. They lack the freedom
Indian sculptors gave to women figures.

It would seem quite possible that Indian sculptor
monks (though very few talented ones) worked at

Yün-kang. Nothing specific can be attributed to them, save perhaps some of the details in Grotto 8. In the *Temptation*, Mara's army and the Buddha seem to have been painted by two different artists. On either side of the door stand Siva and Vishnu, each with several arms and heads. Less importance was attached to Indian iconography than to the sculpting, which is generous, free, a little unorganized and very different from the symmetrical, formal, and more graphic work of the Chinese. Whether the relief is high or low in Chinese sculpture, we are, above all, moved by the quality of its drawing, which cannot be looked at just from the front. It is hardly surprising that the two colossal Buddhas at Yün-kang are mediocre. The local stone is a brownish-yellow color, coarse-grained and easy to polish.

It would be interesting to make an iconographical and stylistic analysis of the best statues but this would take up too much space. It is difficult to establish which prototype inspired certain details in the Bodhisattva's vestments—for example, the short cloak with the ends crossed above the stomach, wider at the hips and shorter in the back. Buddha's drapes also show considerable originality; all the folds were calculated to draw our eyes toward his kindly face, lit up by the "archaic smile." The body counted for little in Yün-kang art. It would be impossible to find a purer expression of such extraordinary spirituality, except possibly in Christian art.

THE SMALL BRONZES AND STELES
Plate 8

We have a very good example of this new Buddhist style of sculpture—which attained its maturity during the early years of the sixth century—in the form of a gilt bronze in the Guimet Museum dated back to the

year 518. It depicts the dialogue between Sakyamuni
and Prabhutaratna, a scene described in the *Lotus of
Good Faith*. One of the Buddhas appeared from the
sky and invited Sakyamuni to take a seat next to him.
Long pointed pinions extend the length of the cloaks;
their rising folds ascend like flames; their beveled surface gives the material a shimmering effect (Fig. 23).

Fig. 23. Bodhisattva. Bronze Gilt. Sixth Century.

The pattern of flames on the halos remind one of the
indecipherable pre-Han *k'uei*.

There are other masterpieces among the steles. They
fall into two categories: the votive steles in the shape
of leaves, which we have already mentioned, and the
commemorative steles, which date back to the Han era.
Sometimes they consist of very tall tablets (ten feet or
more, and in three sections) standing on a tortoise and
crowned by intertwined dragons seated back-to-back.
Their heads and feet stand to the left and to the right

of the top of the stele. The obverse and reverse sides are divided into sections. On one side, the principle motif is a Buddha in all his majesty surrounded by several pairs of divinities. The other sections are in diminishing relief, depicting pious scenes, processions of donors, and inscriptions. The other side is decorated in the same way. The Wei sculptors achieved a remarkable standard of workmanship, especially when one considers the limited possibilities of the stele. We can see on the small, commemorative stele in the Cernuschi Museum, dated 560, three niches of more or less the same size. They are not monotonous, and the manner by which this variety was achieved is subtly disguised.

By using a handsome and somewhat translucent marble for making the votive steles, the sculptors created magnificent works of art full of fervor and luminosity. One cannot help feeling that the new religion inspired the creative spirit and incited the sculptor to yearn for perfection.

Several concurrent styles soon came into being. In a stele dated 547 (in a Japanese collection), we can observe an example of the new way of draping material: the outer layers are draped in an omega shape, with alternate question marks and lozenges. The experts were mistaken at one time in thinking that these folds were characteristic of the Sui epoch, an epoch born thirty-four years later (581).

LUNG-MEN
Plate 9

In 494, the Wei transferred their capital on the southern bank of the Huang-ho to Loyang, the ancient seat of the Oriental Han. In 517, Queen Hou-Che visited the rock sanctuaries that had been moved some ten years before not far from this town to Lung-men (not to be confused with the famous tributary of the same name). Work went on at Lung-men for another twenty years. Then, after a century of slackened activity, the work was taken up again, and continued intensively from 638 to 705. Thus, some of the Lung-men sculpture was executed during the Wei period and the rest during the first third of the T'ang era. Though this enormous collection was almost intact forty years ago, there cannot be much of it left today. Everything was broken up and sold to the antiquarians. The local stone was immediately recognized, for it is a sort of gray-black marble that was easier to work than that of Yün-kang. Some of the grottoes that had been transplanted in 483 and 491 were touched up during the T'ang era, the most interesting of these being the famous Pin-yang-tong (*ca.* 510). In contrast to the happy disorder of Yün-kang art, with its haphazard additions, there was quite obviously a master plan at Lung-men. The side and rear walls of each grotto are occupied by large triads, each fashioned into a statue. The details of the vestments are more refined and precise: eyebrows are raised and eyes are wide open, the archaic smile all but gone. The style is evolving toward a quasi-realism that is, first of all, not really imitative of nature, and secondly, not Chinese. Rather, it is Indian, a style we are getting to know more and more about.

The Pin-yang-tong used to contain a first-rate bas-relief. To the left of the plaque stood the emperor and his courtiers; to the right the empress and her ladies in waiting. It is a superb composition, and the Cernuschi Museum has copies of it. The highly skilled execution of the vestments, hair styles, fly switches, etc., remind us of the best of the French fifteenth-century tapestries. Alas, all the heads from this bas-relief—they were as large as a hand—were sold in Europe before the Second World War.

THE SUI ERA AND THE T'IEN-LUNG-SHAN GROTTOES

During the sixth century, the minor dynasties divided the old Wei empire among themselves. At the same time, South China was uniting under the Nanking Liang. The empire was unified in 581 by the Sui dynasty, which had two sovereigns. The second, Yang-ti, was an ostentatious person. He pursued the expansionist policies that had been forgotten since the Han era, but failed to reconquer Korea. Japan sent him her first ambassador in 607. Yang-ti was unpopular, later assassinated, and his kingdom passed into the hands of the T'ang dynasty in 618.

The rock sanctuaries at T'ien-lung-shan are characteristic of the grottoes of the second half of the sixth century. They were situated in the middle of Shansi, approximately halfway between Yün-kang and Lung-men. The local stone is not particularly attractive; it has a sandy texture and is the color of dust, rather like baked clay. The sculpture had an enveloping and graceful style with unusual incised folded drapery. At T'ien-lung-shan, as at Lung-men, some of the seventeen sculptured grottoes belong to the T'ang epoch. The best are those with a slight relief, closer to drawing than to sculpture. The ceilings decorated with flying angels, the side walls with the two disciples, Lacyapa and Ananda, and a few donors in profile, are all full of life and character. The statues are still frontal. However, in the third grotto the Bodhisattvas are placed at an angle to Buddha, and even have a slightly asymmetrical, leaning posture. In the seventh grotto (580) they are at right angles to Buddha. Balance, always so perfect in Indian sculpture, is never as good in the Chinese. These divinities would topple over if they were not leaning against the wall.

There are several other rock sanctuaries, particularly in the Shantung area. Here the results were even more disastrous than in most regions, because there had been too many sculptors working on the same statue. Thus, we find a handsome head surmounting an ineptly sculptured body. Sui sculpture is seen at its best in the stele, or in the isolated statue found in various temples. Like those of the Wei period, they give the impression of thrusting toward the heavens, some soaring, others restrained. Their silhouettes are either ovoid or cylindrical, the shoulders wide. The heads are of two types: rectangular and oval. The facial expression is sometimes ecstatic. The form, knowledgeably simplified, is highly involved. The only ornamentation is the lively arabesque drawn around either the hem of the garment or the folds of the sleeve. Yet the work as a whole is very uneven: the purity of the seated, white marble Buddha in the Guimet Museum cannot manage to hide its awkward craftsmanship. The Bodhisattvas wear chains of jewelry in a Y shape that come down to the middle of the torso and part again at the thighs to return back up and over the shoulders. This necklace has an agreeable way of accentuating the standing figures (Fig. 24).

The religious fervor emanating from Wei and Sui Buddhist sculpture makes us almost forget that Buddhism was far from being accepted throughout China. However, its position was so strong that Taoism felt the need to create its own art form—incidentally in a rather superficial manner. Sirén cites a Taoist stele dated 587 that a layman might mistake for an uninteresting Buddhist ex-voto. During the T'ang epoch, Buddhist art was more abundant than ever, but its religious quality rapidly disappeared. The next chapter is devoted to the art of this dynasty.

THE T'ANG EPOCH

T'ang art, following the cyclical pattern that occurred frequently in China's history, can be likened to that of the Han era. In the same way that Shih Huang Ti

Fig. 24. Bodhisattva in Stone. Sui Era.

quickly extended and unified an empire which the Han inherited and kept for four centuries, the short-lived Sui dynasty left the T'ang a country that for three hundred years was powerful and whose prestige extended over a wide area. Like the Han, who had dispensed with the last vestiges of primitive mentality, we suddenly find ourselves in the seventh and eighth centuries face to face with an art that has strong affinities with the realism of our modern times.

The historical situation that interests us today is the lack of resistance on the part of the little kingdoms of Central Asia, and even Pamir, under the second T'ang emperor, T'ai Tsung. At this time, China was in close contact with Persia. China's armies penetrated into Tibet, and the king of Tibet married a Chinese princess; one of his other wives was Nepalese. It would seem that this double marriage symbolizes the influence of two cultures in Tibet: Indian philosophy and art, Chinese material progress. Korea was conquered by Kao Tsung because Shigari, one of the three Korean kingdoms, was concerned about the unification of the other two, and had called upon him for assistance. The Chinese occupation did not last long. However, during Korea's nominal allegiance, the peninsula became Sinicized. Japan regularly sent ambassadors to the court of Chang-an. Young Japanese nobles took advantage of this exchange and made their studies in China.

The great Emperor T'ai Tsung, once an intransigent Confucianist who then turned to Buddhism and Taoism, developed into a highly enlightened man. He welcomed the Nestorian Christians in 635, and gave royal patronage to the Buddhists after the pilgrim Hsüan Tsang returned from India in 645. China's influence, her art, and even her form of Buddhism, which was highly individual and subtle, spread to other countries. Her religious thinking and artistic imagination was enriched by her contacts with the Near East and even India. The Near East was even further away than the province of Bactria, since in order to get there one had to bypass Pamir. Among the Chinese who visited India during the T'ang epoch, we will mention only Yi-Tsing, and the diplomat Wang Hiuan-tso, who made two trips. In 662, only thirty

years after the death of Mohammed, the Arabs drove
out the last prince of Persia, Sassanid Peroz, from his
country. For a long time, Peroz hoped that his suze-
rain, Kao Tsung, would help him regain his lands. In
674 he went into exile at the court at Chang-an, and
brought with him the luxury arts of his country, which
were very much admired.

The end of Kao Tsung's reign was marked by rever-
sals. The first was the revolt of the Tibetans, who
occupied the whole of Chinese Turkestan; the second
was the Korean revolt, with the termination of this
country's allegiance to China. The widow of the
Korean sovereign, Wu Hou, a cruel and extraordinary
woman, ruled for twenty years. Everyone, including
the neighboring states, hated her. In the meantime,
the golden reign of Hsüan Tsung ran from 713 to 751.
The emperor founded the Han-lin Academy, which
united the poets, whose verse is still treasured today,
and the painters, whose talents we can, alas, know only
indirectly. In 751, the Arabs defeated General Wu
Pan's army in western China, but did not present any
further threat by their penetration into Central Asia.
Once again, China found herself isolated from the
Near East. The T'ang dynasty gradually declined over
the period of a century and a half, until its fall in 907.

BUDDHIST SCULPTURE
Plates 10 and 11

Han Yü's violent entertaining and critical attack on
Buddhist superstition began in 819. First Manichae-
ism, then Mazdaism were outlawed. In 845, the Buddhists were violently persecuted, resulting in the destruction of many works of art. All that survived, apart
from the steles and a few small temple bronzes were
the new sanctuary statues of Lung-men and T'ien-
lung-shan. Fragments of these statues occupy positions

in collections that far exceed their artistic merit or their interest. Indeed, religious art had fallen into a weak period. Until now, Chinese creativity, despite the peace and prosperity which had turned the elite toward hedonism, had benefited from secondhand knowledge of Indian art. When they had access to the originals, the effect was to the contrary. The essentially sculptural Hindu genius and the essentially draftsman genius of the Chinese were incompatible. The plastic quality of Indian statues became heavy and lifeless in the hands of the Chinese, who were never able to balance a divinity in *tribangha*.

In the meantime, the seventh century has left us a few fairly handsome statues, but we do not find them particularly moving. The ecstatic pose of the Sui epoch suddenly takes on an unsubstantial and awful majesty. The divinities at T'ien, however, are more supple, with a sensual gracefulness. The colossal Lung-men Buddha (approximately 680 A.D., thirty-three feet high, the pedestal and halo adding another fifty feet or so) has a pleasing appearance. But the many figures surrounding him, the Bodhisattva, disciples, Dvarapala and lions, are mediocre. The facial expression of Buddha, and even more, that of the Bodhisattva, became coarser and coarser, sensual and forbidding. The Buddha Gupta was often imitated by exaggerating the eyebrows in a V shape.

The body is nevertheless the same in mass, but no longer well defined. The drapery does not correspond to the facial expression, being realistic in some places and having a somewhat banal symmetry in others. Even the pedestals are conventional. They are covered by Buddha's cloak, which falls in stereotyped folds around them. In short, one has a distinct feeling that Buddhism is now the state religion.

In bas-reliefs, triads are depicted in the same way

as in certain Tunhuang paintings, under a dais of pendants. Trees lend the composition an artificial variety. The small bronzes are now somewhat lax in shape, their gilt being almost their sole attraction. This too-facile design, one of the characteristics of all T'ang art, is, however, very lively in the details, but the over-all plan is never thought out and has little decorative power.

FUNERARY ART

The sculptured groups that encircled the princely tombs underwent considerable refinement. It is said that T'ai Tsung commissioned the great painter, Yen Li-pen, to draw his six favorite horses, and wanted them placed in front of his tumulus. Every emperor began making plans for his tomb the moment he came to the throne. The T'ang sepulchers were destroyed by the rebels during the early part of the tenth century and restored by the first Sung emperor. It is not certain, for example, if the six bas-reliefs just mentioned are the originals, dating 650, or if they are copies that date between 965 and 970. They are indubitably first-rate, but are carved in less depth than the usual T'ang sculpture, and are not unlike the work of the Sung era. Four of them are now at the Si-gnan Museum. The other two were sold to America by C. T. Loo.

During the reign of Kao Tsung, judging from the colossal Lung-men Buddha, official commissions went to both good and bad artists. His sepulcher's statuary is more interesting for its quantity than its quality: next to the pylon archways stand two winged horses sculptured in the round, then two phoenix in bas-relief, ten horses in the round, statues of twenty civil and

military dignitaries, and finally, in front of the tumulus, two colossal seated lions fifteen feet high. The
funerary lions are not seated, and have the canine appearance of Buddhist lions. Our scholars call them
"Fo's dogs" (Buddha's dogs), and the Japanese call
them *Koma-inu* (Korean dogs). Probably introduced
from the south, the Buddhist lions had lost all their
feline characteristics, though the Han prototypes prevented them from becoming the horrible monsters
they became in Khmer art.

It is astonishing that the triumphant Buddhism did
not abolish the use of the *ming-ch'i*, an object that
came into being on account of a primitive materialist
idea of the hereafter. The deceased was no longer surrounded by his belongings and houses. He was furnished with a larger staff than ever before, consisting of
concubines, dancing girls, lady musicians, servants,
bodyguards, grooms, etc., besides many horses and
camels. Although these figures did not have the grace
and polish of the Han period—they are often polychromed or partially covered with a glaze like communal pottery—they were somewhat more realistic. If
we were able to date them accurately, they would give
us a very good idea of the change in women's fashions.
During the sixth century, women were slim and wore
tight-fitting dresses with epaulets. During the T'ang
era, the waists were high, the skirts long and narrow.
The shoes were still large, and turned up at the ends.
The hair was divided into two tall buns worn pinned
to one side only (Fig. 25). On the other hand, during
the eighth century, a fashionable woman had to be a
little plump, her clothes loose, and her hair like a large
cushion worn at the back of the head.

The horses were not the small native breed like
those of Emperor T'ai Tsung. They were larger and,

we believe, came from Ferghana, west of Pamir. Their rumps were always lower than their heads. This period was fond of drama, and the horses were depicted rearing and prancing. The Sui camels had a thick coat which produced unexpected and comic shapes; under the T'ang, the coats were smooth. We have many ex-

Fig. 25. Court Lady. Funerary Terra Cotta. Seventh Century.

amples of an imaginary animal with the head, mane, and body of a pony, and the legs and tail of a pig. Like imaginary animals of all periods of high art, they are impressive on account of their intensity and sprightliness. Let us also mention the polo players, apparently young boys dressed as girls. The T'ang *ming-ch'i* are often compared to Tanagra figurines, though they are not as fresh or universal, and, one must admit, reflect the somewhat dissolute taste of the rich and powerful.

T'ANG CERAMICS

We know the ceramics of the period through funerary and communal pottery. However, these two styles are not representative of T'ang ceramics as a whole. The "three colors"—rusty yellow, green, and a sort of Prussian blue—were painted over stoneware that had been coated with a cream-colored slip. The potters did not know how to prevent these colors from running when they fired their work. The decorators of these vases were often content with speckling them with little dashes of color; rarely do we find pieces where care has been taken to juxtapose the colors without their bleeding into each other. The exceptions are those where the bleeding was stopped by making small crests or incisions. Beautiful specimens have been discovered in Persia. A great deal of ingenuity was required to make something beautiful with such difficult colors. One can see the Persian influence in a variety of objects—bowls, ewers, amphorae—and ornaments—medallions, palmettes, etc. However, elegant contours were not the strong point of T'ang art. We have known for some years now that a porcelaneous ceramics already existed, possibly dating from the Han era, and in appearance like Sung celadon, or a variety of white porcelain, specimens of which, however, are very rare.

THE MIRRORS
Plate 12

During the early part of the seventh century, the ornamentation of mirrors was overcharged and confusing. However, they were already exotic, with vine-leaf patterns in the midst of which were galloping horses, Pegasus, and Hellenistic griffins. The two intertwined dragons are Chinese, as is the tortoise that served as a background around the central hole. On account of a fortunate Iranian influence, everything began to be simplified. For example, we still have the two symmetrical hunters galloping after deer, although they are drawn differently. The background between the two main masses consists of two clumps of simple flowers. The theme of the two dragons was developed during the eighth century; but birds and flowers were more fashionable, delicately and realistically modeled. The birds were often decorated with ribbons, like Sassanian Persian bird designs. The mirrors were sometimes decorated with almost realistic mountains rising from waves, though cosmological symbolism was gradually being abandoned. The mirror was thus becoming a familiar object, feminine and graceful. Instead of always being circular, it was sometimes multifoil. Later, the decoration on mirrors became literary, telling stories, such as "The Cinnamon Tree and the Moon" and "Pong-lai-chan" ("The Island of the Happy Ones"), and showing symbols of longevity. Inscriptions and dates are rarely found.

The essence of a culture is not fully expressed in objects made of durable material such as stone, ceramic, or bronze, materials that the archaeologist usually has to contend with. We are fortunate enough to have the opportunity of knowing something about the most fragile objects of the T'ang epoch, thanks to Shosoin, imperial household comptroller at Nara in Japan, who preserved many luxury objects sent to Emperor Shornu during the middle years of the eighth century. If we did not have the Shosoin collection, we would have never known that apart from the bronze mirrors, the Chinese also made smooth-backed mirrors, inlaid with mother of pearl, malachite, and amber, which were lacquered black or transparent on backgrounds of green or red. The inlay work is not really figurative, and Harada has made an ingenious comparison between this circular pattern and the one found in the "Cups of Chosroès" in the Cabinet Medailles in Paris. In short, this work is similar to that done by Sassanid Persian artists. In certain cases, the medallions were almost leaf-shaped, or like fruit or flowers. Well-drawn little animals were engraved on the mother of pearl; for example, ducks, lions, and rhinoceroses. These last mentioned animals must have been foreign to the Persian artist.

MARQUETRY, STRINGED INSTRUMENTS, LACQUERS, AND FABRICS

The Shosoin also contains a large number of musical instruments in a perfect state of preservation. Among them are several *p'i p'a* (four-stringed lutes); several *kin*; straight, horizontal harps; and one angular harp— an instrument the Chinese soon abandoned. Their decor, like that of the bronze mirrors, allows us to make a survey of the birth of this new style. It consisted of a series of two, three, or five, precisely the same design. Smaller masses are placed between larger ones, etc. The background is also alive, and plays an important role in the composition. Particularly beautiful are the round guitars, inlaid with two parrots in green and purple mother of pearl, holding a chain of jewels in their beaks. A floral design laid out in almond-shaped oreoles with triangular corner designs and free areas between each pattern, exactly like the designs of those exquisite late Persian bindings, is on a ninth-century lacquer box at the Ninnaji in Kyoto. In a Shosoin *kin*, we can see three people partaking of light refreshments in a Persian garden planted with potted trees of different species, the design of which is executed in precious metals inlaid on black lacquer. The scenes are very much like those depicted in fifteenth-century Timurido miniatures, and it is surprising to find a Chinese poem on the other side of the instrument.

No less disconcerting are the plaques protecting the soundboards of lutes. A mother-of-pearl lute player astride a camel can be seen on a five-stringed *p'ia* (Fig. 26); on either side of the camel are trees that look

Fig. 26. Camel Driver. Detail of the *p'i p'a* of Shosoin. Eighth Century.

like banana trees. On two other lutes are depicted vast mountainous landscapes that are typically Chinese, and of a highly developed style for the period. One of them shows a tiger hunt with numerous people in different perspectives, and the other, an elephant carrying three musicians and a dancer.

The extraordinary refinement of these objects is less surprising than the complexity of influence and collaboration. The subject matter, techniques, and materials used come from many far-distant countries. Only the objects themselves are decidedly Chinese. It was thought that stringed instruments and marquetry were the speciality of the Khotan artisans; and it is possible that several Khotan artisans were employed by the imperial workshops at Chang-an. The workshops must also have employed artisans of many nationalities. There exist, for example, several Chinese ten-inch rulers made of dyed ivory, whose ornamentation is Indian rather than Chinese.

At this period, even Iranian art drew inspiration from heterogeneous traditions; we suspect from Central Asia. At Shosoin there is a Chinese checkerboard with two games, which the Japanese call the *go* and the *sugoroku*, respectively. The first is inlaid with ivory silhouettes of camels, birds, hunting scenes, and griffins, etc., juxtaposed, though not strung together. The effect is somewhat Hellenistic. One would not be surprised to hear that they came from Pompeii, which would tie in with the objects we have seen at Miran or Khotan. The *sugoroku* checkers game, however, is decorated with leaf motifs, and little friezes of flowers that look as if they might have been traced from a frame of a sixteenth-century Persian miniature.

The date of the first manufacturing of glass in China is always a subject for argument. The flawless Shosoin pieces must have been imported from the Near East by Hsüan Tsung, who offered them as a gift to Shomu Tenno. Among them are an ewer of brownish blown glass, bowls of white and blue glass decorated with rings, and round cupola-shaped pieces that are exactly like the fragments discovered in Persia.

A study is being made at this moment of 66,800 pieces of Shosoin material. Leaves of folding screens are decorated in batik and other work that is now lost to the Chinese. The famous screen "Six Beauties under the Trees," which is surely Chinese, despite bearing a Japanese date corresponding to 752, was colored with small feathers, except for the flesh which was painted, the background being empty. Out of forty-six felt carpets, thirty-one are decorated with a technique of which we are still uncertain. Once again we have different traditions intermingling in varying proportions: one of these carpets is decorated with medallions laid

out in sets of five, the Hellenistic *putti* of which have
nothing Chinese about them; another has a lotus with
slender stalks that are hardly Persian. On the other
hand, silks with lions, horsemen, etc., standing facing
each other or back-to-back inside medallions are pure
Iranian. The Horyuji treasure contains other samples
of these silks and carpets.

This monastery possesses a subtly shaped bronze
ewer inlaid with gold and silver that is of Sassinid influence. Some experts believe it to be of Chinese make,
because the lid is topped by a dragon. However, we cannot agree with this theory. Indeed, the Shosoin possesses a similar ewer lacquered on a wickerwork base
and decorated with inlaid bushes and flowers made of
precious metals. This style of decoration still copies the
Iranian "landscapes," though the finish is dull, almost
vulgar, and betrays its T'ang origins. Although it is difficult to establish the circumstances of the fabrication
of all luxury Chinese objects with any certainty, it is
obvious that the Shosoin is an inexhaustible fund of
documentary information on all eighth-century Asian
art, and one that is all too often ignored by experts on
Iran and Central Asia.

Also included in this treasure are a few graphic works
of art, some of which are Japanese and others Chinese.
Among the latter, one could mention a series of ten
lacquered wood plaques (sixteen inches square). They
show animals, birds, and even human figures, amidst
trees and wild flowers. These drawings are far from being primitive, and are of the highest quality, drawn in
a dark ocher on a yellowish background. There is nothing exotic or archaic about them; indeed one would not
be surprised if they were attributed to a contemporary
of Ingres or Corot. In his *History of Art* (p. 513),
Pierre du Colombier says: "When Phidias was sculpting the sublime marbles for the Parthenon, China was

making her bronze vases, which Europeans will have difficulty in recognizing as having much human value." We might well ask him where, in eighth-century Europe, he would be able to show us drawings of such maturity and such perfection.

BUDDHIST ARCHITECTURE
Plate 13

Architecture is almost transcendental, depending more upon individual fantasy and fortuitous circumstances than the other arts. Thus, architecture is linked with ethnography and the natural sciences. It is particularly interesting to notice what happens when a universal religion with an architectural style of its own intervenes in a local tradition as solidly entrenched as the Chinese. It has often been said that the great religions, when new, use buildings they find on the spot. The Chinese monasteries, quite different from the Indian *sangharamas,* were groups of separate residential or ceremonial pavilions. The indispensable stupas, which had become multistoried towers, were the prototypes of the belvederes or watchtowers widely built during the Han epoch. However, all Chinese wooden architecture was destined to disappear, and we would have known nothing about early wooden Buddhist architecture if we did not have buildings of the T'ang epoch conserved in Japan and the stone pagodas that remain standing in China.

We will use the word "pagoda" when we talk of the Sino-Japanese stupa. Its Chinese name is *t'a,* formerly *t'ap,* a transcription from the Prakrit *thupa* and a translation of a synonym, *caita* (pile). It is astonishing that the spheric tumulus of the Indian stupa could develop into a square multistoried tower. It is probable that many of the most venerable stupas were protected by a wooden construction when the Chinese visited them, and that they copied the frame for the interior. Furthermore, Perceval Yetts has reminded us that when the monk Houei-Chang returned to the Wei at the beginning of the sixth century, he brought with him a bronze copy of the famous colossal stupa erected by Kanishka at Peshawar. Made of wood, it stood thirteen stories high and measured 197 feet, without counting a 75-foot metal mast, with five 164-foot terraces that formed the sub-basement.

The transformation of the stupa into a sort of tower was already accomplished in India by the second century, and it was this type of pagoda that was depicted in the Yün-kang sculptures.

The oldest standing pagoda in China is at Sung-shan near Kaifeng. Dated 523, it was built during the Indian period we have just mentioned in reference to sculpture. It is quite astonishing that the Chinese architect was able to erect a building with such taste and originality, considering that the forms, taken individually, are authentically Indian while the whole building is not. Built on a dodecagonal plan, the pagoda stands fifteen stories high, including the basement, the first story being the only negotiable one. The other fourteen stories are cornices which give the appearance of being packed with *sikhara* (spires), anticipating the parabolic silhouettes that were to develop in northern India during the Middle Ages. Lettering placed around the main floor supplies the finishing touches to the building—a single storied square stupa with a railed balcony surmounting its dome. Surmounting the attractive hexagonal pillars are lotus-shaped capitals. (The capital was an architectural feature unknown to the Chinese.)

In the area of Sian (the former Chang-an), several T'ang brick pagodas are still standing that have nothing Indian about them. The structure follows the ancient Chinese tradition of using ramparts of beaten earth. The decoration of the casings reverts to an imitation of Chinese brickwork: drain tiles or abaci above pillars, and the omnipresent false lintel. The Ta-yen-t'a pagoda built for Hsüan Tsang in 652 and altered in 701 is rather severe, though not ugly. The ground-floor walls are thirty feet thick, for they had to support the widening upper walls and floors. The building is rather naïve, but quite rational. There is no reason for comparing it, as has often been done, with the tiered buildings found in Ceylon, Egypt, and Central America.

When we get to Japanese art, we will be examining the pagoda and other wooden buildings of Horyuji (670). These buildings lead us to believe that it was a T'ang Chinese monastery. One should mention in passing that Chinese architects, at least in northern China, had not as yet invented the curved roof that to us is so characteristic of their work. The roofs were all rectilinear, save for the consoles that broke up the façade. At Horyuji, however, the tips of the roofs were already slightly curved, as if they were suspended at the four corners by invisible wires, giving the impression that the buildings had gently come down from the sky.

The T'ang epoch resembles the Han epoch in its curious spirit and its taste for the exotic. But perhaps the former was too aware of its civilization's arrogance: China and India shared the honor of being the most civilized countries of the world, and yet China does not seem to have learned anything from the former, outside what was of interest to the Buddhists.

THE SUNG AND YÜAN EPOCHS

After the fall of the T'ang dynasty, China experienced a further period of division which lasted half a century, from 909 to 960. The era was known as that of the Five Dynasties. The decentralization did little harm to art, and perhaps hastened the maturity of Chinese thought, which suddenly seems to have become full of nuances and more individualistic. Confucianism, Taoism, and Buddhism led a peaceful coexistence. The Ch'an sect of Buddhists, the heterodox group that had founded the cult of Bodhidharma (Ta-mo) during the second half of the sixth century, was now the dominant sect, at least among the intellectual elite, and already seemed to be gaining some benefit from a tacit understanding with Taoism. Taoism sprang from a very old form of autochthonous magic which was a metaphysical exercise during the time of Lao-tzu and Chuang-tzu. By now it was a religion that, like the Ch'an, was searching for an escape, a liberation, from this life. It was to become the basis for superstitious belief in modern China.

The unity of the empire re-established by the Sung in 960 was no more than an accident in the great sweep of political elective that had begun exactly in the middle of the T'ang epoch. Barbarians were once again rising near the northern frontiers and China was too civilized to be warlike. The capital was at Pien-ching (actually Kaifeng) on the lower stretches of the Huang-ho. This dynasty, known as "the Sung of the North," seems to have reached the heights of its power during the reign of Hui-tsung when catastrophe struck; the emperor, a dilletante, collector, and painter who spent much of his time with his academy, saw his capital fall into the hands of the Jurchen Manchus. The latter imprisoned the emperor in 1125. The whole of northern China fell to the Jurchen, but by a miracle that was so often repeated during the course of Chinese history, the conquerors became good Chinese. Orthodox Buddhists built some of their best monuments in the area occupied by this dynasty, which had taken the name of Kin.

One of the Sung princes managed to flee south, where he founded at Ling-ngan (actually Hang-chou; today called Hangchow) the Southern Sung dynasty, which for 150 years (1127–1280) reigned over the provinces south of the Yangtze River. Maritime relations with southern Asia became all the more active when Central Asian routes were cut off. Many merchants who were converts to Islam lived in the coastal cities, along with a large number of Jews. Forced to renounce all thoughts of expansion, China underwent a period of withdrawal, a period that proved to be intellectually fruitful.

The final fall of the Sung Empire came about when the Mongols conquered not only the Kin Empire, but also the whole of China (1279), and took the dynastic name of Yüan. Marco Polo was witness to the prosperity and security that existed throughout China under Kublai Khan.

Though detested by the learned Confucianists, the Mongol regime (1280–1368) was a piece of good luck for China, for she was able to reopen commercial relations with the Near East. After more than three centuries of isolation, China was open once more to new ideas.

BUDDHIST SCULPTURE

After the middle of the T'ang epoch, the middle period of Buddhist art became heavy and pompous and seemed incapable of further development. Sculpture, doomed to decline on account of its maturity, took the usual course and became more and more like painting. However, Chinese painting is far from being like Western painting. It is capable of showing an Arhat playing with a tiger; but translated into relief by a Chinese, the theme does not work, and is not a piece of sculpture. (See Plate 603A of *Chinese Sculpture from the Fifth to the Fourteenth Centuries,* by Osvald Sirén.) A stele in the Guimet Museum (approximately 950 A.D.) shows Kuan-yin seated before a cliff, which seems to be some distance away, since the people walking along its top are very small. Only an inadequate bas-relief could be made from this subject. Other faults are even more startling. For example, there exist three large wooden statues (ten feet high) of a standing Bodhisattva, the pose inclining slightly to the side and anatomically incorrect. They look as if they were enlargements of figurines carved out of elephant tusks. There was much of this distortion in small sculpture. A few new themes make their appearance; for example Kuan-yin at the Sintamani—the magic jewel—seated on the ground, one knee tucked under him, his forearm in bhumis-parca-mudra position over this knee. Even more interesting is Kuan-yin in *Maharaja-lila,* the last type being represented by large, imposing, and decorative gilt wooden statues. This new import from India is itself borrowed from Brahman art, for Buddhism was dead by then in its natal country. Statues were also made of cast iron; for example, the guardian kings of T'ai Yuan, dated 1097. The vestment details are almost too carefully executed. The arms and legs are stiff, the equilibrium bad, as usual.

Paradoxically, the progress made by the Ch'an sect is echoed in the statuary. This sect, rigorously atheistic, which refused to see Buddha as a supernatural being and considered him largely mythical, made only hieratic sculpture. Yet the Ch'an quite willingly depicted the legendary arhat (in Chinese lohan), who had been "enlightened," and groupings of sixteen, eighteen, or five hundred lohan were the pretext for making highly realistic statues—portraits of monks in various postures.

Sakyamuni is sometimes depicted before his enlightenment, as if isolated in a sphere on account of his concentration (lacquered statue, 1286 A.D.). The Taoists,
in turn, planned rock sanctuaries by copying Buddhist
iconography. This was a plagiarism similar to that of
the Jainists in India. No one can quite make out why
Taoism, which was purely a Chinese movement and
had such a long history, was never able to produce an
art of its own. In the meantime, let us mention that
between the Sung and the Ming eras, some beautiful
heads of the T'ai Chan goddess were made, with doves
in her headdress. But they look more like noble Manchu ladies than Chinese ladies.

Under the Southern Sung, at Chuanchow in Fukien
Province—which Marco Polo called Zayton—beautiful
narrative reliefs were made. They have the look of work
crafted by goldsmiths, and decorate the exterior of two
octagonal stone pagodas standing five stories high that
were built between 1227 and 1250. The workmanship
is more or less good, but the style homogeneous. The
decoration shows scenes of the life of Buddha, *Jatakas*,
legends—often obscure ones—minor characters in the
Buddhist pantheon, and legendary religions. The
sculpting is fine (even too fine for the exterior of a
building), caressing, and precious. The mixture of sharp
detail with loose masses, the background, the delicately
made observations, all make for a pleasing visual composition. However, from the point of view of style,
these sculptures have no ties with the traditions of religious imagery, and seem to be a continuation of the
"salon arts" of the T'ang epoch. One also senses their
likeness to genre painting of the period and its imper-
fections, for the people shown are not in groups, but
separate from each other, and a little stiff. Clouds are
the conventional indication that a miracle is taking
place. The two *Jatakas*—to be seen in Japan during the

first part of the seventh century—are also seen here, and instructive comparison can also be made to Sanchi sculpture. The elephants clearing the jungle around the stupa at Ramagrama make an extraordinarily graceful picture, though somewhat in the "chocolate-box" style. Orthodox Buddhism was already too old to inspire a religious art form.

In funerary art, the monumental proportions of out-door statuary were not conducive to the "goldsmith" genius of the period. Several statues of people and animals that are on the tombs of the fifth and sixth Sung emperors (mid-eleventh century) are very dull. The *ming-ch'i* disappeared during the Sung and Yüan epochs. Perhaps the elite had come to think that the life of the dead was something other than a repetition of that of the living. The peasants, however, were faithful to the naïve custom: Marco Polo describes how they burned drawings of everything that might be useful to the deceased.

SUNG CERAMICS

Largely due to the increased use of kaolin and feld-spar, the advances made in ceramics were vulgarized during the Sung epoch and are too numerous for us to describe from a technical standpoint. Aesthetically speaking, there is an enormous contrast between the T'ang and the Sung ceramics. The former were con-cerned more with ornamentation than with form, while in the latter, always discrete, the form is felt inti-mately, and ornamentation is reduced to a secondary role. The quality of the materials used played an im-portant part as well. The creamy slips of soft, delicate, indefinable tones appeared in the luxury ceramics in ad-dition to the fine, white porcelains; the distinguished cloudy green "the sky after rain" of which examples are extremely rare, brought great fame to Ju-chou, near

Kaifeng. A green-gray slip, sometimes turning into lavender tones, and of the same quality as the "sky after rain," is characteristic of a large group of this celadon ware (named after the shepherd in Urfé's *L'Astrée* who wore ribbons of this color). Unfortunately there are too many later copies of this type of ceramics, as many Chinese as Japanese, the glossy enamel of which does not have nearly the charm of the Sung celadon ware. The potters knew how to control the flamelike effect that transformed the copper-green metal into glazes of purple-copper color, giving us a crackle in large speckle forms, which are either in tight-meshed net or double lines, or radiate from one spot like a spider's web. The Japanese called crackled celadon ware "kinuta" (the utensil used to beat and press silks). A kinuta-shaped specimen is in the collection of the eighth shogun of the Ashikaga shogunate, Yoshimasa (fifteenth century). It would appear that the workshops situated in the north during the Northern Sung era, notably at Tingchow and in Hopei Province, were in touch with Korean workshops, though this relationship needs further study; in any case Korean ceramics of the Middle Ages are nothing but imitations.

After the fall of the dynasty at Ling-nan, the important centers were in the southeast, between the great lakes and the sea, at Chien-an, Chien-yang, and Fukien. Their speciality was brown-black or rust-colored enamel work that is exceedingly soft to the touch. The Japanese call this type of tea bowl, which was imported by Zen monks from the thirteenth century onward, the *temmoku* (Sky's Eye, name of a place?). The tea bowls have round bases and wide conical bellies. The name of "hare-fur" is given to the enamel where tightly packed tracks blend in brown values. In other *temmoku*, light-toned, alternate stripes of "oil drips" give an iridescent effect to the bowl. This refinement in the presence of mean materials is a new note in Chinese art, a creation of the Ch'an.

Noble, decorative vases were also made with iron or manganese enamels. The most famous are the large ovoid urns, whose black or brown enamel gives off delicate reflections with the appearance of bronze. The peony was the most popular motif, used in black silhouettes over a light background, or vice versa, or as a simple outline incised under the enamel (Fig. 27).

Fig. 27. Mei-p'ing Vase. Decorated with Peonies. Brown and White. Kiln at Ts'eu-Chou (North China).

THE BRONZES AND JADES

The Chinese soul always seems to turn toward the past rather than the future, and even during the most creative periods a certain yearning for the past creeps into the new departures. The Sung epoch was fond of antiques and even of imitations of them. Since a Sung artist could not become a Shang or Chou bronze-caster, his pastiches admirably accentuated the particular traits of contemporary culture, harmonious and benign. For example, an imitation Shang vase decorated with two rams is not ugly, even though it lacks the pride of the original. However, the brutality of the Chou is poorly executed in dull and heavy *ting* vases. The Li-yu style, almost a forerunner to Sung art, does not seem to have been known at the time. Some of the original bronzes of the Sung period are to be found in Japan. They are as simple in shape as the celadon ware and are not very interesting.

The same can be said of the jades. However, jade work is an intimate art, and the Sung genius was more at ease with it. The former Gieseler Collection, now at the Guimet Museum, contains representative specimens of Sung jade, summing up the entire aesthetic of the Zayton pagoda bas-reliefs in abstraction, and objects that were as rich, as finished, as perfectly contained in themselves as the Shang monuments. The art lovers of the past, and even those of today, who find this art too hermetic and abstract, will find at least something to their liking in the small cups and plates of white jade whose modest refinement is exquisite in every way.

PAINTING FROM ITS BEGINNINGS TO THE NORTHERN SUNG DYNASTY

FROM THE BEGINNING TO THE T'ANG ERA

We will now make a study of Chinese painting, whose development presents us with such a remarkable continuity that it is preferable to approach the subject in a separate chapter.

The Anyang excavations bear witness to the fact that

from the most ancient times onward the artists used polychromy for decorating walls. It is as yet impossible to discern whether or not figurative painting was executed at this time. During the late Han era, painting was almost exclusively figurative, with some architectural detail. The carved Shantung stones show that the artist was capable of telling a story in eloquent silhouettes. The painted bricks give us an idea of the artist's flair and dexterity, and we have the impression that the best Chu Wei sculptures can be compared favorably with those of the *quattrocento*. Two or three centuries later, Buddhists imposed new tasks upon artists; sometimes they were required to paint superhuman creatures; they had to depict situations in which humanity found itself more intimately linked to nature than to Chinese myth, which is on the whole urban. The painting was to be edifying, that is to say, directed toward the goal of the super-pictorial. The Chinese of later centuries were not mistaken when they classified figure painting and religious painting well below that of landscape, bamboos and birds, etc. Man was of interest to the Chinese in that he was a thinking being, but they never looked upon him as God's greatest achievement. They had a horror of nudity. Figure painting therefore could hardly develop much further than the limits it attained during the early years of Chinese painting.

All we have of the many paintings executed between the Han and T'ang eras consists of literary references that are a better guide to "the public's mentality" than to the paintings. An eminent master of the fourth century, Ku K'ai-chih is more than a name to us, for the British Museum has a scroll that is thought to have been his work, and is, at least, a very old (sixth century?) copy of his "Warnings to the Palace Ladies." It is an illustration to a fairly brief text written by a third-century author. Nine sections remain, of which only eight contain figures with various accessories. Only one of them, the second, shows a mountain with wild animals and a hunter. The birds and quadrupeds are in proportion to the hunter, though not to the mountain; nor is the spatial relationship clearly defined. The inscription reads: "No beings fly so high that cannot be shot down." The first picture shows the virtuous concubine refusing to climb into the emperor's palanquin, in order not to interrupt the affairs of state. The porters make a very lively group, almost drunken. In another scene, we can see an aged man seated on a cushion belonging to a young lady with whom he is having a conversation. We can see the end of a palanquin bed, the sides of which are oblique but do not converge toward a vanishing point as they would in our European perspective; instead they diverge slightly. Our laws of perspective, which have weighed so heavily on our own art, did not interest the Chinese. Now that our painters have freed us of so many conventions, we can see that the Chinese were right. Chinese painting, which seemed so close to that of Europe during the Han period, turned off the road that European art has followed since the Renaissance. Ku K'ai-chih said what he had to say and nothing more; he said it as clearly as possible, avoiding the superfluous. He painted neither the floor nor the back of room, but the drawing of the figures was so convincing that one feels the presence of the floor nevertheless (Fig. 28).

While Europe slept through the somber Merovingian era, China had art critics and theoreticians. One of them, Hsieh Ho, a fifth-century critic, proposed six principles that the Chinese have always venerated and commented upon. It is almost impossible to make a

Fig. 28. Palace Lady. Detail of the Ku K'ai-chih Scroll. Fourth Century.

satisfactory translation of these principles, and we have not done much better than our predecessors:

(1) The sound of the spirit causes movement to live. (Inspiration.)

(2) When one is using the brush, one should bear in mind the total content or "bone" of the subject matter. (Structure.)

(3) Likeness is achieved by conformity with the object. (Visual veracity.)

(4) Color is used according to type. (Appropriateness.)

(5) Composition is determined by the plan and the elevations. (Unity.)

(6) In copying the masters, one reproduces the originals. (Traditional types.)

The first principle, *k'i yun sheng tung*, which at first sight is rather obscure, has been cited so often by Chinese authors that we are now quite sure of its meaning.

It refers to that indefinable quality found in great art and all its parts. It is to be found in the most insignificant sketch by an old master; it can be a mistake in a work of art whose drawing, color, values, and proportions, etc., are flawless; it is what we call the "life" (animation) in a drawing, quite different from the "photographic life," which captivates the vulgarians. In the Chinese vocabulary, concrete by nature, the "bones" mean the materiality of the object being painted, which one spontaneously expresses with contours. A painting that has no "bones" is one that may have form but has not grasped the essence. Thus the second precept reads: "Know how to depict the difference in matter." The third and fourth principles do not need any explanation. However, duality appears during the fifth century. It had not been very long since China had progressed from the primitive mentality that perceives in each object two forms: that of the visible world, which the Chinese knew perfectly well how to reproduce, and, more important, that of the spirit, determined a priori. The fifth principle, which the West approves of but does not clearly put into practice, commands the artist to have his conception clearly and completely in mind before he starts to paint. The sixth is probably the one that would shock us the most if we knew more about the Chinese point of view at the time. The most important part of the picture was its fundamental idea; its realization, more or less skillful, was relatively unimportant. (This idea, so shocking to us, has been placed in our lawbooks recently under the name of "artistic property.") A copy of a painting must in fact bear the master's name, as long as there is no intention to defraud. This principle, however, seems to be more or less an implicit contradiction of the first. It would be difficult for the copy to have as much *k'i yun*, as much of the "spirit," as the original, and it is

often the only criterion we have for recognizing one
from the other.

In short, we have very few examples of pre-Buddhist
painting (Fig. 29). In the meantime, we can point out

Fig. 29. Detail of a Wall Painting in Manchuria.

that hieratic painting (which the Chinese looked
upon as being purely artisan work) is another form of
profane painting. In Europe, on the other hand, secular painting stems from Christian art. Nearly all we know
about T'ang painting came from the Central Asian
desert. Secular subjects are intermingled with religious
themes. The fragment of the two horsemen is a good
example (Guimet Museum). The scrolls of painting entitled "Women under the Trees" that came from Turfan have an almost Botticellian flavor. In all these fragments the landscape still takes a secondary place, and
is never treated with the same plasticity as the human
figure. Yet it was Chinese landscape art that was to
reach the heights of perfection, making it quite unique.

THE T'ANG MASTERS
Plate 14

During the T'ang epoch, several famous masters
basked in the favor of the court at Chang-an. We have
many written accounts praising their work. Because
authentic works of these masters are very rare, indeed

some of them nonexistent, we are forced to reconstruct the talent of each painter by piecing together ancient copies in rather the same way that one puts a text together by comparing the mistakes made in different manuscripts.

The oldest of these artists was Yen Li-pên, who died in 673. There was nothing revolutionary about his work, though he did his best painting in the tradition of figure painting. He did commemorative and edifying works, which, at least from the mid-Han era on, were encouraged by the aristocracy. His paintings include: "Eighteen Wise Men," "Twenty-Four Statesmen," "The Western Ambassadors" (that is, Central Asian). He was good at characterizing nationalities and animals. T'ang Emperor T'ai Tsung commissioned him to paint the "Foreign Tribute-Payers" so that future generations would be aware of the glory of the T'ang dynasty. There is a scroll of this title in the Peking Museum. "The Thirteen Emperors" is at Boston. Each sovereign is surrounded by a group of people. It is thought that the second half of the scroll, from the seventh group onward, is authentic. The drawing of the faces is first-class, the flesh lightly modeled in pale flesh tones. The perspective of the small platforms is like that in the Ku K'ai-chih scroll: two sides are parallel to the picture, the other two disappearing without converging. "The Collation of the Classic" appears to be a good Sung copy (also at the Museum of Fine Arts, Boston). The composition, scattered and asymmetrical, is truly Chinese. "The Drunken Taoist" (formerly in the Stoclet Collection) does help us out somewhat, because a sixth-century master, Chang Seng-yu, depicted "The Drunken Buddhist," and the scroll attributed to Yen Li-pên seems to be an ironic plagiarism. However, there is a tree in this picture, and an interior with a convincing feeling of depth; in short, an interest in setting that was still lacking in the early years of the T'ang epoch.

Living one hundred years after Yen Li-pên, during the reign of Hsüan Tsung, Wu Tao-hsüan, better known as Wu Tao-tzu (in Japanese, Godoshi), was an imaginative and creative genius. He was an action painter whose work was compared to storms and waves. He painted from memory with lightning speed. A soldier wanted one of the master's pictures. In exchange, Wu Tao-tzu asked for a fencing lesson; the swordsman had to foresee the unfolding of a fight to its victorious end, and the painter had to realize the picture with the same quick reflexes. Less significant is the charming story of the death of Wu Tao-tzu. He invited the emperor to unveil an immense mural he had executed of a landscape with a single grotto. During the unveiling, the artist went over to the grotto, which opened up, let him through, then closed on him forever. Wu Tao-tzu's landscapes were more suggestive than descriptive. Although none of them have survived, we do have, at second hand, examples of some of his religious pictures. He seems to have been the first person to depict celestial bodies flying through space, hence the reason for the Chinese making tracings that were engraved on stones and multiplied by impressing, at a very early date. The divinity of Heng-chan, several Kuan-yin, and the Tortoise of the North are examples of his powerful and dynamic drawing, which are dominated by his sinuous line, sometimes faint, sometimes heavy, and as varied as the strokes of a violinist, rather than with the fine and uniform contours that were considered *de rigueur* in his time. (Though it might sound illogical, contours have always annoyed bourgeois critics of the Far East.)

ANIMAL PAINTING
Plate 15

From the Han period on, at least, the Chinese were
very good at drawing animals. During the eighth century, an urchin employed at an inn, Han Kan, made a
considerable name for himself with his drawings of
horses (Fig. 30). A fragment, considered authentic, in

Fig. 30. Horse of Han Kan. Eighth Century.

which the drawing is good, does not appear to have
been placed on the same level as the horses that were
either sculptured or modeled by several earlier or contemporary or anonymous artists. But during the course
of the next two centuries, until the middle of the tenth
century, animal painting underwent a considerable development. Styles that were to last for a long period
were already being created. For example, one style
showed an animal without any background, but with
such accuracy in its movement and its material (hair

and feathers, etc.) that the subject is still interesting. Another placed several animals of the same breed into an appropriate decor in various poses. A third way was to associate the animal with a human figure—a peasant with oxen, for example—a subject that was full of poetic and philosophical content. The "bird and flower" genre also began to appear at this time. Europeans are not usually attracted to these drawings, being less sensitive than people of the Far East to the symbolism of wild geese (travel, absence, family ties), mandarin ducks (faithful love), the lotus (flowers whose purity cannot be spoiled by the mud they grow in), etc. For the Chinese, subject matter of this sort is a summary of nature, according to the principle "the whole is the sum of the parts," one of the fundamentals of their aesthetic. The oldest paintings of this type—they are represented in European collections, and are usually quite large in size—are astonishing to begin with on account of their severity. They are almost ghostly, on backgrounds that have gone black, though the colors are still fresh but pale. There are no contrasting values, no decorative devices, and the drawing is sensitive, serious, and contemplative.

LANDSCAPE ART

It is somewhat paradoxical that in its early stages— during the T'ang epoch, as far as we know—landscape art was the most developed of all the genres. Bearing in mind that we know almost nothing about the painting of centuries of the T'ang era, it is hard to understand how landscape art managed to develop from the childish schematization of certain scenes engraved on Han sculptured stones to the sophisticated work of the seventh and eighth centuries, done not only at the capital, but also at Tunhuang, on the Shosoin lutes, and in other areas.

Between 650 and 720, there lived at Chang-an two great landscape artists, Li Ssu-hsün and his son, Li Chao-tao, who were closely related to the imperial family. Their painting is distinguished and precious, and all we have are copies. They consisted of vast imaginary landscapes with minute detail that was fanciful rather than observed. Li Ssu-hsün was a specialist of "green and blue" subject matter, with the contours of mountains traced in gold and surrounded with little gold dots, a style that has persisted until this very day and renders fairly well the vibrations of sunlight. It would appear that the two Li were the foremost practitioners of archaic landscape art; but later generations were mistaken in looking upon them as being the founders of surrealist and decorative landscape art.

Wang Wei, during the first half of the eighth century, was much closer to our convention. He was eminently representative of the type of man who was often to be found among the masters of Chinese art. He was highly educated: having passed all his examinations, he was, hence, a functionary, as well as being a fine musician, first-class poet, and highly praised for his writing. Writing (*chou*), a word often translated as calligraphy when handwriting would be the better word, was always looked upon by the Chinese as being as important as painting. As we have already said, they were concerned more with the idea the painter had in mind than with the treatment of the work, and it was particularly in the writing that one looked for the painter's personality. Wang Wei painted many Buddhist subjects that have all been lost. We know of his landscapes through copies that are of very uneven quality. Nevertheless, each one of them leads us to believe that he had a deep understanding of nature, which he studied with the sincerity and humility of a Pissarro. He painted Wang Ch'uan's estate near the capital on a scroll that has been copied and engraved on stone. The interest he brings to the manifest aspects of nature is fascinating. His art is both intimate and universal. There exists such an excellent copy of another scroll, entitled "A Break after Snow," that one wonders if the artist did not accentuate the atmospheric qualities of the original. And yet, this quasi-impressionistic and "meteorological" sensitivity seems to have been characteristic of Wang Wei's talent. He was certainly ahead of his time. Indeed only eight or nine centuries after his death, the painters were hailing him as the creator of intimate and contemplative landscape art. It is almost impossible to know whether or not he used a monochrome wash in preference to color. Two good gouaches, preserved in Japan, which traditionally have been attributed to him, certainly date to the Sung epoch, along with a short treatise entitled *The Secrets of Painting.*

PAINTING IN THE ERA OF THE FIVE DYNASTIES AND THE NORTHERN SUNG DYNASTIES

Giles, Petrucci, Waley, Sirén, and many other translators have given European readers the most important texts pertaining to Chinese painters and painting. There seems to be no better method of gaining a sound knowledge of Chinese painting than by reading what was written at each moment of its history by those praising artists, by critics and by the artists themselves, provided, of course, that we have already assimilated the philosophical and religious ideals that the Chinese were imbued with. However, this sort of study is difficult to make. First, in order to gain some sort of knowledge of ideas that have no equivalent in our language we would have to understand the conventional vocabulary, which is almost as difficult as Chinese. Even though our artists might be perfectly familiar

with these concepts, we should make a choice between
almost incomprehensible literal translation and paraphrase, which will always sound vague and suspect. One
such translation was made of Hsieh Ho's six principles.
It is hardly surprising that Pierre du Colombier wrote:
"We are quite right to wonder if the Sinologists raised
rather than lowered the barriers, or considered everything we cannot understand today as being of the ut-
most importance." More recently in his book *Chinese
Mysticism and Modern Painting*, Georges Duthuit
made a similar complaint. We also believe it is wishful
thinking to imagine we can fully understand the
thoughts of an artist of the past, even if he was a fellow countryman. That is the reason for our pursuing a
different method in the following pages.

The achievement of our artists during the past fifty
years has acclimated our eyes to the extent that we
have acquired a taste for the exotic. Great art is universal, but every generation draws a different enrich-
ment from it. It is considered legitimate to comment
upon Chinese paintings as if they were hanging in our
annual exhibitions without appealing to notions that
demand a long apprenticeship. However, since the Chinese extended the role of painting beyond the position
we normally assign to it, we occasionally have to borrow musical metaphor in order to make reasonable
sense out of criticism.

Sirén cited and reproduced (in his book *Early Chinese Painting*, Plate 45) a picture hanging in the
Peking Museum to which it is difficult to give an exact
date, though it must have been painted between the
T'ang and Sung eras. Its style is somewhere between
the archaic style that we have already seen at Tunhuang, and the surrealist style of the tenth and eleventh centuries. It is perhaps only in China that an obsolete tradition can thus be preserved quite effortlessly,

or rather, never becomes obsolete and outdated, suddenly turning up with renewed vigor. This picture shows a ring of mountains composed of cliffs and pinnacles. Through a hollow, we can see a chain of mountains in the distance. Large trees grow in the sheltered spot, with a river meandering below. A group of horsemen are arriving from the east, among them a man riding a camel. The landscape is fantastical and dreamlike. One could describe its own particular resonant quality by comparing the painting to one by Brueghel the Elder. In the Chinese landscape, however, the human figure is quite small, and totally subordinate to the trees and cliffs.

Thus this imaginative vein, so acclaimed by our contemporary surrealists, and which the Italian influence was quickly to snuff out in Europe, was perpetuated in Chinese art. We come across it again, this time quite free of archaic constraint, among early Sung masters, such as Tao-ning, Kuo Hsi, and many others. Their landscapes (often as wide as seven feet) are prodigious constructions of curiously shaped rocky masses. They give the appearance of being alive, moving. The trees hooked to the cliffside also play a role in the dramatic quality of these pictures. It is as if we were seeing a speeded-up film of the beginning of the world; the life of the mountains. There is nothing in European painting that attains such poetic heights while remaining strictly pictorial. Our early Renaissance paintings often have a distant horizon and peaceful countryside. And yet they look as if they were supposed to make us appreciate even more the human heat of the town, the house, or the oratory. The Chinese artist prefers to turn toward the wilderness, and only finds it in mountains. Vidal de la Blanche tells us why: "In the Far East, the mountain is the still frame surrounding man's activity . . . the smallest relief creates a void that is surprising when one considers the serenity of French hillocks" (Fig. 31).

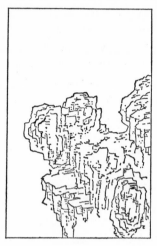

Fig. 31. Manner of Painting Summits. From *The Garden of the Mustard Seed*. Chinese Encyclopedia of the Eighteenth Century.

PAINTED SCROLLS
Plates 16–20

The scroll, in China as in Mediterranean countries, was the first form in which the book appeared. The painters used them not only for illustrations alternating with text (see the Ku K'ai-chih scroll), but also for continuous paintings of considerable length to be unrolled with the left hand, while rolling the sections already seen with the right. Thus, the painting had a new dimension, an extension in time, as it were, and the possibility of developing extended melodic lines, superimposing voices, and varying the rhythm. A fixed drawing, the freezing of movement such as we have in European painting, which is further accentuated by the presence of a frame, would have been an appalling idea to a Chinese. A good Chinese drawing is always a work of art suspended in time; our glance always follows a certain pattern, and even if it is only a momentary glance, we have a vivid impression imprinted on our minds. Rather like listening to a sonata, this is quite different from looking at a European painting, where the focal point was determined beforehand by the artist.

A general rule in Chinese painting (rediscovered by our cubists) is that the artist should always see his subject matter from a distance. What we call the foreground, namely the point at which the picture starts, is always quite some distance from the spectator. For this reason, figures are never placed in the foreground of a picture of mountains. Inversely, in figure painting, they are always placed against an unlimited background. The Chinese artists were careful to maintain objects in their correct proportions, at least approximately. The pseudo Wang Wei treatise states: "If the mountains are one foot tall, then the trees will be one inch tall, men one line high." The "point of view," disappearing in the distance, governs all Chinese perspective; so much so that some Europeans, ignorant of these matters, have called it ridiculously faulty. It is no more and no less a convention than our laws of perspective. Indeed, one should rather be surprised at the remarkable resemblance between them.

It is somewhat foolish to suggest that our different approaches to perspective are the result of the Chinese using the floor, or a low table, to paint on, and our using an easel. The Chinese were not interested in the laws of perspective that produce ugly pictures that, more often than not, bear no resemblance to nature. In short, the Chinese were quite happy with the primitive convention that considered the contents of the background, or the feeling of space, to be the most important part of the picture. They not only see the scene from the distance, but also from above.

From this stems the predilection of Chinese land-scape artists toward mountain scenes that justified a plunging perspective and terraced levels reaching to the top of the composition (Fig. 32). The plain and

Fig. 32. Manner of Landscape Composition. Integrating Mountain and Water. From *The Garden of the Mustard Seed*.

its vast skies were not suited to this ideal. Clouds were accidental appendages, like the shadows, which the artist did not recommend reproducing, a scruple that makes us smile when we think of the dictum attributed to Ingres: "Shadows are unworthy of the painting of history." Therefore, mountains served as support to all the pictorial devices of line, mass, and values, and even to the effects of luminosity. In his lectures at the École du Louvre, Georges Salles was quite correct in saying that mountains played the same role in Chinese painting as did the nude in European art.

Chinese landscape art of the early Sung period (very different from that of the Southern Sung) has a special flavor which would not have found an audience in Europe during the impressionist period, and which today strikes us as being singularly modern. Although it surely derives from Li Ssu-hsün's visions that were "more exquisite than reality," this art is no longer naïve. One gets the distinct feeling that painting has become the means of expression of the intellectual elite, and falls in the same category as poetry. It is also quite natural that the Chinese intellectual and the Chinese language should dislike abstraction. The general idea can only be achieved through a concrete expression, which is the principle common ground shared by the two arts.

King Hao, Kouan T'ong, Sieu Ta-ning, and in the next generation Kuo Hsi are among this group of poet-painters, with whom romanticism never sounds hollow. Rather than taking liberties with nature, Li Ch'eng manages to convey the fantastic by using taste and perseverance, not by stylizing nature's forms. Tung Yuan painted a beautiful scroll entitled "The Sky Clearing over the Valley" (Museum of Fine Arts, Boston). It is as controlled as a symphony; the beginning is slow and majestic, with a rich polyphony. Then follows the lyric adagio, and soft backgrounds slipping gently toward the horizon. He is already more "direct" than his elders, at the same time sharing their almost religious respect for nature. Kuo Hsi is capable of handling a large number of elevations at the same time, correctly placed in the relationship of sky to earth, offering an intricate feast for the eye. Kuo Hsi's painting theories were put into book form by his son Kuo Jo-ssu in a treatise that picks up and develops several pseudo–Wang Wei ideas. Among these is the idea that the observation of nature and the appreciation of its beauty are incorporated in an a priori construction of the phenomenal world according to the hierarchic order of Chinese society and of the cosmos itself. This summary of the progress made by painting, therefore, is not a step toward realism. It begins in praise of the countryside, which can enoble the soul, enlarge it, give it a rest from worldly cares. "There are landscapes to contemplate, others in which we wish to take a walk, others in which we could make a life. The first of these is the best." The painting of a landscape is almost a holy act, demanding sincerity, concentration, and an act of purification. Then come the truths—which seem to us elementary—concerning the change in atmosphere according to the seasons, which are bound by literary conventions rather than by artistic convention. (One must also remember that only the geniuses ignored the conventions.) Thus: "Figures placed on mountains are either showing us the way or climbing a path; buildings simulate the appearance of natural landscapes; ferryboats and bridges suggest human activity," etc. "Water is a living organism; it can give the appearance of being calm and deep, smooth and caressing; it can look like the ocean or it can meander; it can be unctuous and glowing, sparkling, bubbling, jumping, or like straight rain. Rocks are the earth's skeleton; one should sense their depth in the earth; they are not exposed in their entirety on the surface of the ground. Water is the blood of both earth and sky, blood that needs to circulate, and may not remain frozen, inert." There must be tortuous torrents in the foreground, rocks and knotty trees (Fig. 33) "thus making the effect even more exciting if one takes a closer look at the picture." The landscape artist should concern himself above all with painting the high mountain, the master peak, as if it were a sovereign standing in the midst of his ministers. He is to do

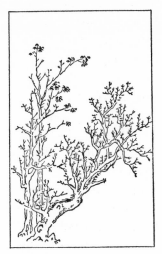

Fig. 33. Manner of Painting Trees. From *The Garden of the Mustard Seed.*

the same with forests; there will be a great pine, looking like a superior being among the peasants.

The pseudo–Wang Wei, whom we have mentioned before, expressed themselves with more naïveté and less assurance:

Men in the distance have no eyes, trees in the distance have no branches, no rocks can be seen on the distant mountain; they blend and are like eyelids (the hairs of which are barely discernible); water in the distance has no waves, like a distant cloud. This is one of the revelations . . . All sides of the stone are visible (one should be able to feel its volume?), the road from its beginning to the end, the trees by their bark, water by the trails of the wind; these are the principles . . . The morning landscape is denoted by the desire of a thousand mountains to light up, the mist is fine, barely perceptible; the moon, still in the sky, is faded over . . . In the evening landscape the mountain swallows the red sun; the sail on a boat wet in shallow water is drawn in. The people walking along the road are in a hurry, and the poor man's door is already half closed . . . When you draw landscapes you should at least bear in mind the four seasons.

The anecdotal characterization of hours and seasons, though obviously adding little to our enjoyment of Chinese landscape art, is a key to the understanding of its sentimental content that is as stereotyped as our own. We would be starting on the wrong foot if we were to think of the Chinese as being quite different from ourselves.

A curious personality of the Sung epoch was Mi Fei. He astonished his contemporaries with his innovations in clothing, his method of painting, and the violence of his passion for collecting, which almost went to the point of indelicacy.

Following in the path cleared by Fan K'uan, who had rejected the anecdotal style for the virtuoso turn, he dreamed of a style of painting that would achieve effects of light without bothering with formal representation. He replaced the paintbrush with a twist of paper or a piece of sugar cane, and painted landscapes of more or less visible mountains in a pointillist style. A bank of luminous mist intervened between these mountains and a foreground of dark forest. Later, the freedoms he took were much admired, though the academy refused to admit him. Also, the Ashikaga of Japan do not seem to have known of his existence. The few works of his art that have survived are of rather doubtful authenticity, for their monotonous style is easily imitated.

The taste of Hui Tsung, the unfortunate emperor and great art collector who was to spend his last years as prisoner of the barbarians, was somewhat conservative, almost Philistine. He liked a picture "that tells its own story," and urged his academicians to depict birds and plants in minute detail. He himself painted some partridge on branches, illustrating in a dignified manner an ornithological treatise. The composition and coloring of his little pictures are, incidentally, rather pleasing. It is interesting to note that in the catalogue of the emperor's collection, of which we still have a copy, 6396 works of art by 230 different masters of all periods are listed. (Many of them, according to Osvald Sirén, were probably reproductions.) There were 2756 bird and flower paintings by forty-six artists, 1008 landscapes by forty-one painters, and 505 figure paintings (excluding religious ones) by only thirty-three painters.

The emperor had dismissed the work of Kuo Hsi, who had been an academician two reigns previously, but admitted Chao Ta-nien, who, apart from the minute attention he paid to objects, had a profound feeling for nature and space. Ma Fên, first master of the Ma line, painted scrolls entitled "The Hundred Horses," etc. His "Wild Geese" in the Honolulu Museum have the charm of consummate ability and an agreeable "phrasing." Li T'ang painted village scenes, a few of which were anecdotal, as did Li Ti, who was also famous as a flower and fruit painter. One can see that there was enormous variety even among the traditionalists, and we are still moved by their great sensitivity.

Bamboo painting is less understood by Europeans. The bamboo was not merely a plant of some sort, but one of the "three friends of the cold season," the others being the pine tree and the plum blossom. Bamboo appealed to the educated person since its silhouette cast by the sun or moon on the paper windows of the Chinese house produced a poetic effect. Its straight stalk was the symbol of the sage, in that adversity could bend, but not break it. The inside of this stalk contained the symbol of the void that must be established in one's mind before thinking of useful ideas. Furthermore, one needed to be an expert with the brush in order to be able to make perfectly cylindrical, smooth, and hard internodes, and thin, translucid, nervous leaves, placed in various perspectives and in dark and light tones. Bamboo was therefore the complete subject matter. Su Tung-p'o (Su Shih), the statesman associated with Mi Fei, liked bamboo painting better than anything else, and his friend Wên T'ung excelled at it. Even today, this genre is still held in high esteem, for though China has not paid much attention to the preservation of her works of art, she never forgets ideas, and, while inventing a new art form, she has no qualms about doing reproductions of successful formulas. Nothing would have more incensed the Chinese of the past than our contemporary demand for originality at any price, no matter how superficial. Other specialities, such as fish and dragons, were already represented in the Imperial Collection, but for us, they are better represented in later epochs. The subjects of genre painting (particularly women and children) mean nothing to us. They are decidedly exotic, even somewhat archaic, for reasons we have already mentioned.

Li Kung-lin was considered by his contemporaries to be the greatest painter of the Sung period. Though very difficult to evaluate—on account of the insufficient fragments that remain of his colossal output—he appears to have been neither profound nor original. He was successful in a large variety of genres, and his work is therefore somewhat eclectic. He was aware of being a second Yen Li-pên, but one gets the impression that he was trying to relive the life of all the T'ang masters. Like Li-pên, he painted the horses the emperor received from Central Asia, and their palfrey. He drew popular scenes in the old manner, without depth or scenery. Like Wang Wei, he painted landscape scrolls; like the two Li he drew imaginary landscapes of palaces suspended between earth and sky. Like Wang Wei and Wu Tao-tzu he was famous for his Buddhist painting, though there is nothing left of this genre. He was looked upon as the creator of a new manner of showing the arhats, primitive Buddhist saints, whom the popular imagination more or less confused with the Taoist immortals. He also depicted old men reading, meditating, talking to each other, although they were not like the strange old men painted by Kuan Hsiu in the tenth century who had become gnarled like trees or rocks. Several series of great paintings of arhats, that Japan had for a long time attributed to Li Kung-lin, are now thought to be the work of thirteenth-century painters. They are well composed, rich in color and imagination, yet despite all this, of a dull realism. Unfortunately, we have no copy of "Reunion of Poets and Philosophers in the Park," in which, if we are to believe Mi Fei, each person was magnificently characterized. The same subject was treated by Li Chao-tao toward the year 700, and was often taken up by later painters.

SOUTHERN SUNG AND YÜAN PAINTING
Plates 21–24

The influence of the Ch'an is felt less directly in the painting of the Southern Sung period, though more so in nonreligious subject matter. It is felt especially in small landscapes, usually painted on a rounded screen of some eight to twelve inches in length, and quite different in style from the romantic dynamism that dominated the previous centuries. They are the expression of a perfect ataraxia, of a contemplative and static condition. One might well say that the only subject they depict is infinity. The distant peaks of mountains peer from under clouds of mist. In the foreground, and marking out the boundaries of the immense vista, we have a few forcefully drawn rocks and a gnarled pine-tree stump with sad-looking branches. The occasional outline of a mountain growing progressively fainter and fainter as it recedes into the background leads the eye to a vanishing point on the far-distant horizon. Or again, one might have an area of water in the middle ground, reflecting the serenity of the sky. One can almost hear the silence.

This scene is best represented in the work of the Ma family, especially that of the two great-grandsons, Ma Kuei and Ma Yüan, who lived during the turn of the twelfth and beginning of the thirteenth centuries. Almost two hundred years later, many of their paintings were preserved in Japan. They have been frequently reproduced in modern Japanese publications, resulting in their being known in Europe. They intrigue people who are the least bit prepared to understand Chinese art. However, we must recognize that they are very uneven in quality. The firmness of a brush stroke is all too often hard and cold, and the transition between planes is too often poorly done. Also, the mountains give the appearance of being like strips of bizarre serrated roofing. At the same time, some of them are masterpieces of concentration and precision. One such painting is "The Fisherman on the Cold Estuary" by Ma Yüan. A small boat floats alone in the immensity of the river. In the background the fisherman is patiently holding his rod. One can almost feel the cold wind and hear the water slapping against the boat. One learns a lot by comparing the later copies of the same motif, in which one sees a distant landscape and an indication of waves, etc. In every case they strike us as superfluous additions to

the original. The same is true of "Lady Ling-chao
Standing in the Snow" (Museum of Fine Arts, Boston) and "Early Spring" (same museum), in a more
pleasing genre: a river winds its way parallel to the tall
cliffs; in the mist one can just make out villages and
woods; in the foreground, one can see two willows not
yet in bloom. They seem to be singing to the gentleness of the new season. A severe critic might reproach
the artist for having been somewhat cunning in his
composition. A hundred years earlier, Chao Ta-nien
treated this genre of human, calm, and melancholy
landscape with as much sensitivity and more ingenuity.
The comparison is easy to make, for the Museum of
Fine Arts in Boston has one of his screens that seems
to have served as a model for Ma Yüan's painting.

Ma Lin, his son (early thirteenth century), painted
in a style that was even more restrained, and several of
his compositions give the appearance of lacking the
basic elements. However, at the Guimet Museum there
is a handsome picture with his name inscribed in
enormous letters down the margin, which is believed
to be an ancient copy of the original. It shows the
immortals walking about on a terrace above a cloud of
mist. According to the legend, the artist died in 926,
reciting the following verses: "Milo, the True Milo
[Maitreya] is reincarnated once every one hundred
thousand years, and each time further away. He makes
himself manifest to the world, but the world does not
recognize him." For this reason he was thought to be
a hypostasis of the future Buddha. The Chinese included him in the group of the eighteen lohan.

Hsia Kuei, a contemporary of Ma Yüan, had a less
formal style. The composition of his "North Wind,"
in the Kawasaki Collection, is highly original, and full
of life; the wash is generous and wet. Kuei quite often
used a thick line with blunt ends, which contempo-

rary critics called his "restrained paintbrush." He was the most admired of the Sung painters in Japan, and it is quite possible that there are some Japanese copies among those thought to be originals. The Japanese painter Sesshu was directly influenced by his landscape scroll in the Peking Museum, and one must admit that the work of the Chinese master is infinitely more sensitive. The unity established in his work—not yet a mannerism—reached a high level of style in his treatment of cliffs, forests, etc.

During the thirteenth century, Liang K'ai, an eccentric academician, retired to a Ch'an monastery near the capital where he had painted, and proceeded to drink excessively. (There were many Chinese painters and poets who were incapable of working except when drunk.) K'ai painted in a variety of styles, and his subject matter was also varied. His "Sakyamuni Coming Down from the Mountains" shows him on the way back from the monastic retreat and the period of denial that preceded the enlightenment. It is typical in every way of Ch'an religious painting. Liang K'ai also painted anecdotal pictures and parables that were one of the means of instruction of the sect. We have, for example, his "Sixth Patriarch Tearing Up the Sutras." (Ch'an was a reaction against the book-worship that was invading orthodox Buddhism.) We have also "Han-Chan and Che-to" (known in Japanese as Kanzan and Jittoku), simple men, one of whom holds a broom, the other a scroll, symbols to remind us to keep our souls free of superfluity and to learn to read the Book of Life. In some drawings of people, drawn with even more synthesis, he seems to have rediscovered the perfectly concise manner of depicting the human figure which formerly had been printed on funerary bricks by the Han (Toronto Museum). "The Ecstasy of the Poet Li T'ai-po" is one of the best known of this kind.

Liang K'ai also painted small screens in the manner of Ma Yüan. Particularly moving is his painting of a pair of herons hovering over their nest.

Another famous painter also lived at the monastery, the monk Mu-ch'i, who had but recently left his birthplace of Szechwan. His "Eight Views of Hsiao and Hsiang" are often reproduced. It was a theme that became immensely popular not only in China, but also in Japan, where it was Japanized (the "Eight Views of Lake Biwa"), and is more or less a parody in the Ukiyo-e ("Eight Views of Edo," etc.). These eight subjects are: (1) nocturnal rain on the Hsiao and the Hsiang (rivers that flow from the great Lake Tungting); (2) the autumn moon on the lake; (3) the evening bell ringing from a distant monastery; (4) wild geese flying over white sand; (5) evening snow on a village; (6) the sun setting over a fishing village; (7) the clearing of the sky on a mountain after rain; and (8) the sails of returning boats from a distance. Although the European and Chinese artists use the same subject matter, their interpretations have nothing in common. The setting sun on the fishing village, for example, suggests cottages dimly lit by a fading sun, or the silhouette of a village against a warm sun. Mu-ch'i painted the eight views without "bones"; the pictures therefore are not drawings, but monochromes. However, sunset is indicated by the mist rising from the low grounds, and even more so by the four or five boats hastily pulling in their nets. It is curious that Chinese painting always depicted the differences of the various hours of the day by calling on intellectual considerations that were literary rather than pictorial. And yet, their effect of night was achieved by purely conventional means.

Mu-ch'i was so skillful at capturing—in a wash—the sudden movements of birds (by rights impossible to achieve) that the small pictures in Emperor Huei-tsung's collection look banal in comparison. The "Arhat Vanavasi" (Iwasaki Collection) is a grandiose composition, its values superb. His "Kuan-yin in a White Robe" is not a hieratic picture of Bodhisattva in his feminine likeness, but an aide for more success-ful meditation, in the sense understood by the Ch'an. The two lateral subjects represent respectively a crane and a female monkey with her baby. The crane is a symbol of longevity and purity, while the monkey sym-bolizes human folly, and also tenderness among human beings. Mu-ch'i's "The Dragon and the Tiger"—also in the collection of the Daitokuji of Kyoto—are the old Chinese symbols of the sky and the earth, while in Ch'an art they became the symbols of spirit and matter.

We know far more about this Ch'an painting of the Southern Sung period than we do about the contem-porary painting based on the same traditions. Some of these paintings were painted in the early Li Ssu-hsün style, such as those of Chao Po-chü (twelfth century), who made highly colored and charmingly in-ventive scrolls. Other painters, among them Yen Tz'u-p'ing and Chu Jui, continued in the surrealist tradition of Kuo Hsi. Their work is among the most remarkable of all Chinese painting. It would be difficult to sum-marize in a few pages the richness and variety of this "renaissance" in Chinese painting.

THE YÜAN EPOCH

We will not be able to do justice to the painting of the Mongol era either. The Japanese had as high an opin-ion of Yüan art as they did of the Sung. However, they knew little about the art of the later decades of the dynasty, which the Chinese of later centuries, less di-rectly imbued with Ch'an art, considered even more important. The general spirit behind Yüan art is less serious, less introspective than the previous period's; but there is nothing new either in the subject matter or in the technique. All Far Eastern painting suffered far more from reproduction than that of Europe, and its qualities are so subtle that photographs cannot do it justice. Yen Hui, whose exact dates are uncertain, painted magicians and Taoist legends. In order to appreciate their fine quality, it is best to compare them to "improved" copies made by the Japanese during the Ashikaga period. There were many fourteenth-century artists who specialized in bamboo painting (Fig. 34)

Fig. 34. Manner of Painting Bamboo. From *The Garden of the Mustard Seed*.

as well as in paintings of orchids, plum blossoms, vines, fish, dragons, etc. We can appreciate these works of art though not with the same passion as the Chinese did at the time.

We give credit to the Mongol conquerors for the presence of a particular development in the painting of Chao Mêng-fu. We know too little about it to be able to say that it opened the door to a new style, or even that it merely marked the beginning of a change. He was twenty-six years old when the Sung dynasty came to a definite end, and after a few years in retreat, he accepted a position under the conquerors. He is reputed to have painted many pictures of horses which might have pleased the conquerors, and his signature can be found on a large number of provocative ones that are not even typical of his era. A fragment in the former Stoclet Collection might possibly be an authentic Mêng-fu: it shows two grazing horses. One can almost feel their weight, smell them, hear their breathing. We are just as uncertain about Mêng-fu's landscape painting. In reducing the words of all contemporary witnesses, ancient attributions, and the supposed copies to their simplest form, we can envisage these paintings by Mêng-fu as having been fairly realistic, and having a faint touch of naïveté forgotten by the Sung. Another trap we have to be careful of is that of painters who worked in the same style, such as Yen Li-pên during the T'ang era, Li Lung-mien (Li Kung-lin) under the Northern Sung, and Chao Mêng-fu under the Yüan. They all seem to have been fully aware of what they were doing. Their versatility, corroborated by texts and copies, makes the reconstruction of their personalities even more difficult.

Perhaps it was the current of fresh air introduced by the Mongols that produced, slightly before the arrival of the Ming in 1368, the revivification that the art of painting was in need of at the time. This "rebirth" came from neither the professional painters nor the Ch'an monks, but from the gentlemen collectors and painters (of whom Chao Mêng-fu was eminently representative), who were looking for a means of personal expression through painting, as others did through poetry and music. One must emphasize that their lyricism does not give the feeling of emotional liberation as does the European. The Chinese were not preoccupied with religion and women. Humanity, therefore, is always given a modest place in nature; it is nature herself who is the most important subject for contemplation. However, the Chinese have never been servile in their attitude toward nature. As far as I know, there is no evidence of a Chinese painter having made a documentary sketch of nature; nor would it be conceivable for an artist to take a sketch pad into the open air and draw from nature. This "imitation drawing" would have even been a hindrance to the artist, who was reaching for an inner truth of greater proportion and depth. Having made these reservations, one can, nevertheless, mention that during the fourteenth century Chinese landscape art attained a feeling of the outdoors that only came to our art during the nineteenth century and which is superior to the little notes made by a Poussin, for instance, to indicate the Roman countryside. "During his leisure time, Kao K'o-kung took his stick, a bottle of wine, some rice, and a volume of poetry, and went out to sit on the banks of the Tsien Tang [the neighboring estuary of the Hang-Chou]. He would contemplate the hills, observe the changing effects of clouds and mist. When he returned home, if he was not too busy with administrative or literary work, he would pick up a paintbrush and express in painting his innermost feelings." We owe our information on the painter to the writing of a friend of his, Ni Tsan, another gentleman painter, the luminosity of whose landscapes immediately seduces us. Ni Tsan's very personal style is not mannered, and we think highly of his work because he was exceptionally skillful at rendering a calm autumn evening and because his rather low-placed horizons, which we are accustomed to in European paintings, do not upset our eyes. It was said that he enjoyed traveling by lake or canal in the company of fishermen. His line is sensitive, like pastel work, and has no virtuoso affectation whatsoever. One might also add that the greatest

Chinese art collectors thought as highly of him as we do. And yet, they went further in their praise because they also had a profound respect for his moral personality. The same atmosphere of serenity and simplicity can be seen in the landscapes of his eldest son, Huang Kung-wang, "a sort of Cézanne of his time" (Sirén), a selfish, obstinate man, who was also on occasion rather maladroit. Among this pleiad of great late Yüan landscape artists perhaps Wu Chen was the most admired by later generations. And yet today he is not considered the most original, despite the richness and expressiveness of his washes which epitomize the greatest masters of all periods.

The whole of this generation seems to have been concerned with an examination of the ancient traditions. The artists had been more or less confused by foreign oppression, though more seriously by the intrusion of Buddhism. The extent to which Buddhism was adventitious can be traced from the early sculptures to the Sung epoch. The Ch'an, so little affected by Buddhism, had a far greater influence simply because it was of Chinese origin. Towards its decline, the old autochthonous Taoism regained some of its previous vitality. Even Confucianism came into its own again; Chu Hsi had just endowed it with a metaphysic that had previously failed to make an appearance. One cannot help feeling that certain European authors have been mistaken in straining their ingenuity to explain Sung painting in terms of Buddhism. In support of their theories they have been forced to invent a Buddhism that never existed anywhere, let alone in China. The Ch'an, which is by no means synonymous with Buddhism, has come to be known to us through well-documented essays Dr. D. T. Suzuki wrote for the American audience. However, when we study his books closely, Suzuki presents quite a different story, a really strange and somewhat forbidding one. In other words, we think that Southern Sung is a product of the global psyche of the period, to which the Ch'an, and not Buddhism, had for some time added a particular flavor. For our part, we know of no text that attests to a lesser contact between the Ch'an and painting.

PAINTING IN THE MING (1368–1644) AND CH'ING (1644–1912) PERIODS
Plates 25–27

In 1368 a new national dynasty, the Ming, liberated China from the Mongol supremacy. This dynasty was to rule for more than three centuries and was responsible for the heights attained by two Chinese art forms: ceramics and painting. Painting was always favored at court; however, this official centralization was much less marked than it was under the T'ang and Sung dynasties. The most exciting painting was done a long way from Peking in the area near the mouth of the Yangtze River, which had been the real repository of Chinese culture since the period of the Three Kingdoms. China is without a doubt the only country that had a nonprofessional art movement that was handed down from generation to generation by her intellectual elite and her art lovers. One hesitates to use the words "art lovers" and "amateurs" because of their current derogatory sense: they are poor words to describe the Chinese genius, and their understanding of the profession. Yet one has the distinct feeling that the particular quality of their painting was due precisely to their cultural background. By a curious reversal of the situation, a few professionals of great talent were considered the outsiders.

The return to the past, which marked the event of the Ming dynasty, was not only a return to naïveté. The surrealist tradition was continued by artists of the first rank, among them Wang Meng, who died in 1385, the subsequent generation, then Che Juei, Ho Ch'eng, and many others. It is difficult to write about the nature of these amazing works of art. Most of them express the remarkable liberation, the enlarging of the spirit, advocated by all Far Eastern thinkers: the moksha of Hinduism, the nirvana of Buddhism and the Chinese philosopher's tao. It is impossible to escape from the journey that nearly always leads us into the depths of a ravine, that forces us slowly, slowly to climb terraced mountains that look like a staircase to the skies, and finally leads us to the summit, where we feel as free as pure spirits. Also, these paintings, of such elevated inspiration, are never cold abstractions. The Chinese artist always thinks concretely, being careful to make a picture whose composition and details are quite positive. The words we have just used were inspired by the paintings of Wang Meng. His works in the Museum of the Manchu Family in Peking is perhaps less ambitious. The whole canvas is turbulent, like the water in the foreground, the roaring of which can almost be heard. We can feel the freshness rising from the torrent; we are blinded by the limpid quality of the sky.

Tai Chin had a style that was new in form if not in spirit. It can be seen in a sketch of a limited landscape, spontaneous, but certainly drawn from memory, and washed with a few tones of water color that are always the same—indigo, Pozzuoli red, and Indian yellow. These few colors are sufficient for our imagination to reconstruct the colors of nature. We now find this technique, where the values are established by India ink rather than color, replacing more and more often the monochrome wash favored by the Sung artists. This was the last technical advance made by the old tradition.

One could legitimately make the objection that the artistry of most of these great landscape painters was full of mannerisms. In Wang's "Ravine," for example (Stockholm Museum), the brushwood attached to the rock formation on the cliffs forms little square packets that give the picture an air of being almost like precious marquetry of some kind. Li Tsai (fifteenth century)—born in Fukien Province though he worked mostly in Yunnan—is famous for his delicate snowscapes, which accentuate slender trees and bushes almost buried in snow. In short, the natural landscape underwent a transposition almost as great as if it were interpreted by a musician.

Chinese painting was ridiculed by Europeans who did not as yet know anything about her masterpieces —particularly when they translated the lists of mannerisms that were made up precisely during this creative period with which we are concerned. In the lists were, for example, the eighteen types of line that could outline a face and the sixteen varieties of "wrinkles" that could be used to outline the substance of a mountain. In actual fact these were not so much precepts as they were the repertoire of styles established by analyzing past masters. In other words, they were susceptible to change, and were indispensable to the transposition we were talking about.

However, there is another "landscape principle" that the Chinese theoreticians do not seem to have made into a formula. At least from the early Sung period, it was noticed that composition always consisted of a few lines, or primary indications, that constituted the "bones" of the picture. All the secondary lines were parallel to the composition. The parallels, which the French École des Beaux Arts so roundly condemned fifty years ago, constitute the decorative force, and almost the *raison d'être* of Chinese landscape art. The proportions and the celebrated "golden section" (that preoccupation of our young painters) do not seem to have played as important a role as this scheme implies.

At this point, our main concern is with landscape art. As we have already mentioned, progress in Chinese figure painting came to a halt very early in the history of Chinese art, and there was no further advancement after Yen Li-pên during the seventh century. His figures were well drawn, and inasmuch as they were portraits, they were perfect. However, the volume, weight, and balance of the body and limbs were never quite realized. This is obviously the reason why sculptures in which several figures are joined together to form a single composition are rare. There is probably no better example than "The Palanquin Porters," shown in a scroll by Ku K'ai-chih. The Chinese were not as skillful in grouping a composition of figures as were the Japanese. This inferiority is evident not only in figure drawing; it also becomes apparent the moment the figure in a landscape plays a more important role than that of a simple intellectual indication. When this happens, the figures seem either too large or too small, superfluous, and often unnatural. Thus, relegated to an inferior position in the arts because of its mediocrity, figure painting was suspect to the great Chinese connoisseurs. "It is good enough to amuse the bourgeois," said one of them. During the first half of the sixteenth century, Ch'iu Ying, a productive and versatile painter, painted all the ancient subjects, giving them grace once again, and modernizing them. There are collections in Paris that contain uneven examples of his work. The best examples of his painting are highly skillful and charming, although they cannot be compared with the landscapes we have already written about. Ch'iu Ying's landscapes are little short of decoration, though he has the merit of being unconventional. This painter was the precursor to a period that was to attain its culminating point during the first decades of the seventeenth century, when painting was, to some extent, vulgarized, and lost much of its beauty.

T'ang Yin's varied work gives the appearance of using the richest and most attractive characteristics of Ming painting. He was not an innovator, but his paintings were full of piquant and personal ideas, particularly his crowded ones. In comparison to his knowledgeable landscapes, his figure work still gives an archaic appearance.

The decorative painters of birds and flowers form a minor though not inconsiderable group among late Ming artists. They worked either in warm and fine color harmonies, or monochrome wash. Rich and detailed, these compositions are as flat as tapestries. We have no equivalent of this genre in our classical painting.

We will see that some restrictive subjects which might have pleased the Sung symbolist period now serve as support for pictorial research. "The Banana Leaves" by Sin Wei (Guimet Museum, sixteenth century) would be of little interest to a botanist, but they make an attractive play of blacks and silver-gray. For some time, in the pictures of dragons, for example, the Chinese painters were even more abstract than our abstractionists, and interesting drawings of this nature were produced in large quantities toward the end of the seventeenth century.

In the meantime, landscape painting, or *Shan-shui*—still "mountains and water"—continued to develop, for the great men of the time poured into it all their imaginative powers, their religious sentiment, and their feelings for beauty. The group of learned and intellectual painters was known as the Wu school. (Wu was the ancient name given to the Nanking and Soochow region). The school of professional painters was known as the Chou (that is to say, of Chou-kang, north of the Yangtze River). Several wealthy members of the Wu school possessed beautiful collections of ancient paintings. They delighted in spending their time studying, comparing the paintings, and trying to classify the masters of the past.

During the early part of the sixteenth century, even the head of the senate was a good painter. Since the T'ang period, we have seen the development of two highly divergent persuasions. One involved the use of color, embellishment, fantasy, and what we have called, for the sake of giving it a name, a certain surrealist manner. The other was concerned with monochrome, with observing nature, though bringing to the latter certain dreamlike mental attitudes that were meditative and introspective. These two styles were named the school of the North and the school of the South, respectively. However, their nomenclature had nothing to do with the vicissitudes of the Sung dynasty; but was borrowed from an ancient subdivision of the Ch'an sect in China.

The term *Wên-jên hua*, meaning the painting of wise men, came into use during the mid-Wu period. This term refers specifically to amateur painting which we know had existed ever since the T'ang epoch. Needless to say, this placing of amateurs in a category above the professionals was in some instances quite unjust. The great Wu Tao-tzu, a professional if there ever was one, was an innovator, while the dilettante Emperor Hui-tsung was rather bourgeois in his tastes. Although it is hard to define the objectives of the art of the intellectuals, we are aware of the value of their individuality and spontaneity.

Elegantly written discussions and commentaries on the past were composed during the early decades of the seventeenth century at Hua-ting, (actually Sung-chiang), southwest of Shanghai. They were held at the house of Tung Ch'i-ch'ang and his friends. These documents have been translated by Sirén along with many other texts of the same period. They deceive the European reader, who expects to learn about pictures from them, almost as much as he is deceived when our painters such as Leonardo and Delacroix write on painting. Furthermore, these Chinese experts strike us as having been neither clairvoyant nor analytical toward the masters of the high periods, examples of whose works they probably still possessed, but which have disappeared today. They repeatedly declared that the old masters—even and particularly the four "greats" of the Yüan period—would never be equaled. Their pessimism was somewhat uncalled for, however, since for another hundred years, first-class painting was still to come out of China.

It appears that they were very much aware that *k'i yun* was to be aimed at; Mo shih-lung, Tung Ch'i-ch'ang's friend, made lucid observations on the incompatability between *k'i yun* and virtuosity. However, they were still rather stifled by the weight of their invention, the "rules of art." It is hardly surprising that the second-rate artists produced paintings that seem to us banal and *déjà vus*; that they reflected, not as in our case, the fashion of a generation, but rather the accumulation of several centuries of painting. Once, during a lecture at the École du Louvre, when we had slides of minor works by artists of the late Ming period, we were shown at the end of the lecture a painting by Claude Lorrain, who was a contemporary of the Chinese Ming. The picture was absolutely first-rate; an Italian landscape without any architecture, without a sunset. The audience received a profound shock. It was as if the French master had raped us, had brought us brutally, far too quickly, toward a dead horizon, and then left us to meander slowly toward the trees in the left middle ground, toward the water reflecting the trees in the middle of the canvas, and then to the superfluous figures. We felt as if we had been cheated of the courteous greeting, the pleasant hospitality, of the Chinese landscape, present even in inferior work. For they not only invite and guide us through their intricacies, but also give us a feeling of spiritual growth, always driving us higher and onward. The few weeks required to grow accustomed to the conventions of Chinese art were sufficient to make a French masterpiece appear almost barbaric to us.

THE CH'ING EPOCH

Plate 28

In 1644, Peking was captured by the Manchus, and the empire was once again in the hands of a foreign dynasty, the Ch'ing, which lasted until 1912. The conquerors had great respect for Chinese institutions. The first Europeans to observe the Chinese vitality and ability to rekindle its genius were wrong to consider the Ch'ing conservative and reactionary. The first emperors of the dynasty, after the second, K'ang-hsi, Yung Chêng and Ch'ien Lung, were great art patrons. On the whole, they preferred the most traditional of the paintings, though the new tendencies did not just fade away in the emperor's court. The flowering of painting was so abundant and so varied that it would be impossible to summarize it here. Therefore, we will just mention a few of the period's important artistic movements.

First, comes the group of painters who, because of the turn of political events, were forced to retire into solitude, or to hide within the "resistance," a period

that lasted twenty to thirty years in southern China.
The absence of social life and the peace of meditation
resulted, for some of them, in a boldness of style like
that of the Fauves, a boldness no other painters had
tried until then. Chu Ta, who took the *hao* (professional name) of Pa-ta Shan-jên, "the hermit of the
eight cardinal perfections," was a most eccentric artist.
Although we have several landscapes by this artist
which, traditional in concept and execution, have a re-
freshing air, he is, nevertheless, particularly famous for
his wash drawings whose originality was not even understood by his contemporaries. This work, and his
contemporary's, Fouchan's, broke completely with traditional styles and the system of masses and values to
which we have grown accustomed in Ming painting.
However, some pages in sketchbooks, quick drawings
of lotuses, insects and birds, etc., have the undeniable
charm of spontaneity and freshness.

Tao-Chi (Shih-t'ao) who, like many fine men of his
time, was both Taoist and Ch'an Buddhist, resembles
Pa-ta Shan-jên in many ways. He painted in many different styles and varied his subject matter. In his writings, highly critical of the rules of painting, he wrote
that the best way to simulate the "heart" of the an-
cients was to be as original as they had been. To copy
their methods which, after all, were established long
after they had first been developed, was self-defeating.
This attitude of revolt is sufficiently novel to merit
mention, and it should be noted that subsequent generations did not copy his work. Another very fine but
less revolutionary painter of the same group was K'un-
ts'an, who worked in the grand manner of Wang
Meng. Traces of Taoist and Ch'an thought can be
found in the many works of Wu Li, who, curiously
enough, became a Jesuit, taking the name of Father
d'Acunha. He went to Rome, a journey that was re-

sponsible for the legend of his disappearance into the West, like another Lao-tzu. During the period that he spent with the Catholics, he continued doing highly inspired and free painting that was purely Chinese. A singular painting, dating 1703, made when the artist was seventy-one years old, has survived. It shows a number of *Jesus naturae* which had previously and mistakenly been thought of as Kuan-yin and his acolytes. His interpretation of rocky pinnacles, like pictures concealed in the veinings of wood, evokes a mysterious fascination.

During the reign of K'ang-hsi, the club of dilettante critics of "Wu" continued to prosper under the leadership of the "Four Wangs": the two elder Wangs, Wang Shih-min and Wang Chien, Wang Hui, and the grandson of Wang Shih-min, Wang Yüan-ch'i. These critics were excellent painters, but their originality does not seem to justify the very important position the Chinese assigned to them in their history of painting. A hundred years later, the "minor Wangs" were numberless. In fact, this school looked upon itself as having a mission to further Yüan and Ming painting. Rather than reproach it for its conservative outlook we might well admire it for its vitality.

Yün Shou-p'ing, who met with tremendous success during his lifetime, is far more representative of the new order. His success continued even after his death, and we find his paintings often reproduced in woodcuts. He might have been a first-class landscape artist, but due to his admiration for Wang Hui, his friend, whom he considered unsurpassable in this genre, he turned to flower painting. His flower compositions, realistic, natural, and highly decorative, must have been the chief source of inspiration to the ceramic decorators of the Ch'ien-lung period.

Shortly before the end of the Ming period, the

movement veered toward a graceful art rather than an essentially poetic art. Toward the beginning of the eighteenth century, this change seems to have been accelerated. Charming feminine subjects, with undertones of gallantry, the speciality of Long Mien, who was appointed court painter in 1713, were very popular. He created an undulating and mellifluous, supple style that had considerable grace. His models were wellborn young ladies whom he painted sitting idle in a palatial interior or in a garden. Or he would paint the lady magicians of the Taoist legends, dressed as Manchu princesses. These paintings, stylistically rather superficial, were, nevertheless, highly original.

Also, during the same period, one must mention the transient European influences, in this same circle, of Jesuit teaching. Toward the end of the sixteenth century, Father Mateo Ricci (Li Ma-tou), astronomer and geographer, demonstrated the laws of Western perspective and modeling. The Chinese admired the engravings of Christian religious subjects, but did not copy them. In 1715, Father Giuseppe Castiglione (Lang Shih-ning) arrived in China. He was a skillful painter, and a great admirer—though somewhat conservative —of Chinese painting. He went to a lot of trouble to found an eclectic school which tried to unite the qualities of the two traditions. He gained the favor of the young emperor, Ch'ien-lung, who commissioned him, in a Yen Li-pên manner, to paint the horses that the Tartars had offered as tribute. He fulfilled his task in an excellent scroll-form water color that can be seen in the Guimet Museum. The formula is more Chinese than European in every respect. Father Castiglione shied from all effects of light, and wisely avoided raising any problems of perspective. For this particular task, his European training was reduced to a very fine modeling which nowhere dulls the luminosity of the general effect.

Father Castiglione finally recruited a follower in the person of his colleague, Leng Mei; no one else seemed particularly interested in the project. Even Leng Mei seems not altogether serious when he draws women in the backgrounds with a perspective that hurtles toward infinity. With reference to modeling, we have another work by the same Leng Mei consisting of illustrations (engraved on wood by a professional) in which, objecting to the use of hatching which has always shocked the Chinese, he devised a double line around the flesh of the body. These two lines were drawn thickly and, with the addition of one or two very fine lines, gave the illusion of being three-dimensional.

The Jesuits stubbornly insisted upon teaching a form of modeling that disgusted the Chinese. Two generations later, under the direction of Father Attiret (Wang Chih-ch'eng), the Jesuits made their pupils paint documentaries of the Peking court in gouache which were later to be engraved in France. The dark values are oppressive and poorly felt. The only mark left by European innovations was in the xylographs, a branch of popular engraving, which were crudely colored by hand, depicting young ladies in luxurious backgrounds. They were perhaps directly inspired by the Leng Mei style of painting; perhaps it was believed that the European perspective might amuse the clients as a curiosity, as it had in Japan after 1740.

Chinese painting created nothing new during the rest of the Ch'ing period. There were more painters than ever before, and their goal was to emulate the Yüan masters, an ambition fostered by the great admirers of the Yüan style, the Wu school. The period produced a mass of exquisite work which Europe is only just beginning to explore.

After the Yüan period, great advances were made in the painting of nature, which became infinitely more varied and delicate than the list of "Six Wrinkles" might suggest. The repertoire of these wrinkles consisted of leaves, rocks, etc., which were often used in illustrated books. During the last few centuries, many Chinese painters have achieved a great sensitivity in the painting of the warm, velvetlike quality of moss and grass under trees. (Courbet is their only rival.) Even in their monochrome washes, the varieties of foliage are more highly colored and realistic than those painted by Western landscape artists. We savor the same pleasant sensation in many of these pictures, even though the subject matter is of little interest to us. For example, we have K'i P'ei's (early eighteenth century) "Fish," in which the waving disquieting movement of the seaweed, the underwater luminosity, the supple and muscled silver belly of the fish, and their slow and darting movements almost give the impression of pulsating.

Another of the merits of the painting of recent centuries is that it has managed to establish the foreground more successfully than did the Sung, who too often were content with just contrasting it to the background. One might say that this was an orchestral advance; the primitive polyphony was sometimes rather hollow. Perhaps the rising mists that so often appear in landscapes can form a steppingstone for the European spectator. Photographs of Chinese landscapes prove that these mists are not imaginary. The good painters used them in a manner that would not alarm us. They strengthen the outlines, introduce restful passages, articulate the composition, and highlight the main parts of the picture by excluding the superfluous. As for the clouds, they were neatly painted somewhat apart from the rest of the picture, appearing only as shadows or reflections in the usual Chinese countryside. The clouds always have supernatural or religious significance.

If we say that many of the grand Ming or Ch'ing landscapes had a dreamlike quality, it must not be interpreted in the banal sense of the word, as meaning "more exquisite than reality." Rather, it should be interpreted as having been a dreamlike experience. For example, in an emotional composition by K'ouen Ch'an (Yamamoto Collection) we have a group of pleasant-looking sun-drenched houses near a lively waterfall. A young servant girl is raking grass under ancient trees. Everything sings of peace and joy. However, much against our will, we are forced to continue our journey. We have several paths from which to choose. We take the first one and it leads to a precipice. So we go by another one, but it becomes impassable. We try to retrace our steps. The innocent-looking rocks we had passed a while ago now seem like ferocious beasts ready to spring. Or again, look at the ravine painted by Kao Ch'i-p'ei (Abe Collection). In the foreground we can see naturalistic rocks and trees leaning over the waterfall. Two people stand on a path that winds around a mountain spur in the center of the picture. What do they see from there?

Dizzying, vast, . . . an abyss bottomless, sublime . . .

(This wash is distinguished by the original distribution of the touches.) Or again, take a look at Fa Jochen's deserted mountain, real enough for trees to grow on it; but as one's glance travels up the mountainside, the rocks take on the shapes of cumulus clouds, shapes that are almost alive, almost terrifying. Suddenly they give the appearance of revolving like suns, going faster and faster. Let us also mention a curious sketch by Huang Tao-cheou (early seventeenth century and in the same museum). In it we can see a small woman seated in the shade of large trees. On the other side of the valley, another person is standing before tall rocks that look like doors. The doors, in turn, look as if they were about to close on him, in the same way as they closed on Wu Tao-tzu.

THE MINOR ARTS OF RECENT CENTURIES

PRINTS

A few pages of prints little known in Europe are to be found in a recently published book. At this point we will mention that though they are less refined than the Japanese prints, they are much more varied in their process. Woodcuts, which were not unlike engravings, were so familiar to the Chinese that they were often preferred to painting. They knew how to vary the effects by using various grains and also different colored inks.

During the Middle Ages, xylography was particularly used for making religious pictures, and like our own, the black-and-white prints were sometimes colored by hand. Even after woodcutting was taught to lay craftsmen, the Chinese rarely made colored plates. Besides, printing was never looked upon as being an art in its own right, independent of devotional, edifying, and didactic connotations. However, during the seventeenth century, handsome still lifes were made, printed with great care in fine colors and even embossed in some sections. A large number of albums were devoted to the vulgarizing of masterpieces of painting, to analyzing the mannerisms of masters, etc. Hardly a European collection is without at least a few engravings torn from the albums *Studio of the Ten Bamboos* and

The Garden of the Mustard Seed, each coming in installments of twenty. They were published from the beginning of the Ch'ing period onward, and were often reprinted, as late as the nineteenth century. It is undeniable that these treatises contributed considerably to the stagnation of painting. During the last century, the Chinese made many lithographs, though not with pencil, as we do, but with thick, undiluted ink. Their work is so neat that it might have been done with India ink. Furthermore, this eliminated the expense of engraving. The most popular art forms, even those on the humblest level, are even in our times engraved on wood and painted either by hand, or by stencil and a few crude colors. However, these engravings do not lack decorative vitality. The French Cabinet d'Estampes recently acquired a famous collection of Chinese prints (given by Atherton Curtis).

SCULPTURE OF RECENT CENTURIES

We have seen that Buddhist sculpture, despite some sublime pieces dating back to the fifth and sixth centuries, remained outside the general area of Chinese art history. When the power of the foreign religion began to diminish, sculpture went back to being purely decorative, which it had been prior to the Buddhist era, and the Chinese did not produce any more sculpture of spiritual import. They excelled in the ornamented bas-relief, rich, full of movement, overcharged and with little variety. When they sculpted in the round, they managed to make disproportionate, often ugly, *bibelots*. The Ming tombs, unfamiliar to most tourists on account of their proximity to Peking, are unworthy of Chinese art. Sculpture played a secondary role for the Ming and the Ch'ing, as if it were merely an accessory to enrich the white marble façades, palace balustrades, and sometimes wooden columns (in the temple of Confucius at Chü-fu [Shantung], for example). The pairs of lions sculpted in the round, the stone lanterns, the petition box, the oil lamps symbolic of the sovereign's justice, all of them made of marble, were little short of being punctuations in a vast architectural plan. G. Ecke and D. Demieville have published pictures of one or two pieces of Ming sculpture kept at Ts'iuan-chou that are more interesting than most, and it is quite possible that there are others in southern China. The supple and enclosed form which was fashionable at the Yung Chêng court appears to have had a fortunate influence on several animal statues, such as the bronze does at the Cernuschi Museum.

The *ming-ch'i*, abandoned during the Sung era (perhaps the most intellectual period of the Chinese psyche), was picked up again during the Ming era. A wave of patriotic enthusiasm called for new ties with the traditions of independent China and the glorious T'ang era. The figurines are now made in series, their clothes enameled in bright green or violet-brown. Despite their obvious quality, they no longer have the smiling and unexpected charm of those of the T'ang era.

ARCHITECTURAL FEATURES

The European preference for Greco-Roman antiquity is perhaps still strong enough for her inhabitants to refuse to give the name of architecture to Chinese construction, which is based on entirely different principles from our own, wood and not stone being the basic material used. The remark has often been made that the methods and techniques of Chinese architecture are re-embodied in our modern techniques of reinforced concrete, for both involve the construction of the entire framework, even the roof, before building the walls. Great attention is given to the vertical and horizontal beams of this framework, with almost complete suppression of oblique and curved elements.

The need to protect the columns, balustrades, wooden frames, trelliswork, and the paper windows from the inclemencies of the weather gave rise to the notable extension of the roof. The overhang, because the roof was always tiled, carried a tremendous weight. Hence the system of brackets so characteristic of Chinese architecture is found even in the most ancient buildings, from the Han period onward. The brackets radiating in four directions stemmed from an abacus or drain tile resting on a column. Each abacus or drain tile supported another drain tile, from which stemmed other brackets. As the centuries went by, the continuous layers of timber multiplied, by two or three during the T'ang era, to seven or nine in recent buildings. These layers play an important decorative role, although a more economical or robust method might have done better. The wooden columns rested on stone pads flush to the terrace. The terrace is highly characteristic of Chinese architecture, while neighboring countries such as Japan and Vietnam used pile foundations.

The layout of buildings, having a religious connotation, including palace reception rooms and audience chambers, is always perfectly symmetrical, if we are to believe the working diagrams of the Peking Palace reconstructed by Europeans. However, we are convinced that even style was bound by certain mathematical theorems. The proportions are large for the Far East, the forms simple, and a wide range of polychrome is used. The roof tiles were enameled yellow; the drain tiles were red and half-hidden in shadow. The terraces were made of white marble.

The building always faced south, the private living quarters north. They were single-storied, for the idea of an intellectually or socially inferior person standing even for one moment above a person of superior quality was intolerable to a Chinese. A palace, therefore, consisted of a series of similar pavilions of varying proportion, some of them connected by covered passageways. Imaginative and asymmetrical styles of architecture were reserved for pleasure houses and were allied to the art of landscape gardening.

The *pcailou* are triumphal arches marking the entrance to certain buildings; for example, the one at the very beautiful Temple of the Sky at Peking, circular in plan, with a blue tiled roof. *Pcailou* were also erected in the center of towns to commemorate the virtues of a particular person. These arches have one, three, or five upper galleries, their piers always rising above lintels.

The construction of ramparts did not change during two to three thousand years. They were built (at least in the north) out of stamped earth; this accounts for their being constructed on a slight incline. They were also faced in brick. Shih Huang Ti is credited with having built the Great Wall, though he probably only joined the scattered fortifications together. The bastions and battlements, vaulted posterns in the middle of each section, and semicircular barbicans have a strong resemblance to medieval fortifications; but ordinary pavilions were erected on Chinese ramparts, serving as arsenals or guardrooms.

The old bridges give the appearance of standing as if by a miracle or by the sheer inertia of the materials used, for only their splendid ornamentation is drafted in arches, and even these seem somewhat irrational. It is true that they did not have to support particularly heavy weights, for freight-carrying vehicles and heavy

chariots had not been invented. In the cities of the
plains like Sou-cheou, canals were spanned by graceful
single-arched bridges, built very high but not strong
enough to support carriages. There is a bridge still
standing at Tsuan-chou which is almost megalithic,
although it only dates back to 1208. The spans are
made of blocks of stone approximately five feet by five
feet seven inches and fifty-nine feet long.

CERAMICS SINCE THE SUNG ERA

We will attempt neither to describe the new techniques nor to name the old workshops; we will try to
enumerate all the genres of Chinese ceramics made in
recent centuries. The subject has been thoroughly
treated by Madeleine David in a monograph that is
readily available. We prefer to single out the forms
that mean something to contemporary taste, and to
defend those that have given pleasure in the past and
are likely to give pleasure to future generations.

There is no new genre that can specifically be called
characteristic of the Yüan period, which lasted under
one hundred years. However, it is probable that the
new Iranian influences arrived during the years when
the commercial routes were safe throughout the vast
Mongol Empire. Cobalt blue (known as Muslim blue)
was imported from faraway places during the early
Ming period; some samples of this pigment were discovered in China, though they were less brilliant and
less pure. In addition to this pigment, the Chinese
ceramists also borrowed nonimitative abstract designs
from the Iranians. We recognize in them the mushroom cloud which Iran herself had borrowed at one
time from China, by confusing the "miraculous cloud"
with the Ling-che mushroom symbol of longevity. A
little later on, the greens and reds appeared. For some
time yet to come, decoration was to have a facile verve

also Iranian in influence. The W*ou-tsai*, "Five Colors," of the mid-Ming epoch represent the heights attained by this art form that was perhaps less profound than the Sung, though even more seductive. Later on, the ceramists became a little too facile. Using a rich palette and having surmounted all the technical difficulties, they went in for extravagant baroque tours de force, such as ewers shaped like cursive characters. Ceramic statuettes modeled in perfect taste and painted Chinese white are almost unpleasant to look at, though they would have been exquisite in ivory, bronze, or wood. The first samples of Chinese white were a little too yellow and too flat. They were nothing like the cold, glowing white developed later. Kuan-yin, the protectress of children, was often depicted. Consequently, the Mother and Child brought to China at this time by the early missionaries were no surprise to the Chinese.

The seventeenth and eighteenth centuries certainly did not see a decline in the art of ceramics. On the contrary, new techniques evolved and new shapes and decorations came one after the other. Most European collectors consider the K'ang-hsi and Chien-lung periods as the greatest eras of Chinese porcelain. And yet, the decorative art of these periods seems quite different in comparison to that of previous eras. The most beautiful of these vases is no longer a complete work of art in itself. It demands that its surroundings be as stately as itself, and this is as true in their country of origin as in our houses, where they seem exotic. They often come in pairs. Singly, they have little decorative power. They always seem to be echoing the forms of past periods, such as the *li*, *tsun*, and *yi* bronzes, and even *ts'ung* jade. There is nothing intimate about them, nothing individualistic.

During the seventeenth century, new effects were

achieved with cobalt blue by using it mostly as a base, with white decoration superimposed. The coloring of K'ang-hsi enamels is exquisite, deep and rich in harmonies, made of pure pigment applied on vases of simple form. On occasion, two shades of the same color are carefully mixed, causing a vibration similar to a tremolo in music. In short this was an adaptation and development of a Sung idea, and quite foreign to the general decorative tendencies of Ch'ing art.

A different spirit lies behind the *famille vert* vases, typical of K'ang-hsi's long reign. Picturesque subjects, often including a number of multicolored figures, are painted in areas of varying size with "frames" of such dense foliage that green becomes the predominant color. To harmonize the whole, the drawing is outlined with exceedingly thin black lines—visible only close up. Without them, the total effect would be drab. The colors of the enamels are now gemlike.

The pinks, with gold glazed background, which were beginning to appear in the *famille vert*, became the dominant colors of the *famille rose*. The *famille rose* is characteristic of the eighteenth century. However, in addition to this inversion of color, the style also changed radically. The dense crowded composition of the K'ang-hsi era is exchanged for light airy schemata that allow the background to breathe. The change in style that occurred during the first third of the T'ang epoch seems to repeat itself during the first third of the Ch'ing epoch. The floral ornamentations (branches of plum blossom, cherry blossom, peonies, etc.) are realistic and so well drawn that they need concede nothing to the better pictures of this genre that were first painted by Yun Shou-p'ing. The figures, if there are any, weave about with ease. The overloading and symmetry are replaced by the balancing of masses, and it is generally thought that this departure was of Japanese influence. Japan had learned the secrets of the art of making porcelain during the seventeenth century, and some of their ceramics, like the magnificent Nabeshima, found their way even into China. The term "orange skin" is used to refer to smooth and granulous surfaces that give life to white backgrounds. The *famille noire* and *famille jaune* were developed under Yung-chêng and Ch'ien-lung. These two colors dominated the background, though the style was the same as the *famille rose*.

After the long reign of Ch'ien-lung, Chinese ceramics produced no new decoration, and the quality of the work slowly declined.

Our own rather blasé era finds a great deal of charm in the porcelains that the Chinese made for the European market and in which they transmuted Christian and mythological subjects in their own manner. These were not even popular in China herself. The Chinese resistance to our art must have astonished the missionaries who were so convinced of its "truth" and superiority. Europe has only now begun to understand the Chinese point of view after finding out about their tremendous cultural and artistic history.

THE OBJETS D'ART

The reader will forgive us for not mentioning at this point the modern *bibelots*—often manufactured for the foreign market—that are still looked upon by many Europeans as Chinese art. Among these are jade and stone copies of ritual bronzes, statuettes, and rock crystal trees. All the motifs that China has produced during three thousand years are to be found in these almost styleless, though nevertheless quite pleasant, imitations.

Unfortunately, this shoddy stuff often prevents us from being just to the art of the Ch'ing period, which had excelled in all that was luxurious, decorative, or sometimes merely pretty. The American museums already prize its embroidery, brocades, and fine silk tapestries, called *k'o-sseu*, which use a stitch identical to that of the Gobelin tapestries. Since the Sung epoch, if not earlier, the Chinese have made small, very delicate pictures in *k'o-sseu*. We all know the enchanting little bags that were made to protect the "Peking glass" tobacco jars, those little flasks of chiseled polychromed glass.

The screens erroneously called "Coramandle screens" have become fashionable again in our era. They were probably at best the ceremonial art of the Ch'ing era. Their surfaces are both flat and monumental. Incisions made on the bias give added vigor to straight lines that form the basic outline of the composition. A generous use of whites and blacks supplies the needed quiet areas in the midst of polychrome.

Chinese furniture does not harmonize very well with our own because of the hardwoods that were used. Also, it is difficult to orient our cabinetmakers toward a similar elegance of line, and away from variations in mass or the richness of surfaces.

Popular Chinese art has yet to be discovered. It is probably not as refined as Japanese. The Chinese masterpieces, unlike the Japanese, as we shall see, were always being produced for the elite—if not for the noble elite, for the intellectual elite.

We have made a rapid journey through three long millenniums, during which Chinese art demonstrated a vitality, richness, and variety that, in our opinion, has no equal in the history of the world—not even in the magnificent art of ancient Egypt and Iran. Is China likely to produce any more art? The violent intrusion of Europe during the nineteenth century caused an evolutionary crisis which has not yet been surmounted.

The Chinese painters who have exhibited in Paris fairly frequently during these past years have proved to be faithful heirs to their national tradition, while at the same time determined to search for new forms. Others have taken over the methods and formulas of European art. None of them seems to have either managed or indeed attempted to synthesize the two traditions, and yet the Chinese art of the future is bound to be influenced by Western painting. However, as we mentioned at the beginning of this section, the rhythm and evolution of China cannot be measured by one generation, or even two or three. In a century or two from now, the present crisis will doubtless be reduced to the proportion of so many others that China has already managed to overcome.

KOREAN ART

Of all the countries stemming from Chinese civilization, Korea is perhaps the country that, over the years, has best preserved and refined her individual genius, despite her having gained nothing from her insular neighbor, Japan. Her maritime climate is generally colder than China's; her geological structure principally granite. Her ancestry is not Chinese, but Siberian. In short, Korea is in some ways like a Britain of the Far East. These characteristics have imprinted a distinctive personality on all her art forms, which—apart from ceramics and, on occasion, sculpture—have both a provincial and an exceptionally robust, logical, and harmonious quality.

Our knowledge of this art stems almost entirely from studies made by Japanese experts. From about 1909, and particularly between the two world wars, they undertook scientific excavations and studied ancient monuments. This very detailed research fills large albums in the series *Chôsen Koseki zufu,* and a number of other publications. The volumes available in a European language are, on the whole, incomplete and uncoordinated, and include only one attempt to produce a general survey of the subject. This was made by the German missionary Andreas Eckardt in 1929 and was translated into English as *Korean Art.* The book is well illustrated but the plan is very confusing and the text not particularly instructive. A comprehensive history of Korean art, describing the native heritage on the one hand, and the borrowing from China and Asia on the other, has yet to be written. While Korean art is well represented in Korean and Japanese collections, there is very little of it in European museums. There is also a linguistic problem to surmount in the study of Ko-

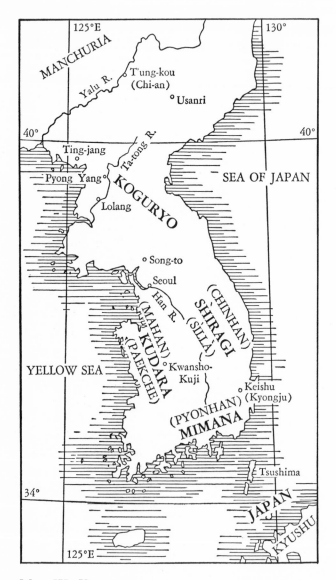

MAP III. KOREA

rean art. Korean proper names are written in Chinese characters. Eckardt cites them in a logical manner, using the Korean pronunciation, which few Europeans have studied. Chinese pronunciation is decidedly more intelligible. However, Japanese writers only use Sino-Japanese, which, on account of the numerous etymons, is extremely confusing. It would be impractical to give each name all three pronunciations, and the reader will surely forgive us certain inconsistencies. For instance, the most important discoveries are known to the entire world by their Japanese names, and we will use these.

There are no affinities between the monuments of the Korean-Manchurian region of precivilization and those of China's high antiquity. On the other hand, we do realize their similarity to the prototypes of the neolithic culture, which is also that of Japan during the present millennium. As we will see in the case of Japan, a culture quite independent of China seems to have existed for some time during the third century in the insular and continental coastal regions around the Sea of Japan. Korean and Manchurian antiquities are also of major interest to Japanese archaeologists. But there is no reason to describe them here since the most typical examples of these objects are well represented in Japan.

In the meantime, during the four or five centuries before our millennium, Chinese civilization was already moving into the Gulf of Pe-chih-li. We have mentioned the degenerate but interesting painted pottery discovered at Pi-tzu-wo. Large quantities of *ming mao*, bronze money in the form of knives with bronze handles pierced with holes, have been discovered in northwest Korea. But we are already in the Han era. Between 108 and 107 B.C. China conquered the peninsula. The permanent Chinese occupation was paradoxical.

(One of the commanderies, Lolang—in Korean, Nang-nang; in Japanese, Rakuro—held out until 313.) The conquerors did not introduce a rustic frontier civiliza-tion into the region—they brought with them the most refined luxury from the capital, and many objects made at the imperial workshops, as attested by inscrip-tions dated from 85 B.C. to 69 A.D. Was it considered an honor for high-ranking noblemen to be sent to com-mand a garrison in the country of the "Morning Fresh-ness" (Chosen)? Whatever the reason, metropolitan luxury-living was restricted to the Chinese colony in Korea. This is why the contents of the Lolang sepul-cher are of interest to Chinese art history only. The tomb construction at Lolang stemmed from the Chi-nese tradition, while at the same time we find a few characteristics that were perhaps regional and cannot be seen in Han or Tonkin tombs. Native Korea was not civilized by the Chinese colony. Her general cultural character did not begin to emerge until her conversion to Buddhism during the fourth century.

THE KOGURYO MONUMENTS

Koguryo was a fairly powerful kingdom established during the first century B.C., to the north of the Chi-nese commanderies on the banks of the Yalu. The cap-ital of this kingdom was moved several times. The most important locations were at Chi-an, east of Yuan-jen, on the Yalu and at Pyongyang in the northwest of the peninsula. There are no traces left of these capi-tals, though there are many tombs still standing around the former sites. One of these, known as the "General's Tomb," is situated at Chi-an, near T'ung-kow on the left bank of the Yalu. It is an imposing pyramid, thirteen feet high, and has nine carved stone steps with three triangular buttresses facing each sub-basement. This tomb is the prototype of a long series of royal funerary monuments of a type indigenous to Korea, but which appears to have been an embellishment of the tumulus of Chinese sovereigns. Building stone was scarce in North China, whereas it was plentiful in Korea. As a result, century after century we find granite and marble copies of buildings that the Chinese built of wood, brick, or beaten earth.

In the meantime, there was an autochthonous tradition that is quite different from that of Chinese underground caves. It consisted of a cromlech rising from the ground and topped by a tumulus. The Koguryo built cromlechs until the fourth and fifth centuries. A very fine example (though almost minus its tumulus) is still standing at Unsanri (Fig. 35). Its roof

Fig. 35. Dolmen of Unsanri.

is composed of a single stone table twenty-nine feet by sixteen feet. The late arrival of megalithic construction techniques and their long use in Korea are among the most interesting archaeological characteristics of this country.

The Koguryo maintained their independence until 689. The monuments erected during these last centuries are witness to considerable Sinification. During this period, the most beautiful sculptures are remarkable for their "Indian ceilings" (corbeling), a purely conventional name given to a system of roofing to be seen in many countries where the materials available were not strong or long enough. Flagstones were

placed at 45-degree angles at each intersection of the
hall that was to be roofed, leaving a square-shaped
block at each corner. Each of these angles was in turn
covered by blocks of stone parallel to the sides of the
hall, and so on up to the top. Finally, the area that
was to be covered was reduced in size so that one flag
was sufficient to close the aperture. "Indian roofs" can
be seen in Brahman temples of the Middle Ages, as
well as in Afghanistan and Central Asia. Albert von Le
Coq reports having seen them in houses in Chinese
Turkestan. Children all over the world have played at
"Indian roofing," its ubiquity proving that it must have
been almost universal.

During the late Koguryo period these same tombs
nearly always had a partitioned vestibule and a square
funerary chamber measuring approximately ten feet,
with the distance between the ground and the top
of the "Indian roof" measuring about eleven feet. Often, by way of decoration, the beams, cushions on top
of Y-shaped columns and brackets, were made of stone
instead of wood. Walls were covered with ornamental
and figurative paintings, and one can find in tomb after tomb the same subject matter in the same places,
just as one can in the Han period (Fig. 36). It was
customary to paint the *chen* of the four cardinal
points on the walls. The deceased and his family were
depicted at the foot of the northern wall. Around
them, and on the walls of the entrance tunnel, other
familiar household objects and people were painted:
women, young girls, sometimes a Buddhist priest holding a long-handled incense burner, warriors on richly
caparisoned horses, and figures seated in covered carts
drawn by oxen. The tight-fitting lay costumes are not
Chinese; they are more like those of eastern Europe
than of Central Asia. The women wear tight-fitting

Fig. 36. Interior of a Tomb.

jackets and bell-shaped skirts. The quality of the painting varies considerably. In one group of sepulchers situated north of the Yalu River, all the paintings were
executed with the same childlike hand. But in the area
around the small river Ta-t'sung, the artisans were
men of great talent. Their four *chen* have particularly
grand arabesques. The White Tiger of the West is a
completely imaginary animal, and hard to distinguish
from the Dragon of the East. The Red Phoenix is twice
repeated on both sides of the door that pierces the
southern wall. The Hiuan-wu, a tortoise intertwined
with a serpent, symbol of the North, is even more
beautiful than Wu Tao-tzu's interpretation of the
same subject some two hundred years later. The two-
pillared tomb is particularly well built. The blocks were
so well worked that the joints are invisible, and the
scenes painted right on the stone and not over a coating of something or other are in a better state of preser-

vation than most. The tumulus is no less than 164 feet in diameter.

SHIRAGI ART

South of the Chinese commanderies during the Han era, the peninsula was divided into three kingdoms which, because they had natural boundaries, maintained their autonomy for a long time under different names: they are the "Three Hans" described by Chinese writers.

The kingdom to the west was called Mahan. Its well-watered lowlands were ideally suited for rice-growing. The kingdom to the east, Chinhan, was mountainous, wooded, and cool, on account of sea breezes coming down from Kamchatka. The kingdom to the south was called Pyonhan; one of its coasts was a maze of inlets. On many an occasion in the course of history the area was occupied by the Japanese. Pyonhan also included the small country of Kara, a name that remains in the Japanese language today and means anything thought to come from faraway. The Chinese possessions were poorly defended during the dark years of the Six Dynasties, and in 389 they fell into the hands of Koguryo. The three Han kingdoms were now called: (1) Paekche (in Chinese, Pei-ts'i; to the west), which the Japanese called Kudara; its capital was not far from Seoul; (2) Silla (in Chinese, Chin-lo; in Japanese, Shiragi; to the east); (3) Mimana, or Imna (to the south). Situated opposite Japan, Shiragi had only hostile relations with the archipelago. Because of an imbalance in the distribution of natural resources, they became a warlike and expansionist people. The Kudara feared them even more than the Chinese did. Some historians believe that the Mimana, who always played an unobtrusive role in politics, were a sort of Japanese

protectorate. The Shiragi finally absorbed the other
two kingdoms and defeated the Koguryo in 668.

During the sixth century a mixed Sino-Korean culture was common to all three countries, although Japanese archaeologists have noticed regional differences,
particularly between the Kudara and the others.
Shiragi art remained specifically Korean. The most
spectacular objects derived from Shiragi sculpture were
the tall, gilt bronze crowns, and in one case, a pure
gold crown. Attached vertically to a band, they each
consist of four conventionalized trees with perpendicular branches crowded with pendants made of hard
stone in the shape of dogs, rather like the prehistoric
Japanese *magatama* (crescent jades). In addition to
the branches, there are also two deer antlers attached
to the base of the crown. Then at the back there is a
cock's tail, arching outward, onto which are hung little
gold disks that sparkle with the slightest movement.
These bizarre and imposing crowns have often been
compared—and quite reasonably, too—with the hair
styles of Siberian shamans (priests). The perpendicular schema of the principle ornamentation of these
crowns indicates a style that was much appreciated by
earlier Koreans, for it is to be found in architecture as
well. Crowns of the same genre found in ancient Kudara have less character; they give the appearance of a
concession to Chinese taste. Umehara mentions
briefly that fragments of similar jewelry, the use of
which is unknown, were discovered in Japan.

From the Han epoch onward, Korea had extraordinarily skillful jewelers, who might originally have
come from China. Chinese tombs so rarely escaped
pillage that today there is no basis for comparison.
The Chinese did very fine chainwork, delicately encrusting each link with pearls. The jewelers of the great

Shiragi era (fifth to seventh centuries) made charmingly inventive pendants and earrings, sometimes geometric in pattern, sometimes animal-shaped. We have already mentioned that Korea seems to have had direct access to North and Central Asian art. It is now established that the T'o-pa empire, which formed the link between these three kingdoms, contributed more than China proper to the early stages of Korean sculpture.

Ceramics of the same period had shown no significant progress since prehistoric times. The formulas were the same; so was the discreetly inscribed ornamentation, consisting of stripes, wavy lines, zigzags, etc. Nevertheless, considering the hard quality of the stone, it is possible that they were influenced by Han pottery. The interesting feature of these pieces lies in the fact that they bring to light subsequent progress: there is a remarkable continuity between the barbaric pottery of Korea and the most refined stage of her ceramic art.

BUDDHIST BUILDINGS

We know the sites and names of the first Korean temples, though they have since disappeared. They were copies of those built by the T'o-pa, and made of lightweight materials. Unfortunately for us, Korea did not have any of the limestone grottoes like those at Tunhuang, Yün-kang, and Lung-men. However, the new religion was soon to use granite, the best Shiragi building material. The ancient Punhwangsa Pagoda, a temple in Kyongtyu, is a very curious monument of the transition period. Only three square stories of this pagoda are still standing, the last two smaller than the rest. It is built out of blocks of granite laboriously fashioned into "bricks," which the Chinese used instead of stone. It would be hard to envisage a humbler imitation of the Chang-an pagodas. (The Ta yen t'a is approximately seventy years later.) The large terrace surrounding the pagoda is paved with wide irregular blocks of stone. At the corners are seated Buddhistic lions, "Korean dogs" (Komainu), as the Japanese call them. Dvarapala monoliths in high relief flank the doors on the main floor. Surrounding the base of the main pagoda are a number of smaller decorative pagodas, simple funerary or commemorative monuments built in approximately 600 A.D. Made entirely of granite, they have a megalithic and rectilinear

Fig. 37. Paekche Pagoda.

character that is to be seen nowhere else in Buddhist architecture. Their floors are rectangular prisms separated by slim, horizontal Shiragi-type stone plaques which are usually thicker in Kudara pagodas. Only their slightly curved profile, which gives them their graceful silhouette, prevents these pagodas from looking as if they were built of dominoes (Fig. 37).

At this point, let us mention a secular building that dates back to 641. An observatory (Ch'omsong-dae) now in ruin, situated in Kyonju, is shaped like a milk bottle approximately twenty-four feet high and surmounted by a square platform made of large blocks of stone.

THE PULGUKSA
Plate 29

The most celebrated and curious of all groups of buildings is the Pulguksa ("the monastery in Buddha country"). The main group of buildings rises from a high terrace built of granite. One gains access to it by climbing a double flight of steps supported by stone arches ("Bridge of Violet Clouds" and "Bridge of Green Clouds") leading to the "Porch of Violet Mists." Of the two pagodas, the Sakyamuni stupa (Sokka-t'ap) is conventional, the other a curious "Prabhutaratna stupa" (Tabo-t'ap) which resembles a square bandstand with four flights of nine steps surmounted by a false octagonal "floor" and a "lantern," all made of granite. The pagoda is not ugly; its proportions are graceful, but the building is disconcerting because it is the only one of its kind in existence. The tall sub-basement and the two balconies are to be found much later in the Japanese Buddhistic *tahoto*.

Above the temple and flanking a low hill is a grotto built to shelter a handsome statue of a seated Buddha, around which believers walked (circumambulation).

This Indian rite of *pradakhsina* was soon to be forgotten by Far Eastern Buddhism (Fig. 38). The walls

Fig. 38. Pulguksa.

are covered with bas-reliefs showing the principal Bodhisattvas (Padmapani, Kuan-yin of the Lotus, is particularly handsome). Minor members of the Buddhist pantheon are depicted on the right and left of the small entrance corridor, which looks as if it has recently been restored. We will not pretend that the statues are in the best T'ang eighth-century style. Clearly, however, the use of granite brought about a fortunate simplification of the forms, in the same way that Breton Gothic architecture simplified the Gothic style.

SMALL SCULPTURE
Plates 30 and 31

Whether in stone or in bronze, the proportions of Korean statuary were usually robust, the forms rounded, and the art work primitive, vigorous, and sincere. However, as in China, and more so in Japan, the talent of the artisans was very uneven, and too many mediocre examples spoil our pleasure in the few good ones. It is curious that the Chinese Wei and Sui have never been represented in any of the books on antiquities. It is even stranger when one considers that their presence is inherent in all the early statues made by the Japanese, who in fact were initiated into Buddhism by the Koreans. Although Korea was converted to Buddhism during the end of the fourth century—and as far as we know, pretty thoroughly—examples of Korean Buddhist sculpture date back only to the early part of the seventh century. Korea's national genius was, fortunately, to prevent her from following China into a soft and decadent period toward the end of the T'ang era.

The famous bell at Shiragi, dated 725, is considered the most beautiful of all the Buddhist bells. Like the *chung* of the highest Chinese period, its sides are decorated with four panels, each studded with four rows of nipples. Underneath, modeled in the delicate bas-relief so full of nuance that is the pride of the T'ang epoch, are exquisite drawings of angelic musicians. Their ribbons float vertically like seaweed at the bottom of a fish tank: an extraordinarily beautiful invention of Chinese Buddhist art (Fig. 39). (It was lost during the recent Korean war.)

With the unfortunate disintegration of the wooden temples, all we have left of the flourishing Korean Buddhist art of the seventh to the eleventh centuries are quantities of small funerary pagodas, park lanterns, and stone fountain basins. All have the same rounded and harmonious characteristics, along with that curious, tender air of rusticity which is absent in both Japanese and Chinese art.

At this time, the Korean ceramists adopted the

Fig. 39. Decoration of Bronze Bell. Apsara.

green or rusty yellow of T'ang pottery. While the latter tended to be ordinary in shape, the Korean vases have singularly subtle and pleasant shapes. The prehistoric method of incised ornamentation continued to be employed with simplicity, ingenuity, and extraordinary distinction—indeed, so much so that we ask ourselves if the great revival of Sung ceramic art was not largely the result of the Korean influence.

NORTHEAST KOREA DURING THE ELEVENTH CENTURY

One must remember that the nominal protectorate that Kao Tsung managed to impose on Korea had little effect on her independence. It certainly inclined her toward a cultural exchange with China. The country then became unified under the Koryo dynasty (they took the name of Korai, origin of our word *Korea*). However, the mountainous northern section of the country was little touched by civilization. At Kwanshokuji, in the northern part of ancient Shiragi, a colossal Maitreya was built in 1006. A really barbaric piece of work, it was sculpted out of several enormous blocks of granite which can only have been put in place by building artificial hills or steps as the Maitreya grew taller. And, judging by the photographs, people are unwilling to climb higher than the statue's stomach. An enormous headdress composed of two immense rectangular pieces of stone with bronze ornamentation further accentuated the weirdness and poor quality of this statue.

On the other hand, beautiful pieces of jewelry were made of gold; they represented animals and plants. They are so well fashioned that they almost look as if they were the last stages of Eurasiatic animal art. The future will perhaps reveal some sort of a relationship between this Korean jewelry and Japanese scabbards made during the Ashikaga period, the latter's spirit being similar to the former's.

THE TOMBS OF THE SHIRAGI KINGS

The last kings of Shiragi copied and further developed the traditions of the funerary monuments of which the "General's Tomb" was one of the first most beautiful examples. Seitoku's tumulus (he died in 737) is around seventy-two feet square and approximately fifteen feet high. Its plan is dodecagonal. Between the buttresses that support the wall, metopes carry bas-reliefs of the twelve hourly animals. They are all anthropomorphic, and we can tell only from their heads that they are the bull, the tiger, and the monkey, etc. They are excellent pieces of sculpture, both elegant and monumental. Around the tumulus one can see the remains of a stone wall, two statues of ministers—one military, the other civil—two lions fore and two lions aft, and some steles of which little remains save the traditional tortoise they once supported.

Seitoku's successors commissioned similar tombs.

They became more and more complicated with an ever
increasing number of statues, but the style had lost
much of its vitality.

The kings of the Li dynasty (1392–1910) built
sepulchers that were similar to those of the Ming
emperors, although of smaller proportions. Li Hiao-
ts'ung's completed sepulcher (1673) is still surrounded
by a supporting dodecagonal wall. It is guarded by four
rams and four lions. The site is of great natural beauty.
The queen's tomb, situated on a slightly lower level,
together with her husband's combine to form, according to Sekino Tei, a very striking landscape.

We should also mention a new type of pagoda
which was first built at Seoul during the fourteenth
century. The sub-basement is in the shape of a Greek
cross. The other stories rise in regular quadrangular
prisms—there are four of them at the marble Seoul
Pagoda and six at the Song-to Pagoda.

Buildings in recent centuries naturally repeated well-
known Chinese styles, with perhaps a few embellish-
ments in the plan and elevation. They can usually be
recognized because they are more squat than the Chinese house. As one example, the tiles on Korean
houses were thicker than those used in China. Also,
the bricks supporting the columns were not always
hidden in the foundations. Rather, they formed a
higher base.

Stone bridges imitated Chinese wooden bridges.
There used to be one at Seoul that dated back to the
fourteenth century. Eckardt also reproduced in his
book a very beautiful stone bridge on Quelpart Island
(Saishu To).

All the ancient buildings formed exceedingly picturesque complexes. During the nineteenth century,
the much-impoverished Koreans did no building. The
Japanese in occupation destroyed nothing; in fact they

piously preserved and studied monuments of the past, performing an admirable service to archaeology. But what remained of all those beautiful things after the occupation?

It would be impossible to make a useful summary of the history of Korean ceramics, which reached its zenith between the eleventh and fifteenth centuries (Fig. 40). It had excelled in the prototype genres, or

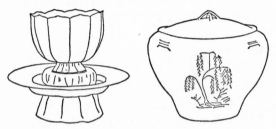

Fig. 40. Korean Ceramics.

those derived from celadon, with enamel work of such sober colors as grays, browns, and blacks. The encrusting of *terres blanches* or *terres noires* on gray backgrounds appears to have been a Korean invention that the Japanese copied in their Mishima-de. The Japanese were always introduced to changes in ceramic styles by the Koreans, not only at the end of the sixteenth century, but more or less throughout history.

There was an obvious incompatibility between the Korean genius and the direction taken by Chinese decorative art toward the end of the Ming period. This accounts for the fact that in the late sixteenth century and the following centuries Korean ceramic art was often of an ugly baroque style that is not redeemed even by the rare quality of the materials used.

The Koreans were good painters. We have ignored many works of art that date prior to the sixteenth century. They have been preserved only because a national tradition did exist side by side with Chinese painting. The best Korean artists were as skillful as the minor Chinese masters. However, the primitive painters are more interesting. They were perhaps not very skillful, but they are delightfully unsophisticated and express themselves with a sincerity and a natural taste that is often lacking in the Chinese painting of later centuries. Korean painters are immediately recognizable by this quality in their work. The high standard of civilization attained by this small country from the fifteenth to the eighteenth centuries inspired respect in the Japanese, and even in the Chinese.

JAPANESE ART

THE ORIGINS

THE NEOLITHIC PERIOD

Japan played no part in the world of Chinese culture until she adopted Chinese civilization and its calligraphy (at a rather late date, the sixth century) as well as the words of the Chinese language that related to the arts, religion, etc. These words doubled the vocabulary of the Japanese language, giving the impression of a linguistic heritage that never existed. During the earliest archaeological era, the archipelago was occupied, at least in the lowlands, by a race of white men who came from Siberia, doubtless via Sakhalin Island. By the beginning of our era, their cultural level seems to have been superior to that of the more recent immigrants, who formed what we now call the Japanese race.

Thus, as A. Leroi-Gourhan shows, the most ancient prehistoric monuments of the archipelago seem, like all those in the North Pacific, to belong to the neolithic culture of these Paleo-Arctic peoples, ancestors of the Ainu. Over the years, the Japanese have gradually unearthed at Hokkaido, the northernmost of the larger islands, objects made of polished stone such as axes, sticks and pestles, etc., of bone, such as harpoons and scrapers; and somewhat vulgar ceramics. There is no reason to believe that they are particularly old. The earliest date one could give them would be during the last centuries of the pre-Christian era.

Somewhat later, they began to develop an interest in artistic design, as seen in the conical-shaped hanging vases with scalloped borders and the almost cylindrical jars with incised decorations and a curiously turned, puddling clay corkscrew pattern. They also made vases that were almost flattened, and furnished with handles and beaks. In the last phase of Ainu pottery, belonging to either the seventh or the eighth century (examples of which are rarely to be found, even in our museums), the paste is hard, fine, and not very glossy, the color brown or dirty yellow, and the ornamentation similar to contemporary wooden sculpture. The Ainu had lost the art of ceramics and never acquired that of metallurgy. When examples were discovered during the last twenty years of the nineteenth century, all this fairly varied neolithic pottery was given the vague name of *jomonshiki* (corded ornamental manner, Fig. 41). By some phenomenon of

Fig. 41. Jomon Pottery.

convergence, this pottery in some of its phases reminds us of certain types of pottery of both South American and Fijian origin.

More indigenous to this culture were the anthropomorphic figurines, two inches high, which we now know represented divinities (Fig. 42). However, the Ainu religious beliefs tell us little about their sculpture, for they let their religion deteriorate as well as their culture. Whether they are clothed or not, these

Fig. 42. Jomon Funerary Figurine.

figurines have the bloated and stocky appearance of Arctic peoples. Vermiform or spiral designs are often found distributed over the body, and are like pseudo-anatomical motifs of shaman costumes (A. Leroi-Gourhan). Apart from the rare "realistic" examples, the heads are disk-shaped. The eyes are either very large and oval-shaped, with lines dividing them in half horizontally, or "owl's" eyes with sunbursts in the middle.

It is curious that such a primitive art should constantly manifest such baroque tendencies. It ignores the restrictions imposed by the technique and materials. In short, they are hardly logical. It attempts to simulate wickerwork and fur in terra cotta. A vase covered with a colonnelted arch of the Katusuzaka variety is loaded with heavy ornamentation that seems to make it thoroughly unusable. Only the pottery of the last phase known as Kamegaoka after the area on the northwest coast of Honshu is really harmonious, consisting of curvilinear areas on smooth surfaces that go well with the robust appearance of the vase. Either there are no animals depicted on the *jomonshiki*, or they are hidden in undecipherable symbols.

MAP IV. JAPAN

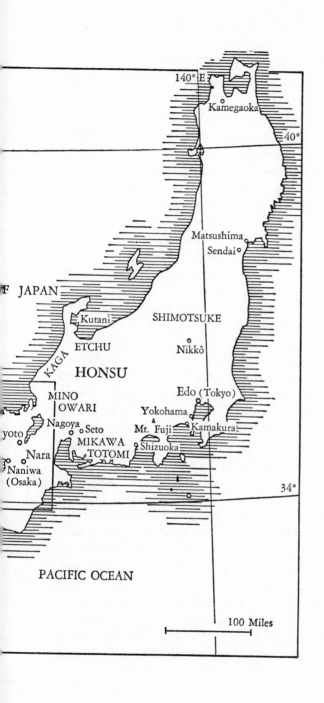

140° E

Kamegaoka

40°

Matsushima
Sendai

F JAPAN

Kutani

SHIMOTSUKE

ETCHU

Nikkô

HONSU

MINO

OWARI

Edo (Tokyo)

Nagoya

Yokohama

yoto

Seto

Mt. Fuji

Kamakura

MIKAWA

Shizuoka

Nara

TOTOMI

Naniwa
(Osaka)

34°

PACIFIC OCEAN

100 Miles

THE APPEARANCE OF THE JAPANESE RACE

Over a period of several hundred years, other inhabitants of the archipelago doubtless arrived in small groups. The first arrivals came from Vietnam and Indonesia, and possibly even from the Pacific islands. The Kuroshiro current carried them from Borneo to the Philippines, from the Philippines to Formosa, and from there to Kyushu via the Ryukyu Islands. Many ancient Japanese customs are reminiscent of Indonesia, notably that of building houses on piles, a system which is still used in Japan today. Matsumoto has listed several hundred Polynesian words in the language. A second wave of migrants came from Korea and were themselves perhaps established for quite some time before the dawn of the pre-Christian era. Although very few Japanese words correspond to Korean, Japanese grammar is based on the same principles as the former, as if the language of the first inhabitants had similar roots to that of the new conquerors. One can still easily distinguish the principal ethnic groups in Japan. The Indonesian Malay has a pale yellow coloring, while the Tongan has a dull brownish complexion. Throughout the centuries, the Chinese were constantly settling in Japan, though their role in creating the Japanese race and its genius seems negligible.

There is no way to establish any correlation between archaeological data and the protohistoric legends handed down by word of mouth, which were finally written down during the eighth century (*Kojiki* and *Nihongi*). They are concerned with only a single line of minor kings. The first "human" emperor, Jimmu Tenno, came from Hyuga (extreme southwest of the archipelago) and his domain was in the central region of the large island at Yamato, south of Lake Biwa. Now that Japanese authors are no longer inclined to accept "official truth" that placed the arrival of Jimmu in 660 B.C., all the experts agree that he could have been a contemporary of Tiberius. The beginnings of Japanese art coincide with those of the bronze age in the archipelago. However, this date is subject to interpretation because Kyushu, along with the mainland, had copper and even iron before the rest of Japan.

NEOLITHIC KOREAN-JAPANESE CULTURE

The pottery of the Bronze age, *yayoishiki* ("germinal"), is named after a street in Tokyo where the first specimen was discovered in 1889. It has a marked resemblance to prehistoric Korean and Manchurian pottery, and is completely different from the final stage of *jomonshiki*, which, as we have already mentioned, was an Ainu art form more than anything else. This Bronze age pottery is logical and simple in shape. The ornamentation is restricted to small incisions, parallel, oblique, and sinuous comb-marks, etc., occasionally with a simple strand of pearls making a ring around the vase. Despite the poor quality of the clay, the shapes are often very elegant (Fig. 43).

Fig. 43. Yayoi Pottery.

The bronze objects are particularly interesting. The weapons, consisting of bayonet-daggers and swords with thick blades (not of Chinese design), were not always imported from the continent, for the stone molds used for casting them have been discovered in Japan. The mirrors are also quite different from those made in China. They are circular, but instead of having one hole in the back they have two or three placed at random. The molding of the frame is a rush design while the flat background is covered with fine parallel stripes, distributed in groups that cross at right angles to each other, giving a most elegant *moiré* appearance. They have not only been discovered in Japan but also in Korea, and even in Siberia at Nikolayevsk of Ussuri, beyond Vladivostok. Vulgar copies of these mirrors made by even less civilized peoples have also been discovered.

In Japan, and only in Japan, another object characteristic of this culture is the *dotaku*, meaning, literally, "a copper sonnet." It is bell-shaped, though it was probably never used as one. The horn is in the shape of a truncated cone with a flat top, and has slightly lenticular segments. A strip of metal binds the bell at its widest point, a halo rather than a handle. The most

Fig. 44. Dotaku. Bronze in the Form of a Bell.

archaic specimen, discovered in the central region (Kyoto), is made of dark-toned thick metal. On it one can see decorations of plants and the fern-leaf pattern, both of which are thought to be fertility symbols. Another type is decorated with water motifs (horizontal broken curves). The third, and the most common, whose patina is always light, has crossed ribbons dividing the sides into rectangles. There is a fine specimen in the Guimet Museum (Fig. 44). The background of this variety often contains childlike drawings in linear relief, in which one can recognize the giant Japanese salamander, a house, a tortoise, the husking of rice, a boat, etc. (Fig. 45).

Fig. 45. Decoration of a Dotaku. Hunting Scene.

Imitating decorated shells, the charming polished stone objects seem to date from this same period (third century). They were also copied in bronze. The *kitsune no kuwa*, "fox-hoes," are shaped like a trapezium pierced with a large hole. We are not sure for what purpose they were used. The *magatama* "curved gems," are carved stones either in the shape of commas, or like the canine teeth of wild animals, or kidney-shaped. They were still worn as part of the regalia by Korean kings during the sixth century (Fig. 46). Were they originally hunting trophies or fertility charms? It is probable that their symbolism changed from century to century and from race to race: the Ainu adopted them too.

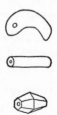

Fig. 46. Magatama. Kudutama and Kirikidama.

This culture, which had been common to all the coastal areas of Japan, was completely forgotten within three centuries. *Dotaku* were discovered by chance in 657 and in 713, and no one in Japan can explain their significance.

THE PROTOHISTORIC PERIOD

The last part of the fourth century marked an important turning point in the history of the archipelago. Buddhism was beginning to spread in Korea, to the great benefit of its civilization. Japan was conscious of its inferiority and sent to Kudara for a few learned gentlemen to serve as teachers and scribes. As they wrote in Chinese, their work also consisted of retranslating these documents orally into Japanese.

THE GREAT SEPULCHERS

The nobility's desire to emulate continental customs was also manifested in the princely tombs of the period (fifth to seventh centuries), which sometimes consisted of immense tumuli. That of Nintoku Tenno, who died in 399, is 1511 feet long. The design is partly circular and partly square in the front and round in the back—or, to be more precise, it has the shape of a key-hole, a design only found in Japan. The design was obviously intended to confer on the tomb the magic properties of *hou*, which imprisoned the demons. On the tumulus itself, and parallel to its outline, stood a row of *haniwa*, closely spaced tubes of baked clay form-ing a fence. The *haniwa* were approximately five feet tall and one inch wide. They may have originally served as guardians, though this idea was obviously aban-doned when it occurred to the Japanese to surmount the *haniwa* with heads made of baked clay, and even with people, standing, seated, climbing, etc. Some-times, they topped them with animals—mainly horses and ducks—and also with inanimate objects such as houses, shields, thrones, boats, etc. It would appear that the Japanese were confusing the Chinese *ming-ch'i* with the latter's guardian animals. The figurative *haniwa* supply us with an amusing and accurate de-scription of the costumes of the period and remarkable masterpieces which we find hard to believe were Jap-anese (Fig. 47). They are well executed, with realistic naïveté which observes the details, though is little concerned with accurate movement.

Princely Japanese sepulchers have never been pil-laged. Our knowledge of their contents results from fortuitous discoveries, for example through landslides. They are the last specimens of cromlechs. It would appear that the cromlech tradition took twelve years to travel from Armorica to Japan, following the south-ern coast lines of Europe and Asia. The Japanese were soon building the sides of tombs out of stones, with-out using any mortar, keeping the large flagstones for the ceilings. The cave is usually long and low, with a transversal tablet in the back. At Kyushu the side walls are covered with rudimentary pictures, in black and white or blue and red, consisting of suns, new "days"

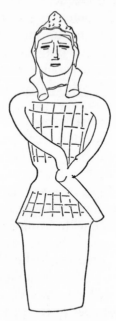

Fig. 47. Haniwa.

for the deceased, spirals placed back to back (fern crosses), triangles, and motifs in the shape of squat pillars with large capitals surmounted by a few parallel lines. The pillars were certainly intended originally to depict archers with their quivers, for it is precisely in the silhouette of several awkward stone statues that the metal armor and other details are worked out accurately.

Inside the tombs, have been found, in addition to sarcophaguses in the shape of houses, a few weapons, cuirasses, helmets, little steles inlaid with silver, and many Chinese, or imitation Chinese, mirrors. Funerary pottery of the variety known as *iwaibeshiki,* "ceremonial vases," was also found. The poor quality of their material is similar to that in our flower pots. A

high foot in the shape of a lighthouse is often pierced
by triangular or trapezoidal windows. There are several spouts on the handle in which were probably
placed artificial globular flowers of white felt, the *tahe*
or *tape* (the Polynesian *tapa*), which are still discussed
in the odes of the *Manyoshu*.

The objects made at this time, very few of which
are really handsome, can be studied only in Japanese
museums. They reflect the culture of a transition
period, in which primitive Japan was doing its best to
interpret a superior civilization it knew very little
about. In this regard the mirrors are worth examining,
for the Chinese motifs and inscriptions were poorly
understood, deformed, and all pirated. The Japanese
casters, on occasion, tried out an original design, such
as the *chokkomon*, a motif consisting of straight and
curved lines copied from the Han · borders. In a
unique specimen, the "stars" of the Chinese mirrors
become bareheaded people miming a hunting scene.
Such a charming and exceptional mirror, probably
made by a Korean artist for a vulgar client, has on each
side of the central square native horses of four different
types; the effect is decorative and the treatment lively.
Of all the objects associated with civilization, the
mirror was the most sought after. Approximately one
thousand authentic and excellent-quality Chinese mirrors have been exhumed in Japan, particularly ones
belonging to the fifth and sixth centuries, along with
a large number of older mirrors, some even dating
to the early Han period, which, old-fashioned and,
incidentally, less handsome, were probably unsalable in
China.

Buddhism, in favor at court since 592, had been
trying to find a means of abolishing the expensive sepulchers. Even so, they were still being built throughout
the seventh century, for the tradition was particularly

tenacious with regard to the funerary rites. This may also be why the contents of the tombs rarely show the influence of Buddhism. Therefore we have both a chronological overlapping and a sharp division between the quasi-savage Japanese tradition and the presence of Buddhism.

We know quite a lot about the prehistoric architecture due to the importance the Japanese attached to the shape of their houses. The support for this idea comes from the pictures we see in a *dokatu* and, later, from the designs of four houses chased either on the backs of mirrors or in the *haniwa* models (Fig. 48). Better

Fig. 48. House. Terra Cotta.

still, we get a good grasp of their real grandeur in certain Shinto sanctuaries, built for the old autochthonous religion that has always been astonishingly conservative; so much so that despite innumerable restorations, the original design has been continued for fourteen to fifteen centuries. The great temple of Izumo (last reconstructed in 1764) is an example of

the most archaic type of all these buildings despite the
disintegration of some of its detail. It consists of a miniature temple made completely of wood, thirty-three
feet square and raised on tall piles. Fifteen feet off the
ground, the floor spreads out into a balcony, the
engawa of an ordinary Japanese house. There are nine
posts at each angle, one in the middle of each elevation and one in the center of the building. The single
door is under one of the gables to the right of the
center post. In order to gain access to the sanctuary
inside, you have to pass around the partition which
joins the central pillar to the left wall. The peak of the
wood is straddled by enormous X's known as the *chigi*,
also made of wood. The *chigi* are the bars which originally were extensions of the rafters. In addition, pieces
of cigar-shaped wood, *katsuogi*, "wooden tunafish," are
placed transversally across the roof, serving to staple
the thatch (Fig. 49). While traveling through Poland

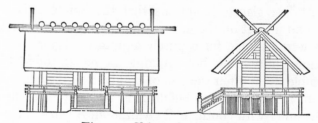

Fig. 49. Shinto Sanctuary.

one hundred years ago, the author's grandfather
sketched the native isbas (log huts) that had the same
characteristics as these Japanese houses. Between the
southern seas and northern Eurasia, Japanese affinities
were always equivocal.

The two famous temples of Ise, which are restored
every twenty years without changing the least detail,
have preserved for us the perfection of a somewhat ear-

lier type. One enters the building through a doorway situated in the center of a long wall on the southern elevation—the result of Chinese influence. There are some differences between the *chigi* and *katsuogi* of the Naigu (inner shrine) and Gegu (outer shrine), but their significance and other details are lost to us today. Each of the small temples is approximately forty feet long and encircled by a quadruple wooden fence. One gains access to these buildings through porches with double lintels known as *torii*, which always denote the presence of a Shinto temple. These primitive *torii* do not have the noble curves with their extremities slightly raised toward the sky that were later borrowed from Chinese architecture. At this point, one must clarify a current error: there is absolutely no connection at all between the *torii* (also known in Korea and in Manchuria in a more rudimentary form) and the Indian Buddhistic torana, unless perhaps in the remote past, which will never be accessible to archaeology.

At first glance, it appears that the Shinto religion had no impact on the history of art. Its rustic sanctuaries were suitable for a purely animistic religion, practicing purity rites, but ignoring all moral codes. Its temples were often the size of bathhouses: they do not seem to have had any buildings at all before their first encounter with continental civilization. A small shelter in the middle of a sacred wood was sufficient to protect the offerings of the devoted. The Shinto religion has always been close to nature and draws its noble character from this intimate association with her purity and authentic savage quality. Indeed, it helps us in understanding the Japanese genius which, throughout the ages, has been able to create something sumptuous and of modest proportions out of the simplest things: to achieve the maximum effect out of very little. Perhaps this is the secret behind the marvelous chawans made

of granite, their two-color prints, their impressive
poems composed of thirty-one or even seventeen syllables.

EARLY BUDDHISM AND THE INFLUENCE
OF CHINESE CIVILIZATION
(Seventh, Eighth, and Ninth Centuries)

THE ASUKA AND HAKUHO PERIODS
(*ca.* 593–710)
Plates 32–35

SHOTOKU TAISHI

Japan adopted the Buddhist faith for political reasons
and with it Chinese civilization. The Korean kingdom
of Paikche, or Kudara, feared the attitude of the Silla
or Shiragi, and hoped to receive assistance from Japan,
the hereditary enemies of the Shiragi. In 552, King
Syong-myong of Kudara sent his ambassadors to the
Japanese Emperor Kimmei. The ambassador was a
priest bearing sacred texts, painted pictures, a Buddhist
statue, and a letter in which the king recommended his
religion as one "that assures unlimited, numberless ad-
vantages." Although his conception of religion might
have been somewhat materialistic, it is still remarkable
that a minor king of that period had the idea of providing a stronger ally with an outline of superior
thought. Yet the Emperor of Japan was far from being
master of his people. He was surrounded by dissident
clans who were constantly revolting. The Mononobe, a
warlike people who dreamed of conquering Korea, and
the Nakatomi, hereditary quasi-priestly officials in
charge of court procedure, were hardly likely to react
favorably toward Buddhism. On the other hand, the
Soga saw in the new religion an opportunity to elimi-

nate their rivals with the help, if the need arose, of one or two assassins. After forty years of seriocomic ups and downs, during which Buddhism was alternately encouraged and persecuted, a young eighteen-year-old prince, whom history knows as Shotoku Taishi, allied to the Soga, called upon the Shitenno—the "Four Lokapala"—for assistance and won a definitive victory. His aunt, the Empress Suiko Tenno, made him her prime minister. An intelligent and virtuous man, Shotoku Taishi understood the tremendous superiority of Buddhism over the completely amoral Shinto. In 607, he issued the seven-article edict in which, with remarkable boldness, considering the era, he posed the idea, in axiomatic form, that civilization and morality should commend themselves to the new religion.

THE HORYUJI

The Prince based his propaganda on charity. The first monastery he built was the Shitennoji at Osaka; it was a sanitarium, dispensary, and medical school. With the help of Korean technicians and monks, several other large temples were built around the year 600. The Horyuji, built in 607, is the only temple which has retained its primitive character (Fig. 50). It was almost

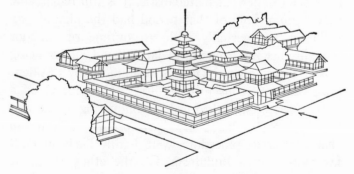

Fig. 50. The Sai-in of Horyuji.

burnt down by lightning in 670, but, until recently, it was believed that a part of the existing structure had escaped the disaster. As a result of further studies, conducted during the war, Japanese archaeologists now admit the building was entirely rebuilt in 670. However, the buildings are still the oldest surviving wooden structures and are invaluable documents for the study of early T'ang architecture, particularly the buildings south of Sai-in.

Apart from dormitories, refectories, kitchens, treasuries, offices, etc., the Horyuji consists of two clusters of buildings: the Sai-in (western foundation) and the To-in (eastern foundation), the latter dating back only to the early eighth century. The Sai-in is a large quadrilateral, oriented in the Chinese fashion from south to north, and surrounded by a cloister, whose roofing rests on columns on one side and on a light wall pierced with windows on the other. The porch (*chūmon*), through which one passes to enter the main building, is four spans wide by three spans deep surmounted by a false floor with a balcony and a "broken roof"; that is to say, a saddleback roof emerging from a lean-to roof of four slopes which is almost a universal form of wooden architecture. The two spans serve as a passageway. Large wooden statues of the Ni-o and Dvarapala, guardians of the door, stand at both ends, and to the left, running along the same horizontal, one can see the wooden pagoda, and to the right, the *Kondo* (golden pavilion), which contains the large iconostasis. The Horyuji pagoda is 115 feet in height including the mast, pleasantly proportioned, and solid-looking. However, like all Chinese architecture, it is nothing short of being a slim silhouette. The building does not invite one's eyes to travel over it, as an Indian sikhara or a Gothic bell tower does.

The *Kondo* is constructed on the same principal as

the *chūmon*. The ground floor measures five spans by
four. The floors above, which are not accessible, meas-
ure four spans by three. Like the Sai-in buildings, it
rises from a flagged terrace. Its ground floor, like the
pagoda's, was unfortunately disfigured during the
eighth century by the addition of verandas, built to protect from the rain the paintings adorning the interior
walls. The buildings of the northern section of the
Sai-in, those at the other end of the *Kondo* courtyard
(the sermon room), consisting of a bell tower to the
east and a library to the west, were built at a later date.

The columns have a swollen shape and are narrower
at the top. They constitute a system of four brackets:
the one that juts through to the exterior indirectly supports the rafters of the overlapping lean-to (Fig. 51);

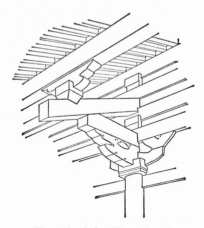

Fig. 51. Detail of the Temple of Horyuji.

the two that are attached to the wall are exposed and
their beautiful profile enlivens the façade. The second
column supports a tie beam. Although old Japanese
buildings were occasionally destroyed by typhoons or
earthquakes, this happened less often than one might

think. The carpenters, who did not use a single piece
of metal, were excellent craftsmen. The Sai-in buildings
are rigorously but subtly individualistic, so that they
are harmonious without being monotonous. It is unfortunate that neither China nor Korea have preserved
their own comparable monuments.

The interior of the *Kondo* includes a covered walk
as wide as a span. In the center there is a space twice
as wide and three times as long which is free of columns
and covered by a roof raised by four rampant vaults.
This space is occupied by the iconostasis. The southern
end contains three bronze Buddhas. The middle and
the right-hand Buddhas date from the Suiko period
(also called the Asuka period, after the location of the
imperial court). The Buddha on the left is of the thirteenth century.

EARLY BUDDHIST STATUARY

The central Buddha, a Shaka Sakyamuni, is seated between two small, standing Bodhisattvas. We learn from
the inscription on his halo that the statue, executed in
honor of Prince Shotoku when he died at fifty years
of age, was made in 623 by Tori of the Saddlers' Guild,
the most highly skilled metallurgists in prehistoric Japan. Tori was descended from a southern Chinese family that had immigrated to Japan one hundred years
earlier. Although they were Buddhists, they were not
proselytizers. The statue is undoubtedly a Japanese
work of art, though it was inspired by Chinese art that
dates back approximately three-quarters of a century:
the sinuous ornamental scroll around the halo (which
the Chinese copied from Gupta art), the edges of Buddha's coat forming fringes of capital omegas and question marks, all of which were well known in China
since the year 550. But the elongated and full faces,
which have no sign of heaviness and are of a simple

and sensitive modeling, bear absolutely no resemblance to any known Chinese statue. The only tie to their ancestors, the Wei and Sui masterpieces, would be the ecstatic, smiling fervor they have in common.

The Buddha standing on the right-hand side is a Yakushi, Bhaishajyaguru, the "Master Doctor," curative god to whom the Buddhists always attached special importance when they were in the process of converting a country. He was probably the principle deity when the Horyuji was founded. The statue is dated 607 and is almost certainly the work of the talented master, Tori.

The Bodhisattva Avalokiteshvara, kept in the Yumedono, the small To-in octagonal *Kondo*, was discovered toward the end of the nineteenth century. This Bodhisattva, known as Yumedono-Kwannon, was the statue that enchanted the American E. F. Fenollosa, the author of a book entitled *Epochs of Japanese Art* (1887), and converted him to the art of the Far East. Almost monoxylic, and yet deserving to be seen in profile for the beauty of his gesture, this Bodhisattva is perfectly charming. The pointed folds of his coat remind us of the mannerisms of Wei sculpture around the year 510. His elongated, oval face, small eyes, and gentle, archaic smile are almost identical to the Buddhas of Tori. Another even more unusual statue of a famous deity, mysteriously known as Kudara-Kwannon, could have been the work of an eclectic amateur, dated approximately between the years 640 and 650.

The Horyuji used to have some fifty-odd gilt bronze statuettes which are now in the Tokyo Museum. They all belong to the seventh century, and many of them are exceedingly handsome. However, we have no means of telling whether they were made by Japanese, Chinese, or Korean artists (Fig. 52). In a neighboring convent, the Chuguji, there is a charming, wooden statue, hardly larger than life-size, of the compassionate Bud-

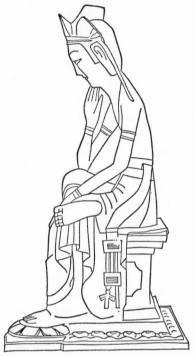

Fig. 52. Buddhist Sculpture. One of the Forty-eight
Buddhist Statuettes of the Imperial Treasure.

dha, of Maitreya (in Japanese, Miroku), in the pensive
pose of the divinities, many examples of which can be
seen in the Yün-kang grottoes. In our opinion, the
pure, somewhat flat grace of this youthful form is truly
Japanese. Similar statues found at Koryuji, west of Kyoto, are thought to be slightly earlier than the Chuguji
masterpiece.

On the iconostasis of the Horyuji *Kondo*, there is an
exceedingly interesting object, the Tamamushi tabernacle. This Tamamushi is the Coleoptera beetle, whose
hard blue sheath serves as a background to bands of
jeweled gilt copper. Its major section is an exact model

of a temple like the *Kondo*, whose details we will not mention here. The interior is carpeted with the "Thousand Buddhas" made of embossed copper. The exterior walls are decorated with exquisite and original paintings. Three guardian kings, considerably less military-looking than usual, stand above the three doors, with a number of Bodhisattvas, of a style never seen in China, but certainly to be seen in Central Asia at Bezekliq (J. Hackin). Among the other panels, all of which are interesting, we will only mention the sides of the base which contain two *Jatakas* (*Jatakas* are rarely seen in Sino-Japanese art) in which the future Buddha is shown three times at different stages of the action. The forest vegetation is decorative and the rocks become a kind of ornamental foliage rather like the Louis Quinze *rocaille* (Shell) pattern. A fairly large number of objects decorated in this style, starting with the Han period, have been found in Korea. Others at the Shosoin date from the eighth century, after which the process was more or less forgotten. The Tamamushi tabernacle is probably the result of collaboration between Korean and Japanese artisans, a collaboration attested by the inscriptions on several other pieces of the Suiko period.

All this early Buddhist art in Japan reflects a faith both ardent and naïve, a belief still innocent, that makes a clean sweep of the burden of pedantry accumulated through the centuries and finds within itself the freshness of early Buddhism. One must remember that throughout the first half of the seventh century, all that Japan knew of Buddhism came from Korea. In the meantime, the first Japanese ambassador arrived at the Sui Yang-ti court in 607, young Japanese nobles went to study in China, and Chinese specialists arrived in Japan to teach writing, astronomy, chronology, etc. With the usual profound Oriental indifference to historical dates, the Japanese adopted the Chinese method

of counting years according to the sexagesimal cycle
and by eras of a very few years. The Hakuho period
was named after the era of the White Phoenix (673–
686), the interval which separates the Suiko or Asuka
period from the Tempyo period; in short, the second
half of the seventh century and the first half of the
eighth century.

Imperial power was only gradually consolidated. The
civilizing work conducted by Shotoku Taishi was to dis-
integrate in 645. The cause was saved by Nakatomi Ka-
matari, whom the dying Emperor Tenchi rewarded
with jurisdiction over Fujiwara. Buddhism took roots
gradually but deeply. It was genuinely tolerant of the
ancient Shintoist. Buddhism was decidedly in good
standing, for toward the end of the seventh century
many large monasteries were founded and considerable work was undertaken at Horyuji.

The most notable of the new buildings at Horyuji
was the *Kondo* mural. It could be seen on the wall until January 20, 1949, when a disastrous fire, started by
a copyist's electric heating pad, broke out. At this time,
the main part of the building was dismantled and the
objects it contained were put in a safe place. The far
traves of the *Kondo* (the room measured only forty
feet in length) being narrower than the others, the
paintings were on eight narrow panels in the corners
and four large panels (east, west, with two on the
north side)—the six large remaining traves being on
the double doors. Each picture was about ten feet high:
the four larger ones showed Buddha in all his majesty
surrounded by a fairly large group of people in the style
of the Tunhuang formula. The corner panels showed
the Bodhisattvas, seated or standing. The paintings
were not all done by the same artist. The one of Amitabha on the west wall is perhaps the most beautiful.
People have often mentioned the Indian appearance of

the faces: the long eyes, the noble and languid gestures of the "Divinities." They evoke the "handsome Bodhisattva" at Ajanta. Jeannine Auboyer has, once and for all, established that comparisons cannot be made with Indian mural painting regarding composition and detail, but can be made with the murals at Tunhuang. Still, we believe it unwise to conclude that this masterpiece drew its inspiration from Central Asia. There is an air of order, a symmetry, a certain Chinese quality to the Horyuji murals; the master artist in charge must have been a Chinese who was well versed in Indian Buddhist art. It is surprising that there is no mention in contemporary texts of such an important work of art, or of the presence in Japan of such an important foreign artist.

The ground floor of the pagoda was also decorated with paintings no longer there today. In addition, there were four bas-relief models made of unbaked puddle-clay that depicted scenes from the life of Buddha. They must have looked like dioramas in relief set back-to-back to the framework of the pagoda's mast. The background was blocked in with conventional mountain-scapes, and many figures sculpted in the round stood in different perspectives. Similar compositions still exist at Tunhuang. They are of little interest, apart from their rather vulgar realism that neatly places them in a category outside the hieratic tradition.

The Yakushiji, founded in 698 at Asuka and transferred to the new capital at Nara in 718, has preserved several bronze statues that were probably made by Chinese masters. They are of finer quality than the best T'ang stone statuary found in China today. The Sho Kwannon (Avalokiteshvara) is a highly inspired piece of work, despite a certain stiffness, and its ornamentation does full justice to the beauty of the material. The famous Yakushi triad, dated 726, is an example of mature T'ang art. The bodies are plump but well constructed. They have almost overpowering majesty, perhaps betraying that Buddhism had by then become the state religion of Japan, as it had in China. The bronze base of this Yakushi is particularly curious, with its distinctly Indian appearance. The lotus root, which had already seduced the Miran painters, is here confused with the serpent, entwined around the Meru, the pivot of the globe, who, according to the Indian legend, churned up the ocean. As in the *Kudu*, realistic savages are depicted under the arches. They could almost pass for the "Hayato" from the extreme southwest of the archipelago, who had just been subjugated.

The Tamamushi no Zushi, another tabernacle at Horyuji (in the *Kondo*), belonged to Lady Tachibana, daughter-in-law of Fujiwara. It still contains a small gilt bronze triad of Amida, the drapery of which was fashioned during the year 700. The three figures are supported by lotuses, whose sinuous stalks rise from a horizontal plaque that represents the surface of a pond. The figures stand in front of an iridescent apse-shaped backdrop ornamented with charming Buddhist angels. The pictures on the outside walls of this tabernacle have all but disappeared. As for the *Zushi's* roof, it is very much like the canopy suspended over Tori's Buddha. However, this one has wooden phoenixes about to fly off, and small musician Bodhisattvas which have a naïve charm, a realistic plastic quality, and are sculptured in the round.

THE NARA EPOCH
Plate 36

During the precivilized era, the imperial Japanese court changed residence each time an emperor died. Finally, copying China, a permanent capital was founded at Nara, situated north of the Yamato Plain. Here, the imperial government remained from 710 to 784. The "Nara" century was therefore the eighth century. It can also be divided into three rather different phases. The first, lasting from about 710 to 730, was generally an optimistic period, enlightened by a benevolent religion, internal order, and a civilization that was avidly absorbed. However, the loss of a child at an early age caused Emperor Shomu and Empress Komyo, daughter of Lady Tachibana, to become excessively pious. And an outbreak of the plague carried off a great number of people. The Japanese considered abandoning Nara. They built new temples and then erected a colossal Buddha which they completed in 751. Shomu Tenno's only pleasure during his later years in life lay in religious ceremonies. The second phase of overpowering piety, disastrous for the nation, gave us the religious art treasures preserved in the monasteries. Secular art died out. The third period, lasting from about 760 to 784, is marked by a wave of anticlerical and even anti-Buddhist feeling. The leaders of the revolt were the Fujiwara, and one of the chief instigators was Shomu's daughter, who twice ruled the kingdom and dreamed of raising her bronze lover Dokyo to imperial dignity.

The Tempyo era, which lasted from 729 to 748, was prolonged by three other phases up to 766, with the result that the era known as the "Tempyo period" implies the middle period of the Nara epoch.

Contact with China was maintained, despite the great dangers involved in the voyage. The whole of Korea had fallen into the hands of Shiragi, and the temperament of the nation was bellicose. In order to get to China one had to sail straight to the mouth of the Yangtze River. Imperial power now extended over the whole of the archipelago, except in the north, where the Ainu were later to fight for their independence. Monasteries were endowed by statute in every

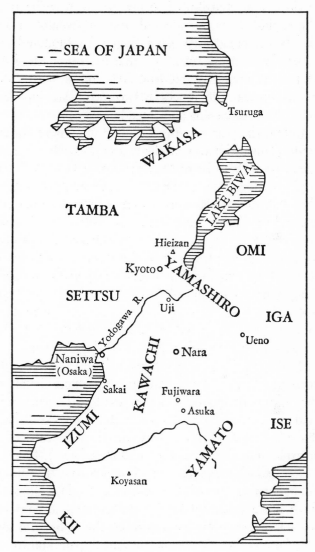

MAP V. CENTRAL JAPAN

province, and contributed to the spread of civilization. The capital, however, was still the only center of art. The Nara monasteries gave shelter to thousands of monks. It is hardly surprising that each monastery developed its own characteristic style, quite apart from the ideological differences between the six Japanese sects (three Mahayana and three Hinayana).

Around the year 730, the Kofukuji monastery, for example (Hosso, Dharmalakshana sect), excelled in realistic statues. Its series of the "Ten Great Disciples" and "Eight (categories) of Deva" are distinctly Japanese. The realistic heads were often sculpted from life, whereas the limbs were never well observed. Bronze and wood were usually replaced by unbaked puddle clay made over an armature, or by dry lacquer (*kanshitsu*). This method consisted of drying a clay statue by plastering it with rags dipped in lacquer. The lacquer was then scraped off, leaving a light but solid shell that could be painted, gilded, or ornamented in relief, etc. The *kanshitsu* did not lend itself to realistic effects.

At Todaiji (Kegon, Avatamsaka sect) between approximately 736 and 750, the style was more dynamic. The statues of guardian deities were particularly successful. In the building known as the Hokkedo or Sanguatsudo (because it was used for three months only for explaining the "Lotus of the Good Law"), there is a large *kanshitsu* statue of Fukukenjaku Kwannon (Amoghapaca, one of the forms of Avalokiteshvara) which has a beautiful head, superior even to contemporary Chinese examples. However, the eight arms are stiff. Among the divinities, the small pair known as Brahma and Indra (supposedly made on the site, but probably coming from the Todaiji workshops) are usually admired for their flowing shape. One can feel the grim heaviness of the last years of the Nara era in the large pair (thirteen feet high) depicting the same couple. The standing statues of Kichijoten and Benzaiten (Sridevi and Sarasvati) are well modeled, although today they are in a rather shabby state. Many Lokapala and Dravapala statues exude strength and hatred. Their partial state of preservation is due to their layer of polychrome.

The colossal Roshana Buddha, the "Great Enlightener," was erected in the park of the Todaiji. It was made of five hundred tons of copper, almost the whole of the country's output. The statue, fifty-two feet high, was cast in the temple grounds, layer by layer, in much the same way as we would build a structure in concrete. The head collapsed during the next century, and after other accidents and innumerable repairs, the huge Buddha was replaced during the eighteenth century by the ugly statue still standing on the site today. Nothing remains of Tempyo's Buddha save a few lotus petals from the base, engraved with drawings depicting the Buddhist cosmos. The pavilion that sheltered this statue was, along with the Kanishka stupa near Peshawar, the largest wooden structure the world had ever seen. Its façade was approximately 285 feet long, 167 feet deep, and 118 feet high. The Daibutsuden is at most half as large.

THE SHOSOIN

In order to provide shelter for the offerings sent to the colossal Buddha from the provinces and from foreign countries, a simple warehouse was built in the Todaiji park. It was called the Shosoin. After the death of Shomu in 756, the objets d'art that had belonged to the pious emperor were also placed in the building. The warehouse is a type of isba measuring ninety-eight feet by twenty-nine feet, and is raised on thick piles.

The walls consist of tree trunks squared out in three chamfered isosceles prisms, with the bases turned toward the inside. Rarely opened from the ninth to the nineteenth centuries (it was once closed for 103 years), the Shosoin has preserved its contents with remarkable efficiency. During the humid summers, the wood swelled and became watertight. During the dry seasons of autumn and winter, the walls automatically contracted to provide a system of ventilation. Since 1873, the Shosoin has been opened every November, the most beautiful time of the year in Japan. The variety of these treasures is quite extraordinary. Among them are large pieces of furniture (one wardrobe belonged to five emperors from the seventh to the eighth centuries), elbow rests, screens, T'ang pottery and imitation Japanese T'ang, Sassanid glassware, parlor games, musical instruments, clothes, hats, shoes, hunting weapons, mirrors, sculpture, a few drawings, paper, India ink, paintbrushes, rulers, drugs, documents, and autographs of all kinds. Of particular interest to Chinese art history are the objects imported from China.

The art of the final Nara period is well represented at Toshodaiji, a monastery that was founded by the Chinese Kien-tchen sect (in Japanese Ganjin), a band 293 strong, who arrived in Japan in 754 after twelve years of all sorts of misadventure. T'ang art was already in decline, and the Japanese painters of the period did poor copies of this ponderous style. But those artists who managed to avoid the Chinese monitors were able to make majestic standing statues which had a certain static and haughty grace, and draperies of undulating folds that do not appear to have been copied from Chinese originals. Wood was also used again. The *kanshitsu* were abandoned by the ninth century in favor of lacquered and gilt wood.

PORTRAIT STATUES AND MASKS

Perhaps the most interesting features of Nara sculpture
are the statue portraits of monks and the dance masks.
The sculptured or painted portraits, usually posthumous, were already being made in China, and the Japanese did not change the formula. Thus we have portraits that are likenesses of the famous Nara monks. We
will only mention two: that of Roben, the founder of
Hokkedo, whose likeness is inclined to be photographic,
and that of Ganjin, a sublime picture showing the face
of this holy man, who was already blind before he arrived in Japan.

The dance masks of this period, of which we have at
least two hundred specimens, are vaguely classified as
"Gigaku masks" (Fig. 53). We do not know much

Fig. 53. Gigaku Mask.

about them, or what they were really used for. The court at Nara, which had a passion for folklore, imitated the Chang-an court by collecting "music" (which also included dances and chants) from the provinces and from other countries.

We can be reasonably sure that most of the masks that have come down to us are Japanese. There are often signatures or other inscriptions attesting to their authenticity. They completely cover the face, and should not be confused with the much later no masks. Many of them are tengu masks, obviously descendants of primitive bird-masks. Cousins of the Indian Garuda, the Japanese tengu were jovial genies who laughed at mankind. Another common one is the old man with a long nose, sometimes with phallic implications. It is astonishing to find that the old-man mask always has Indo-European features. There are also masks of young people and androgenous Bodhisattvas. They are all sculptural masterpieces.

There is very little left of Nara painting, except for Chinese copies, such as the fragmentary examples of "The Sutra of Cause and Effect," of which we still have a much more piquant copy at Tunhuang. It has the same frieze of very naïve water colors above the text, showing a paradise highlighted with embroidery known as *taemamandara*, a Kichijoten (Crideri), or simply a small elegant lady in the style of the mid-T"ang epoch, and the screen that was mentioned in the Chinese chapter entitled "Six Beauties under the Trees." This was given a Japanese date of 752, though the ample and lucid drawing is actually Chinese. The Japanese talent for caricature is particularly noticeable in quick brush sketches found on surfaces normally hidden from sight, such as the pedestals of statues at Toshodaiji, or on the upper reaches of arches near the ceilings of the *Kondo* at Horyuji, etc.

Venerated by the Japanese as a golden age of their civilization, the Nara century has left us an accurate picture of the times in its poetry, in the enormous anthology of the *Manyoshu*, as well as in its plastic arts. It was only the religious imagery, a little removed from life, and the objets d'art of this period that failed to have a lasting and enriching effect on the Japanese tradition.

THE EARLY HEIAN PERIOD (Ninth Century)

It was decided in 784, largely on the initiative of the Fujiwara, who wanted to flee the monks, to build a new capital in the valley of Yodogawa, a natural road between Lake Biwa and the sound. The capital had barely been completed when a new site was chosen further north. This was called Heianjo, "the Stronghold of Peace," better known as Miyako or Kyoto, "the Capital" (794–1868). Japan was beginning to feel that her apprenticeship was over. She no longer asked China to send her professors or technicians. She was, however, still feeling her way regarding religion. She had acquired good taste, reacted against the crudity of T'ang art during its decline, and looked for livelier and more stylish shapes (Fig. 54). In architecture, she tried

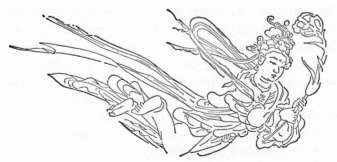

Fig. 54. Fresco of the Heian Period.

to refine the forms she had learned, and sometimes included autochthonous elements. Reciprocally, Shinto temple-huts unobtrusively acquired a few Chinese elements. Under the aegis of the Buddhists, who stated that the Shinto deities were but hypostases of their own, the sculptors of the Heian period made statuettes of historical personages who had been deified, rather than the ill-defined, indistinguishable wooden statuettes of ancient *kami*. Their sculpture is almost peasant work, very involved, and fully sustains the polychrome.

A few priests continued to go to China, but only to study new Buddhist doctrines. The most famous travelers were Dengyo Daishi and Kobo Daishi, who returned to Japan in 805 and 806 and founded respectively the Tendai and Shingon sects. These gave to Japanese Buddhism its special flavor which was to last until the Middle Ages. Tendai Buddhism is particularly interesting for its doctrine, whereas Shingon is treasured for the works of art which it inspired. The Tendai monasteries spread out over the Hieizan slopes between Kyoto and Lake Biwa. They were unfortunately burned down during the sixteenth-century civil wars. The Shingon, who were in favor at court, were endowed with a large monastery known as Toji or Kyoogoko-kuji, which was built in the new capital. However, the motherhouse and largest seminary was at Koyasan, approximately sixty-two miles to the south in the Kii Mountains. Kobo Daishi could read and write Sanskrit and had studied the rites and symbols of pre-Buddhist India. These he adapted to his system of Shingon, giving it a new and highly exalted aura. Although Shingon drew on the ancient sources of tantrism, no link between the two can be assumed. The new sect gave painters fresh and difficult subject matter. The Shingon sculptor-monks made beautiful primitive and expressive

wooden statues, most of which have unfortunately
been lost during recent years. Large paintings (approximately ten by thirteen feet) show angry gods with a
remarkable feeling for the simplified expression required for mural work. In a quite different style, the
mandara (in Sanskrit *mandala,* meaning "circle") visu-
ally symbolize the links between spiritual activity and
a multitude of deities. They are large hieratic miniatures, executed with tremendous self-confidence and a
perfect sense of decoration either in color or with ink
on an indigo background.

MICHIZANE

In short, the Japanese genius appeared ready to fly with
its own wings. An internal political incident favored
this. In 894, the brilliant Sinologue Sugawara no Michizane became tutor to the young Emperor Daigo.
Jealous of the influence he might acquire over the
young man, the Fujiwara tried to have him made ambassador to China. Michizane let it be known that Japan had nothing more to learn from the great country,
and that she might as well break off diplomatic relations with the T'ang regime, which was about to col-
lapse. As a result, he was made viceroy of distant Kyushu, in effect a sentence of exile, and he died there of
chagrin in 903. We know that in order to appease his
angered soul, the Fujiwara deified him with the name
of Temman Tenjin. The embassy to China was closed
permanently, an action of great importance in an era
when an exchange of presents took the place of a nonexistent international commerce. For the next three
centuries (tenth, eleventh, and twelfth) Japan closed
her doors and developed her own culture and institutions.

JAPANESE CALLIGRAPHY AND ITS CONNECTION WITH THE GRAPHIC ARTS

The ideograms, signs that express a recurring idea or situation and a very practical construction in Chinese, were at the same time impractical for transcribing the language. Japanese knowledge of Indian calligraphy via Shingon inspired the creation of kana, which proved useful for rendering the sounds of the Japanese language. The kana signs were drawn from Chinese characters—for their phonetic value only—by using two methods: the first, by tracing the entire running character (hiragana); the second, by removing only part of the square character (katakana). We can see the supple, sequential, very lively hiragana in graphics and in scrolls dating from the Middle Ages up to the engravings of the Tokugawa period. We can also see Chinese characters intermingled with the Japanese.

The invention of kana had an enormous influence on Japanese culture during the Fujiwara era. The educated Japanese put all their skill into drafting serious texts into Chinese, just as our scholars wrote in Latin. The women, who were too ignorant to know Chinese, were nevertheless able to read and write in Japanese. The glory of this period was the abundance of literature written either by or for them. This literature consists of stories, novels, diaries, and, later, romantic chronicles and an infinite number of *waka* or tanka, poems of thirty-one syllables, which have fed the Japanese imagination for thousands of years, and as a result were the source of inspiration for most secular art.

Poetic expression is most natural to the Japanese. Indeed, the ninth-century poem *Ise Monogatari* is far more mature than prose. No other country has had such a close relationship between poetry and the graphic arts. We would need much more space and many more photographs in order to explain this close relationship. We will be seeing that the lacquer decorations, for example, nearly always had an allusion to a well-known poem; and the allusion could vary from being a simple paraphrase to being a commentary, and from there to two or three double entendres. This began during the Fujiwara period; but a few centuries later, and particularly during the thirteenth to the seventeenth centuries, the collaboration or the confusion between the two was pushed even further.

THE CLASSICAL PERIOD OF JAPANESE CIVILIZATION (*ca.* 930–1350)

THE FUJIWARA PERIOD (844–1185)
Plates 37 and 38

During the ninth century, the Fujiwara pursued with determination their simple, family game of politics by placing their daughters in the imperial harem and giving their sons all the important posts—notably that of regent during the minority of the monarch (*sessho*), and soon that of regent even during the monarch's majority (*kwampaku*). For more than two hundred years, from the disgrace of Michizane in 894 to the Taira *coup d'état* in 1160, the Fujiwara were absolute masters of the empire. Neither fanatic nor sanguinary, nor particularly warlike, they were fond of city life, ostentatious display, literature, and the fine arts. Although they were not especially religious, they were highly superstitious. They donated generously to both the Shinto and the Buddhists. (Let us remember that the two religions were not rivals.) Thus developed one of the most refined civilizations the world has ever known, but one that benefited only the entourage at court. The provinces were still impoverished. People of quality divided their time between ceremony and pleasure. Affairs of the heart were the main preoccupation of the court. One might well say that the culture and the aesthetic of the Fujiwara era were essentially feminine. The best writers were women, and the spoken language of the period, somewhat simplified, remained the written language—the use of which was *de rigueur* until about 1900 in the writing of every kind of book, article or letter. This frivolous society had a great taste for painting. The palace interiors were decorated; the nobility amused itself by going through portfolios of drawings; noble men and women painted miniatures themselves.

SCULPTURE

Sculpture was bound to be at a low ebb in this self-indulgent atmosphere. It followed the same fatal road that Chinese sculpture did when China found herself in isolation. In short, sculpture became dangerously close to painting, making excessive use of polychrome and producing a picturesque baroque style that paid too much attention to detail and ignored spatial relationships. By now, the Buddhist pantheon consisted of numerous deities whom the painters were permitted to depict in a less hieratic manner which was almost caricature. It is important to notice that this was the final development of Japanese Buddhism. After the tentative overtures to sects which we have already mentioned, we have the work of the eleventh-century Jocho, who created the Buddha who was neither too realistic nor too human, with an expression that was both agreeable and serene. This Buddha is just short of being like the one that was shown in religious imagery until the nineteenth century. The portrait statues did not develop any further. However, the second half of the twelfth century saw the unfortunate fashion of en-

crusting the eyes with jewels, an innovation that
spoiled many statues of the period.

RELIGIOUS PAINTING

We still come across hieratic works of art brought back
from China by the monks. Among the many pictures
of Mahamayuri (Kujaku-Myoo), the goddess mounted
on a peacock, whom one called upon in the event of
drought, there is one that has been traditionally attributed to Chang Ssu-kung (tenth century). However,
the one in the former Hara Collection seems to us to
be really Japanese on account of the extreme grace of
its shape and the somewhat purist treatment.

The painting of the Fujiwara period is hardly painting in the real sense of the word—rather, it is miniature painting on a grand scale. The intense colors are
highlighted with kirikane, minute cutouts of gold leaf.
The smallest detail of costume or furniture is as important as the lines of a face. Everything is meticulously
described and nothing is real.

The Toji has a handsome screen of which we know
neither the date nor the origin. It shows a noble visiting a hermit. The right-hand side of the picture shows
the small procession arriving. The sage's hut is in the
middle of the screen standing at the foot of tall flowering trees. From there our eyes search the distance
where a smooth expanse of a lake completes the composition. This composition is both rigorous and calm.
The fact that the costumes are Chinese seems, in con-
junction with the composition, to confirm the artist's
debt to an ancient Chinese painting of the same subject. On the other hand, the central portion of the
screen is very much like certain Japanese paintings
made around the year 1200.

We have numerous pictures of the death of Buddha.
At both ends and on either side of the funerary bed,

there stand *kala* trees, which more or less cut the picture in two. The Bodhisattvas stand around the dying
man; the disciples and the "grand auditors" are in the
foreground. The best-preserved and the oldest of the
Nehan-zu is that of Kongobuji at Koyasan (1086 A.D.).
A lion (symbol of Buddha's sovereignty) is rolling
about like a cat in the right-hand corner. Later, the
artist included more and more animals, making the
painting look as if the whole of creation was taking
part in humanity's mourning.

Let us also mention the large and beautiful composition entitled "Amida and his Bodhisattvas" (approximately seven by thirteen feet), which is dated 1587 and
attributed to Eshin Sozu or Genshin, a monk who died
at Tendai in 1018. All the people shown are seated
upon a bank of clouds; below them and to the left we
can see an infinitesimal corner of a terrestrial landscape. The same motif was used again later in a somewhat less static composition that shows the divine procession moving. Also, in the later ones, the Buddha is
standing with some of his acolytes kneeling on wind-
tossed clouds (*raigo* of the Kombuin). Finally we even
see the faithful praying, toward whom the divine procession is descending like a slow-moving meteor (*raigo*
of the Chionin).

EARLY YAMATO-E

The Taira, descendants of a ninth-century emperor, relegated to the rank of provincial nobility, neglected no
opportunity to acquire a place in the sun. In 1160, due
to a favorable situation in the palace, they quickly
stripped the Fujiwara of their privileged position and
for a whole generation emulated the Fujiwara in their
taste for ceremony, if not for their morals. During this
period, one of the amusements of the nobility was copying and making drawings for sutras—thus acquiring

spiritual merit. Therefore, the frontispiece of a scroll
executed around 1165 by some thirty members of the
Taira family is more than interesting. The subject matter is not always hieratic, but often borrowed from daily
life. Secular painting had been done for quite some
time, more independent of Chinese examples than in
the case of religious paintings. However, those remaining to us today—incidentally, there are quite a few—
do not date back prior to 1140 (Fig. 55). Apart from

Fig. 55. Court Lady. Early Yamato-e.

sutra frontispieces, whose influence was often secular,
and which are attributed to amateur painters of the
Fujiwara family, the four scrolls depicting a "Genji
Monogatari" have been traditionally ascribed to Fujiwara no Takayoshi, head of the Imperial Collection
and of the Kasuga workshops. (Kasuga is a Shinto temple northeast of Nara, with which the family had
strong ties.)

One immediately notices a certain affinity to the

anecdotal painting of the deities and the eighth-century margins that show scenes of paradise. Even the plunging perspective, the angles of perspective, and the convention of doing without the roofs in order to show what was going on inside the house are the same in both pictures. The architectural and household details (matting, screens, curtains, etc.) give "bones" to a composition that is otherwise somewhat diffuse. The scale of the people is measured by the importance of their activity rather than by their proximity to the spectator. The contours are very fine, the colors opaque and intense, though limited in range, with sumptuous and unexpected harmonies. The faces are more often than not three-quarter views and treated in a fairly conventional manner, with eyes like commas and with hooked noses. These scenes give us a very good idea of palace life during the Fujiwara epoch, where everything was ordered and beautiful.

There are several other scrolls which again evoke the Kasuga school whose characteristic is a miniature style with dense coloring. But near the year 1200—the dawn of the Kamakura reign—a new style came into being. It too was similar to the Yamato-e style, a narrative form that owed almost nothing to China, included a system of perspective, and had the same interest in daily life though with a freer, more confident style of drawing with suggested highlights of water color and occasional dashes of opaque and brilliant coloring. Credit for this innovation was given to the most famous painter of the time, Fujiwara Tsune-taka, who took the name of Tosa after the province of which he was governor general. However, Otto Kümmel believes that the name was adopted by a long line of painters who appeared sometime after Tosa was dead. Incidentally, the last-mentioned painter vacillated between the somewhat miniaturist style of the

Kasuga and the "high-lighted" style of the first Tosa—
so much so, that we look upon the Tosa style as being
synonymous with Yamato-e. In the meantime, let us
remember that Sherman Lee wanted to reserve the
name of Yamato-e for the style known as Kasuga.
Whatever it may be, it is a fine tradition that was livelier than ever. Its masterpieces were executed during
the Kamakura period.

During the twelfth century we also see the beginnings of a monastic style of painting that has no ties
whatsoever with China although it does not belong to
the Yamato-e tradition. It consists of brush drawings
of human beings or animals with a few cursory indications of trees, water, etc. (Fig. 56). The Kozanji mon-

Fig. 56. Fragment of One of the Kozanji Scrolls.

astery seems to have been the center of this essentially
caricatural and satirical art. These scrolls were once
attributed to a man called Kakuyu, *sojo* (an ecclesiasti-
cal title) of Toba, who died in 1140 a very old man.
They were in fact executed by several artists. Those
scrolls caricaturing monks and simpletons in the shape
of rabbits and frogs are particularly famous. The lines
are confident and admirably vivacious, the animals remarkably well constructed, and their humor still makes

us laugh today. During the following two or three centuries, this tradition continued with anticlerical drawings in which the monks were depicted as tengu.

FUJIWARA ARCHITECTURE

A few isolated buildings, which once formed part of a considerable complex, are all that remain of the architecture of this period. One of the most characteristic examples is the Hoodo (Pavilion of the Phoenix) at Byodoin of Uji, situated between Kyoto and Nara. It used to be a villa belonging to Fujiwara Yorimichi who made it into a temple in 1051. The ground plan is T-shaped. The long gallery gives onto the lake in the form of a square pavilion. To the right and the left of the pavilion, smaller galleries lead to secondary pavilions that jut out slightly onto the lake. This fantasy plan seems to have been inspired by the celestial palace painters conjured up in the paradise of their minds. It also demonstrates the taste for rhythmic architecture that was common at the time in the Far East. The decoration of pillars and beams can also be compared to contemporaneous Khmer art. In Japan, however, these highly stylized botanical decorations were encrusted and not in relief. The interiors were iridescent with mother of pearl and precious metals. The paneled ceilings at Hoodo are painted in vivid color.

The Hoodo *honzon* is an Amida by Jocho, who probably also sculptured the charming figurines of Buddhist angels that were somewhat awkwardly attached in the areas above the walls. The Amidist murals by Takuma Tamenari have almost completely vanished from the walls. Akiyama Terukazu has been able to reconstruct them, thanks to a copy made during the early part of the nineteenth century by Tanaka Totsugen, a copy that was not very faithful from a spiritual point of view, but otherwise quite exact in detail.

THE KAMAKURA ERA (1185–1333)
Plate 39

While the Taira were supplanting the Fujiwara, other nobles of imperial descent, the Minamoto, were nurturing similar ambitions. The Taira *coup d'état* did not act in their favor, but the two young Minamoto, Yoritomo and his half-brother Yoshitsune, who had led sheltered lives, came into their majority. The political genius of one and the military audacity of the other were ultimately to oust the Taira. This struggle, which lasted from 1181 to 1185, is known as the famous war of the Gempei (Sino-Japanese transcription of Minamoto and Taira) and was to become the national epic struggle of Japan. Yoritomo accomplished in ten years what Taira no Kiyomori had not even attempted during twenty years of despotism. His military government was the first *bakafu,* "government of the tent" or shogunate, and his military headquarters were at Kamakura, ninety-three miles east of Kyoto.

The repercussions of these political events were felt indirectly, though immediately, by the arts. They were translated into a perfect clarity and pragmatism which caused a change even in religious art. The resumption of relations with China, at least through the mediations of the monks of the two countries, introduced new styles of architecture that were at that time the ideas expressed in the Ch'an sect, called Zen by the Japanese. Zen on the other hand learned about watercolor painting of the Southern school and the rite of tea-drinking. Four or five generations each elaborated the tea ceremony, the famous *cha-no-yu,* which was to have a profound influence on Japan's culture and aesthetic.

In this new, more realistic, and humanitarian atmosphere, narrative painting produced its greatest masterpieces. For example, we have the three scrolls describing the history of "Ban Dainagon" (a judiciary error, the reversal of which consolidated the supremacy of the Fujiwara in 866); the "Shigizan engi," the legend of a hermit who had a particular devotion to Bishamon (*Kuvera*); and the "Taema-mandara no engi," an Amidist legend which dealt with the paradise of 755 which we have already mentioned. These works of art, including many others, are traditionally attributed to the oldest aristocratic families, which is more than possible in the case of the twelfth-century "Genji Monogatari." But here, the painter is so familiar with the life of humble country and city people, with street scenes and field scenes, fhat one wonders if the teachers of these noble amateurs were not popular artists who remained anonymous. Details of these scrolls, which were usually ten to twenty inches high and three and a half to five inches long, have often been reproduced in *Kokka*, in the *Kokuho* (National Treasures), and in the *Shimbi Taikwan* and other famous publications. But their beauty and originality can only be seen properly in the ·new photographic facsimiles, larger than the original. Several of these were given to the Guimet Museum by Japan when René Grousset was visiting the country in 1947 (Fig. 57).

In these scrolls, the continuity of the pictures, their rhythm—sometimes relaxed, sometimes taut—and even the silences are expressive, which would not have been possible if they had been executed in any other fashion. The scene of a crowd of people running toward a veranda in flames is typical of a section of the "Ban Dainagon." This group of rather odd-looking people, wearing black hats which are almost equidistant from each other, strike a somewhat discordant note which is resolved a little further on in the left-hand side of the next picture, where the first arrivals are being

Fig. 57. Life of Honen. Detail of a Scroll of the Kamakura Period.

driven back by smoke and sparks. In the second scroll we can see two children fighting in the streets. A door is opened and a brutal porter beats them so soundly that one of them drops dead. The other is hurriedly removed from the scene by his mother. Some of the passers-by turn their heads for a moment, not daring to intercede. Others ignore the scene, continuing on their way. The "Shigizan engi" contains the famous scene of the barn that, due to Myoren's miraculous power, is flying, while the astonished villagers watch on, hoping to get back their bags of rice which are whirling through the air like a flight of pigeons. The old sister of the hermit sets out on her search, questioning the peasants, who are both curious and fearful. Details of country life are so accurately recorded that one can almost smell the stables. The old lady falls asleep and dreams she is standing before the Daibutsu of Nara; one can see the colossal golden Buddha through the giant doors. The universality, the profound humanity of this art, its extension into areas that we do not ordinarily assign to painting, make the thirteenth century Yamato-e really unique.

The "Heiji Monogatari," which comes in three scrolls (the first of which is in the Museum of Fine Arts, Boston), illustrates the events that took place during the Heiji era (1160). The style, once again, is different; the artist is not particularly interested in the setting of the picture, though he excells in composing picturesque and teeming groups of people with lively colors that stand out against their empty backgrounds. This rather superficial formula was frequently imitated by the Tosa of previous centuries. Chinese Buddhist legends and other foreign subjects were treated in a fairly Sinicized manner and are full of spirit. The suffering of preta, souls condemned to wander starving among living people who cannot see them, and the pain of hell and illness, are treated well. This same vein of realism inspired the illustrators of one or two romantic novels. The four series of the legends of Tenjin (Michizane) are different interpretations of the same composition, one being a richly colored miniature, another a line drawing, etc. We have two late thirteenth-century scrolls which depict the second attack of the Mongols against Kyushu (1281). Particularly numerous are pictures depicting the legends of holy places and biographies of famous preachers. We have two completely different and equally good pictorial versions of the life of Ippen Shonin: one of them concentrates more on the countryside, the other is more anecdotal. The life of Honen Shonin is mentioned several times in forty-eight different scrolls. "The Miracles concerning the Divinity of Kasuga" (1308; twenty scrolls) are delicate and charmingly inventive, although there is a little too much insistence on the minor details of the scenes.

Portrait painting, which had not been further developed since the beginning of the ninth century, now
showed the influence of the new realism and used it
to create a formula in the grand style. The fashion
in clothing was for garments of silk with starched
creases forming polygon-like designs. Fujiwara no Tak-
anobu has left us, among other things, a beautiful
portrait of Minamoto Yoritomo, the austere politician.
His son Nobuzane painted scrolls of the thirty-six poets
(*kasen*) using the same formula, which for a long time
remained traditional for this favorite subject.

RELIGIOUS PAINTING

Among the several highly prized paintings of Fudo,
the "Red Fudo" by Koyosan is a good example of the
transition period between the miniature work with
gold leaf of the Fujiwara era and the more pictorial
style of the Kamakura; the composition is asymmetrical
and highly original. Numerous eschatological subjects
(scenes of hell, kings of hell, the Six Worlds, the Lake
of Ice, etc.) reflect the pessimism that was widespread
after the violence of the "Gempei" epoch. The Amida
cult was clarified, simplified, and popularized by Honen
Shonin and many other preachers. Following the series
of *raigo* (the descendant of the divine procession to
meet its faithful) there appeared the moving subject
of Amida crossing the mountains, from which rises
Buddha, gigantic and radiant, like a sun of justice and
pity, over the edge of the Yamato which is plunged in
shadow.

Although the outlines are still drawn with a line as
fine as a hair, and the colors painted absolutely flat,
even the most hieratic painting is now clearer, more
eloquent, more "real" than that of the Fujiwara period.
The cutout gold leaf is now usually replaced by gold
ink. There are many examples of pictures of Jizo, the

Bodhisattva who is the protector of children and compassionate toward warriors. He is shown as a monk with a shaven head.

THE SCULPTOR UNKEI AND HIS SCHOOL

The general tendency toward realism was almost fatal to sculpture. However, thanks to Unkei, a sculptor of genius, who in the year 1200 was already an old man, sculptors produced some works of extraordinary freshness. These sculptors were the sons of Kokei, members of the Jocho family of painters seven generations removed. Commissioned by Yoritomo to make the statues for the Nara temples, which the Taira had burned down, Unkei worked in the same realistic vein as Tempyo, whose work is so well represented at Kofukuji. He had a knowledge of anatomy lacking in Nara artists. He executed some statues which Houdon, for example, would not have disowned ("Patriarchs of the Hosso Sect"). Furthermore, he had a good understanding of the decorative and monumental role of statuary. "Fudo's Twelve Acolytes" is one of his best series. "The Thunder and the Wind" (acolytes of Kwannon) are outright baroque, but so highly successful that later painters unsuccessfully attempted to copy them. For a long time now, the Japanese have had uncritical, wholehearted admiration for the Unkei workshops, for Unkei's disciple Kwaikei, for his elder son Tankei, and several other highly capable sculptors. Today, Unkei is thought to have been far superior to all of them. He also seems to have left several pupils whose names we do not know and who, having inherited his audacity, are responsible for several remarkable statues in the Kamakura temples.

The colossal bronze Buddha at Kamakura dates from 1253. We do not know the name of the sculptor. Travelers have always been of two opinions as to its quality. However, though not a masterpiece, it is incontestably a plastic as well as a technical success.

ARCHITECTURE AND THE MINOR ARTS

In order to be able to make a useful study of architectural innovations introduced in Japan during the Kamakura era, we would have to illustrate it fully. Everything was soon reabsorbed into the tradition we call Wayo, the "Japanese style," which was nothing but the T'ang style with a certain amount of Nipponizing. The numerous tiered brackets unite to form a sort of continuous cornice. They built several relatively large Prabhutaratna stupas, *tahoto*, the main floor of which is covered with a roof squared with four slopes, themselves surmounted by a circular floor, also covered by a square roof. One can often find wooden or bronze models of these strange buildings.

We have many Kamakura masks. They are less subtle than the Tempyo ones. The bronze objects— ewers, mirrors, gongs, etc.—are usually rather austere. The Chinese incised lacquer in a new way by covering wooden sculptured objects with a layer of monochrome lacquer (*kamakurabori*), later used in architectural decoration. On the other hand, the traditional *maki-e* process of sinking precious metals into black lacquer became much more supple, and changed from simple ornamentation to an almost sublime form of painting which had a noble air. On the interior of the Kongobuji sutra chest, we can see a severe *vajra* decoration, indicative of its religious contents. Yet, the lid is ornamented with a landscape (three pine trees on an island, water, rocks, and two ducks) and the sides with small birds and irises. Symmetry has been completely replaced by equilibrium, one of the principle tenets of the Japanese aesthetic. The abuse of this formula in modern times should not cause us to forget its profound originality. During the Kamakura era, the designers began to spread inscriptions over the drawing as naturally and as easily as the kana with supple and infinitely varied forms. There is only a short step between the kana and the picture puzzles that run all the way through a poem, and their decoration was to become more and more a kind of graphic poetry.

THE ASHIKAGA AND MOMOYAMA PERIODS
(Fourteenth, Fifteenth, and Sixteenth Centuries)
Plate 40

After the fall of the Kamakura regime in 1333, the court hoped that it would be given back the privileges it had enjoyed during the early Heian period. However, times had changed and the ancient regime was no more. For more than half a century, the two branches of the imperial family had been fighting each other for the throne, supported less by conviction than by the personal ambition of their partisans. Fishing in troubled waters, the *condottiere* Ashikaga Takauji paved the way for his family's supremacy, with the result that this confusing period, known as Nambo-kucho, "court of the North and court of the South," ended with a second *bakafu*, that of the Ashikaga.

Politically weak, they maintained themselves nominally amidst a period of anarchy until 1573. The arts took refuge in the Zen monasteries. Because the word Ch'an is a transliteration of *dhyana*, meaning contemplation, Europe often calls Zen a contemplative form of Buddhism, which is a poor characterization of a doctrine that is, perhaps, the only one among the Eastern philosophies to accept active life and struggle on a temporal level. It immediately became the warriors' religion.

The constant exchange of Ch'an or Zen monks between China and Japan once again opened the archipelago to new Chinese influences. Japan gave a special welcome to the poetical washes of the Southern school, and of the Southern Sung and Yüan periods, but not to the Northern "Surrealist school," genre painting, and the young Ming school. Large colored pictures of arhats, grouped in fives or tens, were much admired and even copied by Takuma Choga, as were the bronze Mincho and other styles. But the most important influence was the monochrome wash of Ch'an inspiration, which was to have a lasting impression on the later development of Japanese painting. The court patronized the traditional Yamato-e, whereas the first Ashikaga shoguns, particularly Yoshimitsu and Yoshimasa, were admirers and collectors of the avant-garde. Hence, many contemporary Chinese paintings found their way into their palaces in the Muromachi and Higashiyama eras as well as in the Zen monasteries: the powerful Gosan "Five Sanctuaries" of Kyoto and the five others of Kamakura. Many Chinese fleeing the Mongols had sought refuge in Japan. As their religious names were the same in that country, it is sometimes difficult to establish which paintings were executed by Japanese monks and which were painted by the Chinese.

ASHIKAGA WASH PAINTING

In the beginning, one recognizes the inadequacy of the Josetsu apprenticeship which was nevertheless sincere and delicate. His contemporary, Mincho, versatile but more superficial, whom we have just mentioned, made the first wash landscapes in Japan, and excellent colored or monochrome portraits of his fellow monks (Fig. 58). We will not discuss the quantities of Zen subjects executed by painters whose names and identities we are unsure of and who added nothing to what we have already seen in China. The more successful the copy, the less interesting it is. During the early part of the fifteenth century, Shubun had a firm

Fig. 58. Portrait of the Emperor Gohanazono.

quality to his brush which is just as good as that of Ma Yüan, but which does not prevent him from being inferior to his austere and almost homonymous contemporary Cheou Wen-tsing. His subject matter is charming but insufferably monotonous. It is always a cottage at the foot of a cliff, standing amidst tall trees that dominate a lake. Three popular secular painters at the shogun court—Naomi, his son, Geiami, and his grandson, Soami—had a free style of bravura brushwork that fails to disguise their small talents. All this Sinicized painting has been overpraised by the Japanese and does not warrant our spending too much time discussing it. Soga Jasoku is a capable, thoughtful, and fairly intellectual painter. Chokuan is highly respected for his paintings of hawks, which are of little interest to us. Oguri Sotan is a good painter of birds.

Sesshu catches our attention more for his personality than for his painting. As he was in charge of the appraisal of art imported from China, he was in a position to see the work of the new Ming painters who were at that time turning from the Sogen tradition (Sung and Yüan eras). He himself spent six years in China between 1494 and 1470. His work, inasmuch as we can sort it out from those paintings wrongly attributed to him and those which are forgeries, cannot be placed in a chronological pattern. He made screens of birds and flowers, rather delicate and austere portraits, free washes with "splashed" ink—which have little to recommend them except the force of the improvisation—and portrayed simple, rather brutal religious subjects with lengthy texts as taught by the Zen masters. He also painted symbolic landscapes ("The Fisherman and the Woodcutter") which are rather ugly washes, though nevertheless the work of an artist. The small, highlighted water colors are as charming as those done by Chinese painters. Hsia Kuei's brittle line is particularly noticeable in his landscapes, which are intellectual rather than sensitive. These landscapes are curious for their perfectly balanced construction which nearly always consists of a system of oblique lines stabilized by a small horizontal placed in the middle. This irreproachable but nevertheless monotonous framework is the main interest in two scrolls and several *kakemono* (hanging paintings). And yet we are bothered by the artist's contempt for his composition and his materials. His forceful line silhouettes the form but never suggests its volume. The sky stands in front of the cliffs; roofs dotting the composition are badly defined when placed in the background. Furthermore, trees, pathways, rocks, boats, etc., are so schematized and so little felt that the picture ends up by being a calligraph. The picture would have been as eloquent, if not more so, if the artist had, instead of drawing, inscribed corresponding characters in those spaces. Sesshu's personality is best expressed in his signatures. Even someone unable to read the language is struck by the power. (And yet, let us mention here that the Japanese were not overly concerned with the signature.) For more than two centuries, painters who had none of his temperament worked in the style of Sesshu and his "Unkoku workshop" ("vale of clouds").

During the mid-sixteenth century, Sesson made drawings that are full of movement and on occasion have considerable grandeur. We should also mention the astonishing birds painted during the seventeenth century by the warrior Miyamato Niten. They are almost better than those of Mu-ch'i.

Before moving on to the most interesting school of the Ashikaga period, the kano, we should remind ourselves that the Yamato-e, particularly that of the Tosa, only just managed to survive in aristocratic circles. It often became somewhat dry and conventional. The religious sects continued to commission narrative scrolls, glorifying their patron saint. The Amidist Yuzu Nembutzu sect asked several artists to collaborate on a large work of art which, according to certain writers, was engraved on wood so that it could be repeated, the engraving serving as a surface for ordinary paint. In order to fill the demand for screens and *fusuma* (sliding doors), the Tosa made highly colorful compositions with a great deal of calligraphy (Fig. 59). Those paintings attributed to Tosa Mitsunobu, the head of the school, are of doubtful authenticity. It would appear that toward the end of the fifteenth century there was a school of quasi-popular anonymous decorators, which we shall speak of in a moment.

THE FOUNDING OF THE KANO SCHOOL

During the later Ashikaga period, among the painters who worked in the Chinese style (*kara-e* or *kangwa*) was a certain Kano Masanobu, born around 1453. He

Fig. 59. Horse and Groom. Muromachi Period.

left us some wash landscapes of uneven quality and figure work painted in opaque colors, lacking in grace. His son, Kano Motonobu, a highly gifted person who fully understood the requirements of decoration, made excellent panels in India ink, with or without highlights in color. He made scrolls in the Tosa manner with extensive empty gilded areas, always taking care not to make a "hole" in the painting. In fact, he was responsible for the fortunate eclecticism that made the Kano school famous for two hundred years, although the two tendencies are not quite as intimately blended together as they were in the work of his successors. He married Tosa Mitsunobu's daughter, and succeeded his father-in-law as court painter. From a Chinese point of view, it would seem that he exploited the variety of line we praise in Wu Tao-tzu of the late T'ang period. He draws flesh with fine, light pointed brush strokes, using diluted ink; and clothes with bold accentuated strokes; rocks have rectilinear and angular shapes that suggest their hardness. (The "Three Vinegar Tasters" in the Guimet Museum might well be one of his last works. He was concerned with the unity of the three religions, Taoism, Confucianism, and Buddhism, a subject that has always fascinated Japanese thinkers.) Motonobu also painted landscapes without "bones" in the manner of Mu-ch'i. His "Eight Views of the Siao and the Siang," placed two-by-two on four panels, are poorly executed. His many screens and *fusuma*, without being extraordinary, are generally good decoration. He was surrounded by several painters whose style is indistinguishable from his own, among them Yukinobu (his younger brother, son?) and his nephew, Gyokuraku.

Japanese painters were still not in the habit of signing their work. Apart from the Zen washes, which often are loaded with numerous eulogies, poems, and colophons inserted by other monks, the majority of names we find on paintings are attributions that would not stand investigation. Many works of art which were not part of a noble family's treasure, or that of a monastery, are anonymous. The often rather naïve style causes us to believe that they were executed by non-aristocratic artists who worked for the bourgeoisie and who naturally copied the styles that were popular at court. Their repertoire, to begin with, was limited, consisting of the four seasons, the sun on a spring or summer screen, the moon in silver on the left panel, autumn, and winter; or pine trees standing by some water with *momochidori*, with flocks of gulls flying about; or the Uji Bridge with its willows and Persian wheel, etc. The main part of the composition is usually found on the right panel of the left-hand screen, on the left of the right-hand screen. Toward the center of the screen are vague suggestions of distant scenes that seem to lead to the section opening out into the two side panels. This same symmetry was used by the Kano until the middle of the seventeenth century.

THE MOMOYAMA PERIOD (1570–*ca.* 1610)

The feudal anarchy which erupted in Japan and lasted two and a half centuries was finally suppressed by Oda Nobunaga who, in 1573, chased out from kyoto the last Ashikaga shogun and severely punished the politician and warrior monks by burning their temples. Relative peace reigned, at least in the central provinces. Nobunaga was stupidly assassinated in 1582, but his lieutenant, Toyotomi Hideyoshi, an exceedingly gifted statesman, carried on with his late master's work. He made the mistake of getting involved in continental wars; the Korean expeditions were disastrous. He was justifiably alarmed by the Catholic missionary activities, and took the first steps to have them suppressed. When he died of an unknown disease in 1598, he had succeeded in imposing his authority over the whole of the archipelago. However, this was a precarious unification, for the great feudal lords were always prepared to take up arms again. Tokugawa Ieyasu, whom everyone agreed should be his successor, defeated at Sekigahara the people who had tried to remove him from power, and, founding the third *bakafu*, which lasted until 1867, occupied himself immediately with the daimyo, rendering them impotent so that they could no longer disturb the peace.

The period, which lasted thirty to forty years and was a fruitful one for the arts, is called the Momoyama epoch (named after a Hideyoshi palace). Religion played a minor role: Buddhism, compromised by its role in temporal affairs, was no longer a moral force. Although a few members of the nobility arranged profitable business connections, it was a new class of financiers and merchants who, between 1566 and 1572, providing the artists with a new clientele, slowly began to grow in influence. These clients preferred the decorative or anecdotal paintings to the art of either literary or religious allusion. It is hardly astonishing that the schools of art most honored by the learned, that of the Tosa and the Kano, had been developed by popular, anonymous painters who had found a formula which was neither too literary nor too realistic, which had dense coloring yet was refined, and which was far more in harmony with home decorations than delicate water colors.

The Kano of the second and third generation after Motonobu are far more interesting to us than any artist of the Ashikaga period. They have left us charming interpretations of popular scenes such as "The Visit to Takao" (neighboring temple of Kyoto). In a screen by Hideyori, second son of Motonobu, we can see an arched bridge in agreeable relation to people strolling about: on the left, a few samurai, on the right, seated young women are watching over their children, and a traveling salesman is offering them cakes. Hideyori's nephew, Kano Eitoku, is eminently representative of the new style in his *fusuma* of flowers, in his imaginary lions (*karashihi*), and in his screens decorated with great simplicity with trees in sober and powerful colors. A pair of screens shows views of Kyoto laid out in seed fields encircled by large areas of golden *ambiance*. Even though these views have no depth, they make pleasing decoration. His brother Naganobu (Fig. 60) painted lovely *hanami* (picnics under cherry-blossom trees); and Kano Naizen, the celebrations in the year 1604 in memory of Hideyoshi, in which we can see hundreds of well-drawn and well-grouped

Fig. 60. Detail of a Screen Painted by Kano Nagan-obu. Popular Dance.

people. In addition to the painters permitted to use the name of Kano, there were several first-class masters who used the same formulas; for example, Hasegawa Tohaku ("The Uji Bridge," "The Fishing Nets").

It is not a very long time since the Japanese began to take an interest in the paintings of manners and customs which they had formerly considered somewhat vulgar. Many marvels of this genre have yet to be discovered. Europeans will find in it an aspect of the Japanese genius of which they still know very little. A particularly interesting category of these everyday scenes is found in screens showing Portuguese sailors and European merchants disembarking from their large ships and walking in procession to the Catholic Mission. (The Guimet Museum has a fine specimen.) We know that the Portuguese discovered Kyushu in 1543 and that Saint Francis Xavier came to preach the gospel in Japan in 1549. However, it was somewhat later that the Jesuits were permitted to preach to the nobility, and for the first time, European customs were the rage in Japan (Fig. 61). The rigorous persecutions

Fig. 61. Detail of Lacquered Box. A "Portuguese." Momoyama Period.

did not come until after the death of Hideyoshi. It is curious that the screens depicting the Portuguese were made precisely at the time of the persecutions, although we should remember that the Japanese of this era were not in the least religious. The painters were most certainly not Christian and their lively observations were not particularly kind.

It is hard to determine the reciprocal influences between the popular painters and those of the established. The popular painters gained much from the Kano, and the Kano repaid the compliment. However, the Tosa influence was predominantly in those paintings of scenes from the early secular theater, of which the favorite subject matter is *Tagasode*: the rich cos-

tumes laid out on easels preparatory to being per-
fumed; the charming faces of dancers, male and female;
several screens—the most beautiful of all—which present us with a grandiose picture of courtesans in their
misery and vulgarity. We now realize that these Momoyama paintings of customs were the main precursors
to the Ukiyo-e, which was to triumph during the
second half of the seventeenth century—at least at
Edo.

THE ARCHITECTURE OF RECENT CENTURIES

In order not to interrupt constantly our study of
Japanese painting, we will at this point make a few
notes on secular and religious architecture from the
fifteenth to the eighteenth century.

In the Shinto religion, the conservatism of the villages was often satisfied with a humble cottage sufficient for the local parishioners; as a result, we have a
number of picturesque and unexpected buildings.
However, the large sanctuaries under the protection
of the nobles, like the one at Kasuga near Nara and
that of Itsukushima Jinsha in the Hiroshima region,
adopted many characteristics of Buddhist architecture
—for example, the multistoried porch, the cloister
forming a surrounding wall, and even such a typically
Buddhist building as the pagoda; neither did they omit
the *torii*, nor the pavilion of sacred horses, nor the
votive tablets. By the end of the Middle Ages, the
main building was usually composed of three halls
grouped together in the shape of a horizontal H. However, the details were the same as those in contemporaneous Buddhist temples.

In the Zen temples of the Ashikaga period, a large
porch called the *sanmon* looks, on first sight, like the
chūmon of the old Horyuji, though the floors were accessible. It was really a long, low hall with an iconosta-

sis, the imposing beamwork of which was exposed and which had a dragon inscribed within a circle on the ceiling. In the cities, the general plan, more complicated, was nevertheless squeezed into a small space. It consisted of several buildings with rectangular and symmetrical pools of water. Emperors and princes who had abdicated often retired to temples situated in the country; this explains why we sometimes find a temple that is actually an aristocratic secular villa with a well-planned garden, such as the famous Daidemboin of the Daitokuji.

NIKKO AND OTHER SHOGUN MAUSOLEUMS

When Tokugawa Ieyasu died in 1616, a council was held to discuss the question of funerary rites. According to reports, the meeting was most amusing. Buddhism had lost its authority; Shinto, considered popular superstition, was vegetating in the background. The Tokugawa saw in Confucianism a religion that would consolidate their regime and they decided, therefore, that the deceased should be honored by the building of an *otamaya*, the Chinese *miao*, the ancestral temple. However, most people would have been baffled by this exotic idea if the service had not been conducted in the accommodating Shinto style. One mausoleum was erected in the Kunozan (under Shizuoka jurisdiction). In 1635, the Nikko mausoleum was built on a magnificent site sixty-two miles north of Edo. Each of the succeeding shoguns had his own mausoleum, but the enormous cost was incompatible with the poor financial state of the country, and after 1730 they stopped building new *otamaya*. Those already in existence each contained the tombs of several members of the shogun family. The Nikko mausoleum and others belong, therefore, to a form of artificial religion created to intrigue the ignorant European.

Confucian and Chinese in spirit, they are only Shinto-ist in their exterior. They are unfortunately a disgrace to Japanese art.

The famous Yomeimon porch at Nikko represents the summit of this architectural decoration developed from approximately 1550 onward; yet, it is over-charged, extravagantly heavy, and covered with poly-chrome. A process much like our "fumed oak" was in common use, giving a creamy yellow appearance to certain parts of the building. The façade, consisting of doubled curve arches known as *karahafu*, "Chinese gables," in spite of there being no such thing in China, here look heavy and decadent. The humble Shinto palisade has been turned into a wall of panels sculpted in high relief, too realistically and with every available space covered with polychrome. The subject matter consists of flowers and animals, all reduced to the same proportions, whatever their size might be in reality—the height of a misguided aesthetic. The guidebooks call our attention to an analogous work of art (in the sacred stables) where we can see three monkeys (*saru*) that see no evil, speak no evil, hear no evil, in appropriate postures. But they usually for-get to add that *saru* is the negative expression of the verb *kikazaru*, in classical language meaning "to not hear," etc. This is one example among many thousands of the play on words which often inspired decorative art.

The decoration inside the halls is also too sumptu-ous. Yet, there is a little more control, a well-managed graduation, while the profusion of gilt re-establishes the unity. The panels are embellished with floral and other compositions which are similar to the work of the Kano executed in delicate bas-relief. In the cornices one can see twin ribwork which is due probably to

European influence. The Dutch donated the bronze lantern in the courtyard.

In the last of the *otamaya*, dating from the beginning of the eighteenth century, there were some more or less fortunate, fairly interesting innovations, such as the striped columns with convex grooves, *ryugutsukuri* porches, "dragon palaces," or a pavilion of ordinary wood surmounted by massive pieces of masonry pierced with an arch. This form, borrowed from southern China, had already been introduced in Japan by a new Confucianist Zen sect (the Houang-mo, Obaku). This sect encouraged painting and played an appreciable role in the eighteenth-century artistic movement.

SECULAR ARCHITECTURE

Our knowledge of the Fujiwara palaces comes to us from literary references and from the pictures of Yamato-e. There are a few rare Ashikaga buildings still left standing, such as those near Kyoto, the Kinkakuji, dated 1397, and the Ginkakuji, built during the following century. (The first mentioned, alas, burned down in 1950.) Formerly they were villas that had been given to the Zen monks. A small house standing in the same park as the Ginkakuji, known as the Togudo, contains a small room set aside for the tea ceremony. During the sixteenth century, the *chashitsu* was by preference built on the outside, a few steps from the house, simulating a cottage lost in the depths of the woods. The famous aesthetes of the period did sketches of these teahouses which are still much admired. We do understand the search for perfection and good taste through simplicity, though we have little admiration for this vaunting display of poverty, for which the *chajin* ruined themselves. They sent to far distant places for fascinating small stones of unusual shape and color with which to pave the pathways, for round pieces of knotty wood to make a base for the *tokonoma,* and they fought among each other for the privilege of buying at fabulous prices thick sandstone cups and rusty, battered hot-water bottles. The houses of the rich became more and more intimately linked to the art of the garden, which actually dominated the floor plan. The style was known as *shoin-zukuri.* The Japanese garden had nothing in common with the French garden, nor with Persian gardens, though they could be compared to the eighteenth-century English garden, obviously without either recourse to the antique or the taste for artificial ruins. One might compare these gardens to Japanese landscape painting: they consisted of a carefully studied composition and various vantage points with which nature collaborated for further variation at all hours of the day. Though it still survives in Japan today, all this art is as foreign to us as Versailles would have been to the Fujiwara. Even the third-rate restaurant has a small garden as large as a "cat's forehead," which deserves to be admired even in its detail.

MILITARY ARCHITECTURE

On every page of the chronicles written during the Ashikaga period, there are references to fortresses which we know little about since we do not have further documentation. The introduction of firearms during the sixteenth century created notable changes. The great feudal lords built themselves fortified castles rising from rounded hillocks and surrounded them with ramparts. One entered the manor by a narrow postern; then came secret passages and another rampart which divided the interior into *maru* (circles) or zones that became increasingly difficult to penetrate. In the center of this labyrinth was the *tenju*—or dungeon—a tower of three, four, or five stories crowned by a broken roof of the usual variety. There was no ornamentation, but the Japanese used the numerous windows, some surmounted by triangular pediments, some by *karahafu*, to make compositions of perfect taste. Nagoya castle, which contained very interesting decorative paintings, was destroyed during the last war. Osaka castle was merely a modern reconstruction of a fortress built by Hideyoshi. During the early part of the seventeenth century, the Tokugawa prohibited the construction of new castles, and the architectural form developed no further.

Although many rivers cross the natural routes in Japan, the bridges were not very sophisticated. There was too much vested interest among lords, boatmen, porters, innkeepers, etc. The few bridges were usually simple wooden stepladders, often seen in engravings, rather like those at Edo. But there were others also made of wood and built on the quite different principle of the corbel arch. The most curious of these was at Kintai Bashi of Iwakuni, not far from Hiroshima. It consisted of five units rising from some forty feet above the water, each ninety-eight feet long. There were also several stone bridges at Nagasaki attributed to the Chinese, although so rational in design that one should probably give credit to the Dutch for having built them.

THE TOKUGAWA EPOCH

FIRST PERIOD (1602–*ca.* 1740)
Plates 41 and 42

No period in the history of Japan is as interesting as the Tokugawa epoch. The Tokugawa formulated the totalitarian state, with the sequel that our generation knows only too well: the closing of frontiers, espionage and inquisition, financial dishonesty, a central authority controlling all activities from the arts and letters to amusement and debauchery. However, we cannot deny the impartiality of the Tokugawa statesmen (with a few notable exceptions) nor their success in establishing a long peace both at home and abroad. At least their adoption of Confucianism, which appears dry to us, once again gave Japan an ethic, which it had not had since the Buddhists relinquished their power. Although they were suspicious of Kyoto circles, they greatly respected the art of the past.

Ieyasu decided that the seat of the *bakafu* should be at the foot of the castle Hideyoshi had given him in the village of Edo, which was to become Tokyo. The city grew in size and population with incredible speed. As Tokyo had no past, she built a cultural center which was to be as different as possible from all the others. Her attitude toward old Japan was somewhat like the United States's toward Europe: respectful and tender, though a little mocking at the same time. Apart from the old aristocracy, stripped of its former powers, and the new nobility consisting of the Tokugawa vassals, who were kept strongly in check, the population was divided into four classes. These were the samurai, commoners who considered themselves superior to the other castes, farmers, and merchants. Only the last two led relatively happy lives during the Edo epoch.

BIRTH OF THE UKIYO-E

Circumstances explain the birth of a new artistic movement which was not a "school" as such, since it never had its own workshops and famous masters, like the Tosa and the Kano. Rather, this movement was brought into being spontaneously by artists stemming from the most diverse backgrounds but united by the desire to capture the bourgeois market which was steadily growing. As we have already seen, this movement began during the Momoyama period. Our first Japanese scholars made the mistake of translating the word *ukiyo* as meaning "the floating world." The word was in current use during the Middle Ages to denote "that world which only inspires revulsion" (from the word *uki,* which could mean either fastidious or miserable). However, they ended up by using a homophonous character which actually means to "be above," "in relief," to be "in a state of euphoria." At the same time, the old expression with Buddhist overtones took on the quite different meaning of "beau monde" or "high life." The word was soon bastardized into a commercial slogan equivalent to the word "modern," "select," etc. It could be applied to anecdotal or gallant subjects which titillated the semieducated bourgeois. The subjects included celebrations, excursions, shop scenes in the Yoshiwara (the red-light district at Edo), and later the secular theater, which was born, along with the new regime, around the year 1600.

When Momoyama painting had been forgotten, the founding of Ukiyo-e was traditionally attributed to a certain Iwasa Matabei or Shoi, who died in 1650, and who was a somewhat enigmatic character. Those of his works to have been positively identified can be counted on the fingers of one hand. Furthermore, they are all quite different in style. In one he imitates Liang K'ai in quick wash sketches; in another he depicts the voyage of the "Virgin of Ise," using a refined classical Yamato-e formula. Delicate miniatures of members of the professional classes have also been attributed to him. He was soon given the name of Ukiyo Matabei. No work was as aristocratic as his. He had no contact with the new movement which the elite had for many years branded as vulgar. However, before going any

further into the history of Ukiyo-e, we will summarize
the evolution of the old schools of painting.

THE KANOS OF THE TOKUGAWA EPOCH

We have now reached the fourth generation of the
Kano family after Motonobu. The head of the school
also, on occasion, conferred the name on artists who
were not related to the family. Three brothers each
founded a separate workshop at Edo. The eldest, Kano
Tanyu, occupied a very important position in the artistic world of the time. He made wash compositions
(screens, *fusuma*, etc.) of Chinese subjects, with highlights of gold powder which had been in fashion since
the end of the sixteenth century. He also painted pictures of Bodhisattvas which are Zen in spirit, and
scrolls in a style that is a cross between Tosa and Kano.
(Among these is a posthumous glorification of
Ieyasu.) He made large murals, somber in color, with
gold backgrounds which are irritating to the eye. He
wanted very much to be the Motonobu of his century.
He was the Lebrun of Japan, as gifted as the French
woman and no more passionate. Conservative and au-
thoritarian, he was responsible for the academic tone
which has weighed on the school ever since. His
brother, Tsunenobu, a highly prolific artist, has left us
some rather drab water colors. The other brother,
Eino, is particularly admired for his history of Japanese
painters. Another Kano workshop, known as the "Capital" because it had not moved from Kyoto to Edo, fostered two great artists during the seventeenth century:
Sanraku, whose qualities and defects were almost similar to Tanyu's; and his son Sansetsu, who was more
distinguished, more original, and more open to influences not associated with the eclecticism of the first
Kano.

THE TOSA SCHOOLS OF THE TOKUGAWA EPOCH

During the Momoyama epoch, the Tosa had been forced, in order to make a living, to transfer their main workshop in Kyoto to Sakai, a very busy port until it was superseded by a new center which was built near Osaka by Hideyoshi on the site of the old city of Naniwa. The Tosa also had to make certain concessions to the taste of the period by drawing closer to the hybrid style of the Kano. However, Ieyasu made a good strategic move when he presented a statue to the imperial court. This flattered the old and somewhat neglected aristocracy, which once again became the patrons of the Tosa. The school's most important master during the seventeenth century is Mitsuoki, who painted scenes of the Japanese Middle Ages, as well as Chinese subjects. His younger brother (?) Hiromichi, was encouraged by the emperor to revive the name of Sumiyoshi, formerly made famous by the painter Keion, whose best-known work is the *Heiji Monogatari*. Under the name of Sumiyoshi Jokei, and with his son Gukei, he founded a dissident school with a style that is hard to distinguish from that of the Tosa. During the years that preceded the fall of the Tokugawa, the group of painters sympathetic to the old imperial court championed a return to the Yamato-e style. Their leaders were Tanaka Totsugen, Ukita Ikkei, and Tametaka Reizei (who was assassinated by a *bakafu* fanatic), together with several other good painters.

THE DECORATORS

The early sixteenth century marks the beginning of a dynasty of universal artists who were at the same time painters, lacquerers, potters, etc., and who could be called scholarly decorators to distinguish them from the popular decorators, to whom, however, they were much indebted. The popular decorators were always thought highly of in their own country, and Europe has learned to appreciate their talents. Lacquerware was Honnami Koetsu's specialty. He broke with the traditions of the *maki-e* to invent a highly original style which was suggestive rather than descriptive. In addition to gold, he also used lead, which by some miracle he managed to make even more attractive than precious metals. He also went back to using *ashide*, which gave the characters a very important decorative role. For the Chanoyu sect he made granite tea bowls, whose rustic modeling suggests autumn, the Mount Fuji snows, etc. In collaboration with his friend Tawaraya Sotatsu he painted scrolls, whose main theme appears to be a text in kana. Drawings in light wash depicting plants, animals, etc., play a subordinate role. Like many masters before and after him, Sotatsu penetrated the old Yamato-e. However, he had learned sufficiently from the style to be able to detach himself from its formulas and techniques. Koetsu and Sotatsu can be compared to a double star in a constellation, the major star of which, two generations later, was to be the illustrious Ogata Korin, a great nephew of Sotatsu on his mother's side.

Korin's genius lay in his ability to evolve a harmonious and lively formula from the various traditions that abounded in the artistic world toward the end of the seventeenth century, which is the reason Europe considered him the most Japanese of all Japanese artists. As son of the shogunal court fabric painter, he had (through his family connections) access to the sketches of Koetsu and Sotatsu. On several occasions he borrowed their ideas—the use of lead, mother of pearl, etc.—and even their subjects. His brush stroke has a thick and velvety quality to it which has never been imitated. One of Korin's more astonishing inventions was his application of India ink to gouaches that were still wet. The black merges extraordinarily effectively with the red ocher and the green. He brought a new system of values to colored composition. Snow-capped peaks under gray skies had been painted before him, but we gasp at his view of Mount Fuji seen from another hill. His profound and quiet humor is unique. He never seems to be serious about either his subject or his interpretation of it. The Japanese writers do not mention his sense of humor, as if they were uncertain of the artist's intentions, or as if a hint of a smile were incompatible with a tone of respect. He is the most successful of all the painters in depicting the refinement, *joie de vivre* and sense of fun that is germane to the Genroku period (1688–1704). Independent and original, Korin never had a patron among the nobility, and was almost unknown during his lifetime. He was, however, appreciated by people of taste, and for a long time his studio produced both signed and unsigned works of art all worthy of the master.

Korin's brother, Ogata Kenzan, painted in the same style, though perhaps with less freedom and less fantasy. He is particularly well known for his pottery. Like his brother, he too managed to achieve a perfect synthesis of all previous styles, from the old Japanese Seto to the Ming porcelains. Let us also remember that Korin and Kenzan were both born in Kyoto, and spent most of their lives there. In his old age, Kenzan followed a princely monk, who was his patron, to Edo.

Oga Haritsu, their contemporary, was a somewhat eccentric poet. His name means "torn straw hat." He painted with lacquers, using diverse materials, such as ivory, bone, hard stone, ceramics, and several metals. Though his taste was Chinese and rather graceless, he was nevertheless an admirable artist.

THE UKIYO-E AND THE FIRST PRINTS

We may now return to Edo and the Ukiyo-e, which
was to reign supreme for two hundred years. It is hard
to show any enthusiasm for this style, so greatly admired by the Japanese (although less than all the other
schools and only because of a sentimental attachment
to the period). The favorite subject is *bijin*, "pretty
woman" (Fig. 62)—almost courtesan—treated without

Fig. 62. Woman. Ukiyo-e Painting.

style and usually anatomically incorrect. There is nothing new about either their appearance or the technique
of putting opaque colors over faint drawing. During
the second half of the seventeenth century, several
painters seem to have hesitated between the ancient
traditions and the new ideas. Among these would be
Hanabusa Itcho, whose work is agreeable, though superficial. He painted popular scenes and, although a

tactless person, made every effort not to burn his Kano and Tosa bridges. In 1698, he shocked the *bakafu* with a drawing of "Asazumabune," an allusion to the boat trips that the fifth shogun made with his mistress. As a result, he was exiled for eleven years on one of the Vries Islands, where a butterfly came to distract him in his solitude (Itcho means "unique butterfly"). In a painting showing a man leading his horse over a bridge, there are, for the first time, reflections in the water. However, these reflections are not where they might be expected to be. Although Miyagawa Chosun was one of the most eminent Ukiyo-e painters of his time, his *bijin* appear feeble to us; and we find his genre and pseudohistorical subjects unpleasant.

In order to reach a wider public than the wealthy middle class at Edo and Osaka, many Ukiyo-e masters were forced to make inexpensive prints. Despite the limitations of the technique, and the reduced format, they almost all turned out to be very good. Since their *nikupitsu* (paintings and drawings as opposed to engravings) are never superior to their *hangwa* (prints), we will be able, in the few pages we have at our disposal, to discuss the history of Ukiyo-e as a branch of engraving.

Since the Tempyo period, xylography (Fig. 63) had only been used for religious purposes—even more exclusively so in China. Simultaneously in China, and doubtless because of the influence from European books, xylographs began to appear in Japan as illustrations in secular books. After the publication of the *Ise Monogatari* in 1608, short illustrated novels and good-sized picture books appeared in large numbers. The idea of issuing individual prints is attributed to Hishikawa Moronobu around 1673. The son of an embroiderer (the fashion at the time was materials embroidered or painted with picturesque subjects, even entire land-

Fig. 63. Portrait of Sugawara Michizane. Mikkyo
Hanga Xylograph.

scapes), this great master was in no manner naïve, having a sound knowledge of Chinese painting, including
that of the Kano and Tosa. Like a great many other
artists of the early Ukiyo-e period, he signed his work
"master of Japanese painting"—a pretentious claim of
belonging to the Tosa. This was done because the public had little taste for Chinese painting. He painted
screens and scrolls that gave an accurate picture of the
theaters of his time. His numerous books of engravings contain above all many pictures of women going
about their daily tasks—not only those in the Yoshiwara, but also women of every estate. His drawing is
characterized by a largeness of spirit resembling Dau-
mier's, with simple and unbroken lines. His many pupils perpetuated his style for twenty to thirty years after

his death in 1695. We know their names, though it is hard to tell their work apart, for the paintings are rarely signed. All the xylographs of the time were printed in black ink, though they are quite frequently highlighted with one or two superimposed colors painted in by hand: a faint opaque orange called *tan*, a transparent Indian yellow called *kuchinushi*, and indigo. Prints that are colored by hand after having been processed are called *tan-e*.

Nishikawa Sukenobu, supposedly harassed by the state police, went to Osaka and Kyoto in order to paint and engrave his paintings of gallant ladies and gentlemen. It is perhaps he who has given us the most gracious and the most faithful portrait of Japanese women. During the mid-eighteenth century, Nishimura Shigenobu followed in the same tradition. Although not particularly original, he is thought to have been the master of several innovators.

During the lifetime of Moronobu, new grounds were explored in engraving. Toward 1687, Torii Kiyonobu I, the son of an actor, created dynamic and original theater posters. He subsequently did engravings of actors in their best roles. It was precisely at this moment that a genuinely "dramatic" art was born, for up until that time the public had been attracted mainly by the physical appearance of the actors (we know that since 1629 women had been forbidden on the stage). Kiyonobu I's successor, Kiyomasu I (Fig. 64), and several other collaborators whose identity is unknown (Kiyonobu II and Kiyomasu II, etc.), were no less talented than Kiyonobu I. During these two generations, the Torii workshops specialized almost exclusively in theater prints. It is hardly surprising that engraving, which owed its success to the glorifying, if not to the advertising, of courtesans and play actors, was for a long time not popular among the Japanese elite. Europeans

Fig. 64. Actor. *Tan-e* Hand-Colored Engraving by Kiyomasu.

were the first to recognize their great artistic value—only recently recognized by the Japanese.

Between 1715 and 1725, the mysterious Kaigetsudo workshop occupied itself solely with the making of *bijin:* the famous courtesan, either alone, or accompanied by a *kamuro*, a young girl who was her little servant while waiting to be a courtesan herself. There exist so many superb though similar paintings and engravings of this subject that one asks oneself if the various signatures—Ando, Anchi, etc.—were not pseudonyms of the one and same draftsman.

Okumura Masanobu, a powerful publisher, was also an excellent artist. He increased the variety of engravings by depicting scenes of not only the Yoshiwara and the theater, but also of anecdotal, legendary, and true stories. During his long career (the same name was actually used by the father Gempachi and his son Genroku), he seems to have been the first to perfect some of the engraving techniques. The *tan-e* was already being enriched with gold dust, and certain blacks were intensified with varnish (*urushi-e*). In either 1740 or 1743, they invented the two-tone print, and since one of the tones was nearly always *beni* (a very pale pink), these engravings are called *beni-e*. The other color was usually either green or slate blue. Japanese engraving reached its most enchanting stage during the *beni-e* period. It is astonishing to find that the last improvement in the technique—printing the colors desired by increasing the number of blocks—was only invented some twenty years later.

The workshops gradually became less specialized. The Torii factory, under the leadership of its third master, Kiyomitsu I, used the same subject matter and designs as the Okumura establishment. The same can be said for Ishikawa Toyonobu I, whose style was noticeably virile. Printing was often done in three colors in addition to the black. Formats became standardized. The tendency was toward abandoning the *hoso-e* (twelve inches high, six inches long, the most frequently used for the early *beni-e*) for more ample formats.

From 1730 to 1750, the general quality of engraving was extraordinarily high. To the European, its refinement is at once astonishing and unbelievable, considering the humble clientele for whom it was made.

THE MID-TOKUGAWA PERIOD
(*ca.* 1740–1800)
Plates 43–46

After a century of construction and consolidation, the middle period of the Tokugawa regime was one of such stability that it gave the impression of having always existed. Since the seventeenth century, the Dutch were the only Europeans allowed to enter a Japanese port, and even they had to drop anchor at the minuscule island of Deshima in the port of Nagasaki, where they hardly attracted any attention at all. Glass mirrors, binoculars, and imported clocks were in use at that time. (It is thought that Japan started to make her own glass during the eighteenth century.) We know little about the works of art imported by the Dutch. European influence in Ukiyo-e began to appear in approximately 1740. However, the Japanese believe that European perspective, badly understood, came to them via Chinese art. Chinese junks were permitted to anchor only at Nagasaki where their merchandise was scrupulously examined by high officials, the *mekiki,* who acted more as censors than customs officers. Many of the Chinese painters who spent some time in Japan seem to have traveled no further than the area around Nagasaki. Diplomatic relations with China had not been re-established; in contrast, the receptions accorded to the Korean ambassadors were "the news of the day," and were commemorated with engravings that were made for a period of 150 years. The state religion of Confucianism was bearing fruit, the Confucian virtues sincerely honored. As for Buddhism, it led so quiet an existence that people no longer jeered at it, and the monks were already looked upon as "cemetery keepers."

Repeating the attempts made in the Asuka period, the famous shogun sage Yoshimura (1716–1745) tried to lower the barriers between Japan and the outside world by entrusting two or three learned men with the task of asking the Dutch some questions about science, particularly medicine and astronomy. However, except for specific missions, intercourse with the Dutch was not encouraged. Elementary education was sufficiently widespread to keep the printing houses busy. In the cities, theater and engraving played an educative role comparable to the cinema's today. A few Chinese and Japanese historical facts and the great masterpieces of literature, though abridged perhaps, were available to a large mass of people who would have never seen a book. At Edo, the marionette theater (*joruri, gidayu*), for which Chikamatsu had written lively and colorful masterpieces, was not as popular as the legitimate theater, which, unlike that of other countries, did not act as a simple "escape." If one makes a close study of the dramatists' artifices and of the theater's technique, one realizes that the Kabuki has succeeded in creating a continuously imaginary world side by side with the real world, engravings of which convey a sense of intimacy.

THE SINOMANIA OF THE ELITE AND THE BUNJINGWA

For four centuries, Japan had thought that Sung and Yüan painting—which, incidentally, they did not know well—were the only Chinese styles worth copying. A Chinese from Wuhing, Yi Fou-kieou, who arrived in Nagasaki on a business trip, and who was an amateur painter, brought with him the *Wu-jen-hua* (lettered paintings), which had been flourishing in his country for more than a century. The intellectuals—who were united in a common admiration for Basho, the *hakai* poet—were most enthusiastic about this new mode of expression. The ground had already been somewhat broken by the new Zen-Confucianist sect of Obaku: one might have just as well have been in China as at his monastery of Mampukuji, near Kyoto. The Sinomania of these young people was not without a certain amount of childishness. If, on an excursion into the country, they had climbed three hills, they would call themselves "The Hermits of the Three Peaks." They would boil the water for their tea over dry maple leaves; they brought a bottle of water from a Chinese river in order to blend it with the Yodumaga; they amused themselves by taking three-character Chinese names.

The poet Yosa no Buson was the center of this movement. Like his companions, he has left quick sketches, straightforward souvenirs and notes of the pleasant days he spent in their company. We particularly admire his more important washes, certainly traditional in their form and manner, in which one feels the personal touch. The Japanese have called him the "down-to-earth" poet. He was actually extremely fond of horses, which are present everywhere in both his paintings and his verses. His technique was also perfect, and his *fusuma* among the most successful. His great friend, Ikeno Taiga, was perhaps more knowledgeable, more bold. At the Mampukuji, he painted "Arhat on the Waves," a superb composition. Of all the Sino-Japanese painters, he is perhaps the most versatile and piquant.

We will not mention the large number of *Bunjingwa* painters whose work is of uneven quality. By the end of the eighteenth century, and during the beginning of the nineteenth, the aesthetic and dilettante world around Kyoto was dominated by Tani Buncho, who undoubtedly wanted to be the Tung Ch'i-ch'ang of his time in his country. A great connoisseur, a highly influential and discerning critic, an able and often agreeable painter, he made his start by chanting his admiration for the painters of his time in the famous pleiad of the late Yüan, and it was only in his old age that he became interested in the various styles of the antique. During his lifetime he enjoyed tremendous prestige, which has continued until this day. As proof, one of our contemporary novelists noticed a fake Buncho hanging on the wall of the *tokonoma* in an expensive public house! Rai San-yo, the famous historian and a member of the same group, was, according to Buncho, too much of an amateur to be honored as a master, and the ceramist, Aoki Mokubei, painted badly composed landscapes. Among the next generation of painters, let us mention Watanabe Kwazan, who was venerated more for his exemplary and miserable life than for his admirably sincere but dull painting. He killed himself in order to escape the *bakafu* persecutions, despite his having been their staunch partisan. Tanomura Chikuden, a prolific though somewhat facile painter, had pupils who were still working during the early years of the Meiji. Even today, this tradition of *Bunjingwa* and *nangwa* (Southern painting) has managed to resist all European influence and, from time to time, produces a charming piece of work.

SHÊN NAN-P'IN

A professional Chinese painter who was not among the best known in his country spent two years at Nagasaki from 1730 to 1732. Also a native of Wuhing, this able man, known as Shên Nan-p'in, had many patrons and pupils and was selling his paintings to the Japanese twenty years after he had returned to China. He painted animals, particularly birds, with backgrounds of plants and rocks. They were executed in fine sonorous colors, with sober or gray-tinted backgrounds. His technique was excellent, his pigments especially pure and permanent, his compositions both decorative and in the high manner. They justifiably delighted a most knowledgeable clientele. They inspired Ito Jakuchu, an artist of the next generation, who painted birds, particularly cocks, in vivid colors, but who was, nevertheless, an overrated artist in his own country; to us he seems vulgar and lacking in sensitivity.

Not wanting to be left behind, state propaganda fi-

nally succeeded in creating a Confucian school of painting. The output was enormous, but so uninteresting
that not even Japanese scholars rise to its defense.
Furthermore, it was not too different from the Kano,
who were now divided into several workshops. Their
names would be forgotten today if it had not been for
rebel students who distinguished themselves in livelier
artistic movements.

THE MARUYAMA AND SHIJO SCHOOLS

After a long period of prosperity, the middle class was
sufficiently refined to insist upon an art as accessible as
the Ukiyo-e, with either artistic or intellectual overtones, with a background of Chinese and ancient Japanese civilization, and with, perhaps, to boot, a touch
of "exotic Southern barbarity," that is to say, of the
European. We are by now in the middle of the last
quarter of the eighteenth century, when the "optical
views" were to have a great vogue. They found their
man in a young painter perceptive enough to find exactly the required formula. Maruyama Okyo was a
gifted, little peasant whom the prior of a monastery
had sent to Kyoto to study painting. He rapidly became
an exceedingly able artist, and was always conscientious
about his work though, alas, entirely superficial. In
every format, subject, style (the latter subtly eclectic),
his work is irreproachable, but it will never move us. It
is significant that he drew optical views of Kyoto and
other cities, of which the European perspective is, for
once, astonishingly correct. One might have attributed
them to a capable artist of no genius. Okyo believed
himself endowed with a gift for covering large surfaces and from time to time would go with his pupils
to a monastery where he would paint the walls of an
entire room out of gratitude to the monks for their
protection. His eclectic painting was particularly popu-

lar in the Kamigata region (Kyoto, Nara, and Osaka).

The damage done would not have been so great if he had not had as friend and pupil Matsumura Goshun, a painter endowed with startling facility and who, still very young himself, had many pupils. His school was known as the Fourth Street School (Shijoha). His eclecticism resembled Okyo's: Kano and Tosa styles, Ukiyo-e, *Bunjingwa*, and Chinese decorative work, some of Korin's technique, were all reunited into a conventional and cold purism. There was, incidentally, no sign of European influence in his work. He repeated over and over again the same carp in fast-running water, the same doe standing under maple trees, the same tigers in bamboo plots, the same Japanese or pseudo-Chinese *bijin*. His pupils were guilty of vast production which was much admired by the Kamigata merchants and disastrous for Japanese art. Furthermore, this Shijoha style infected all the other schools of painting, and even the allied arts, such as lacquer work, sculpture, and ceramics. This style is also mainly responsible for the mediocre quality of the Meiji (1868–1910), and its ravages are still with us today.

At first sight, Mori Sosen appears to belong to the same school. Yet he remained independent, specializing in a study of monkeys, and succeeded in painting them with such acuity that they warrant our respect.

During the middle of the eighteenth century, the Korin school considerably reduced their output. Sakai Hoitsu, a nobleman and son of the chatelaine of Himeji at Harima—one of the few fortresses still standing today—was excited about the school's style, and dedicated his life to copying and glorifying it. He published the *One Hundred Korin Drawings*, celebrating the one-hundredth anniversary of the artist's death. As a painter, Hoitsu had the personal qualities of charm, elegance, and good taste, but he never managed to surmount the purism of Fourth Street, having none of Korin's bonhomie, generosity, or humor. Despite all his qualities, he is nevertheless the third luminary of the "decorator" constellation.

THE PRINT AT THE END OF THE EIGHTEENTH CENTURY

We may now return to the very different atmosphere of the Edo, and the progress being made in Ukiyo-e, or, to be more precise, the progress made in prints. All the masters we have mentioned so far are called primitives, for the sake of giving them a name, for colored xylography was to be something quite apart from the meteoric career of Suzuki Harunobu, which lasted for no more than eight years, from 1762 to 1770. He seems to have invented the *nishik-e*, "brocade picture," toward 1764. One might almost say that he was the only engraver to benefit from a literary, dilettante clientele to whom a bargain was not a prerequisite. A samurai by birth, he usually avoided the so-called "vulgar" scenes of the theater and the Yoshiwara. He mostly drew honest, middle-class women, young girls, and children. He transposed spiritually in feminine terms the old Chinese and Japanese legends, giving his people a grace, a virginal gentleness, immediately recognizable, even if unsigned. Nevertheless, like most Ukiyo-e masters, he also put out erotic and highly obscene albums. The theory behind his researches lay in the idea that xylography could achieve effects similar to that of the old Kasuga miniaturist Yamato-e style. Harunobu copied the layout, the fine contours, and the coloring that was both dense and restrained, frequently covering the entire page. Until then, engraving had been little more than a feeble "reduction," a suggestion of painting; it now rose to equal heights. The favorite format was the *chuban*, measuring eleven inches by nine inches. Many examples are dated with disguised inscriptions of the year 1765, a few 1766, and have different signatures (some of well-known literary figures) followed by the word *ko*, meaning work. It is necessary to understand that "so and so suggested the idea for the composition" is a concept which, in fact, is always piquant, humorous, or gracious. Sometimes the work is also signed by the engraver, the colorist, and the printer.

The parody of subjects considered sacred by scholars, which had always been an Ukiyo-e specialty, became light and witty in the work of Harunobu. In "Eight Views," for example, the "Evening Bell" is a clock attached to a wall, and "Return of Distant Sails" is suggested by a napkin! Harunobu excelled at grouping people in a natural manner with style. His decor is always simple: an interior, a corner of a garden, the minimum needed to indicate the setting. Possibly, due to the high prices his work fetched during his lifetime, there were numerous forgeries made, recognizable by their poor figure drawing, superfluous decoration, and careless execution. As for the modern forgeries, which have managed to creep into the best of collections, they can be nosed out because of their poisonous coloring and their brutal goffering. Harunobu's pupils imitated their master's style, but captured neither his gracefulness nor his spirit.

Only his friend and collaborator Isoda Koryusai, also a student of Shigenaga, was as talented as he. After Harunobu's death, he made further progress in the art of engraving. Using an older, less luxurious technique and simpler colors, he turned engraving away from imitating Yamato-e—which could only have led to an impasse. Instead, his black lines, always in varying thicknesses, give a quick turn, a realistic volume to his figures in space which they would have lacked without. He was the first artist since Moronobu and Kiyonobu who knew how to introduce the elements of distant landscape into his work. In his last period he adopted the *oban* formula (fifteen inches by eleven inches, which would be henceforth the usual size), using it to make grandiose compositions which sometimes extended over three consecutive pages. In them we can see processions of the *oiran* of the Yoshiwara in their sumptuous clothes, escorted by adolescent *shinzo* and small *kamuro*. In these scenes, each branch of flowering cherry reveals the unrivaled quality of his drawing. Koryusai also excelled in compositions of *hashirakake*, long narrow engravings (thirty-three inches by six inches), which, mounted on *kakemono*, could be hung indoors on square pillars. The portrait of one of the period's "phenomena," a giant deformed head, is one of the first real portraits in the history of Japanese prints, for the so-called portraits of the Torii actors did not have much individuality. These innovations, and others that Koryusai introduced over a period of ten years—for, he, also a samurai, stopped making, in 1780 the engravings that were considered vulgar—were sufficient to keep the most famous xylographers of the younger generation fully occupied.

Katsukawa Shunsho, a direct professional descendant of the mediocre painter Miyagawa Choshun, has the credit of developing the anecdotal portrait and the landscape with figures. He had the idea of showing actors in their dressing rooms, surrounded by wigmakers, wardrobe masters, etc., or walking in town with their beautiful mistresses. The pictures are lively and well composed. He also made paintings of geisha girls and courtesans in their rooms, even at nightfall—light is always rendered in a conventional manner, though Shunsho does at least give a suggestion of the luminous aura of the "lamps"—or taking the air along the banks of the Sumidakawa (Sumida River) or in Asakusa

Park. Without using any tricks, he excelled at the art of placing a head against a clear sky or in front of a background of distant trees. At this period, all the planes of a landscape are connected as they move toward the horizon.

Shunsho had many pupils who were no less talented than their master: among them were Shunko, Shunjo, and Shunei, all of them still active during the first two decades of the nineteenth century. He dismissed one of his pupils by the name of Shunro, the future Hokusai. With great success, the workshop exploited a new subject, namely professional wrestlers, mountains of fat flesh with stupid faces which were, nevertheless, full of character.

Shunman did not belong to the Katsukawa workshop. He was a distinguished artist (though less known in France than in Germany) and immensely talented at suggesting depth. He was also the first person to grasp the fact that night blots out the values.

Kiyonaga, the fourth head of the Torii workshop, went back to painting processions of courtesans whose beauty had already been shown in the works of Koryusai. He painted them with less grandeur, ignoring their flaws. He gives the Japanese women willowy, graceful figures which are quite unreal. His coloring is rich, though sometimes a little sweet. He also composed landscapes behind his figures. In "Pleasure Party at Shinagawa," the sunlit sky above the low tide is quite extraordinarily accurate. The triptych had existed for quite some time, though it was composed in such a way as to make a single picture. Kiyonaga and his pupils even managed to make a series of five plates, in addition to which each is a complete picture in itself.

Ippitussai Buncho (who died in 1793, and was no relation to Tani Buncho) belonged to the same generation and remained faithful to the tradition of painting actors in *hoso-e*, which had been done since the time of the first Torii. However, his are so varied and unusual in coloring that we are always delighted to look at them.

Kitagawa Utamaro had been Kitagawa Karamaro's protégé, and pupil of the somewhat romantic Ukiyo-e painter Toriyama Sekien. In 1788, the latter wrote an enthusiastic preface to a colossal book of drawings and paintings by his pupil entitled *Selected Insects*. The charm of these compositions, the refinement of tones, the extraordinary quality of the engraving (which must have been executed by Fuji Hazumume) make this book one of the marvels of engraving. During the next four years, Utamaro published several other albums one after the other, among them *The Silvered World*, containing snowscapes of exceptional quality, and *Memories of the Tide*, including a fine view of a beach which was ahead of its time. The young master proved himself astonishingly original and gifted in the most varied of genres. Later, he was to devote most of his time to drawing women. His compositions are never facile; they are always somewhat deliberate, somewhat haughty. Dancing pinks, yellows, and blacks give them a tremendous éclat.

There are a large number of signed Utamaros in existence, though we can be certain of neither their authenticity nor their chronology. Many of these come from his workshop, though perhaps some are counterfeits made at the time; the best stand with the worst. Utamaro's heads and shoulders of women strike us as being unique, without peer, drawn with a superb monumentality and a feeling for masses that has never been surpassed. He was able to make astonishing use of the piled black hair coiffure, of the "lacquered" hair styles, etc. One might say that Utamaro uses the "color black as a real color"—perhaps the most beautiful color of all.

His pin-point line fully expresses the curves and the weight of the flesh. These qualities were not fully understood by his contemporaries, who made many superficial copies of his work. The two fine series of "Yamauba and Kintoki" must date back to 1795, for the legends (those which are decipherable) of the "Old Lady of the Mountain" and "The Small Japanese Hercules" were transposed for theatrical performance in the same year. The heavy sensuality of these engravings is powerful, indeed irresistible. In the series known as "The Twelve Hours of the Green Houses," barefooted women, not too well drawn, give the appearance of having been produced by the workshops. For two or three years, Utamaro successfully employed pearly backgrounds; however, this innocent luxury was banned during the autumn of 1794 and it is thought that the yellow backgrounds date from that year. He lived for a long time in the house of the famous publisher Tsutaya, in a street that led into the Yoshiwara. Edmond de Goncourt describes the artist as a frequenter of brothels. Actually, it is more likely that he was an untamed character, harassed by the volume of his commissions. He had in the neighborhood of ten pupils who did not sign their names until after his death. Thrown into jail for having depicted Toyotomi Hideyoshi and his five mistresses, he was fined heavily and died soon after.

One of his pupils married his widow and used the signature of "Utamaro." Utamaro II's work can easily be recognized by the almost lozenge-shaped heads and unpleasant stripes in the backgrounds; they are not bad pictures, merely dull.

Utagawa Toyokuni I, Utamaro's rival for popularity, was the pupil of a highly original artist, Toyoharu, member of the Ishikawa Toyonobu line of painters. He was a skillful artist whose relatively original innova-

tions were copied by all his contemporaries, such as
Shunsho, Kiyonaga, Utamaro, and Sharaku. His early
work has a curiously modern look to it, rather like our
own nineteenth-century painting. He was spoiled by
success; the mannerisms seen in his work executed between 1790 and 1805 prevented him from making large
xylogravures, and he gave up engraving twenty years
before his death. Toyokuni II only imitated his mistakes. Toyokuni III was the fine artist Utagawa Kunisada (who also signed his name as Toyokuni II, *ni-seir*,
in order not to be known as the pupil of his immediate
predecessor, whose work he disliked). He died in 1864,
with the result that we have the Toyokuni signature on
paintings dating over a period of at least three-quarters
of a century. The workshop became a semi-industrial
outlet working for a large popular clientele.

Tsutaya Yusaburo, friend and boarder of Utamaro,
was also the printer of another first-rate master, Toshusai Sharaku, whose work flashes through the artistic
world like a meteor; he produced approximately 135 engravings in less than a year (1794–1795) and then disappeared without a trace. His *hoso-e* of actors (rarely
to be seen in French collections) have a remarkable
quality of perception and grandeur. However, the
twenty-eight *oban*, which he presented either alone or
in pairs, are great masterpieces of synthesis, decorative
power, and psychological penetration. They were
looked upon as being caricatures and it was thought
that the public and the actors resented this, hence forcing Sharaku to abandon engraving. This is certainly
an error, for he was a successful artist. We have a much
better idea of his work now that we can identify the
roles the actors were playing when he drew them.
These roles were infinitely more subtle and more varied
than is usually thought. The women were not all young
and beautiful; the men were not all heroes or traitors.

In addition to the actor's personality, which the public knew intimately, Sharaku was good at making us understand the complexity of the character he was portraying. Thanks to the fine taste of Baron Camondo, the French national museums possess perhaps the best collection of Sharaku's *oban*. The coloring has an intensity and vigor which the modern facsimiles do not even attempt to render.

Surrounding these masters whom we have just mentioned, there were a few remarkable eclectic painters who were not particularly original. One of these is Hosoda Eishi, one-time functionary at the shogunal court, who had many pupils. This group resuscitated the Kiyonaga formula, using a new system of colors in which cool violets, green, and grays played with yellow-greens and mustard yellows. Choki (Nagayoshi), who during various stages of his career signed his name as Shiko, used mica to achieve the misty atmosphere of night and the full moon. Several artists, of whose backgrounds we are not certain, took the name of Kitao. Kitao Masanobu was none other than the famous humorist writer Santo Kyoden. Masayoshi, who was born in the same year as Santo Kyoden (1761), was rather an undistinguished person; Masahiro, probably the youngest, is responsible for two plates of engravings which would have done honor to Utamaro.

The reader will excuse us if we tell the story of another experience we had at the École du Louvre. During a lecture devoted to Shunsho and Kiyonaga, we projected originals, not reproductions, of good etchings by Moreau the younger, Eisen, and Gravelot, contemporaries of the two Japanese artists. The European paintings seemed conventional and dishonest in comparison to the Japanese xylographs, particularly, of course, in outdoor scenes. At that time, some of our painters were incapable of observation the moment they left their studios. The Japanese,. who lived in brighter interiors, were much more familiar with the effect of changing light.

THE END OF THE TOKUGAWA EPOCH (1800–1860)

During the last years of the eighteenth century, a harmless incident woke the Japanese out of their dream. A fleet of Russian ships led by Admiral Laxmann appeared off the northern shores of the archipelago. Among the Japanese, a few wise men foresaw the danger the empire was running into by isolating herself from the outside world and by refusing to participate in the progress made by science in Europe. The grand minister, Matsudaira Sadanobu, a stern Confucianist whose virtue was a source of trouble to the Ukiyo-e artists, was only too delighted to recruit painters who came from the entire country and were not particularly interested in European arts. Their job was to inspect the shore line and to make maps and defense plans. The people had no warning of any danger, but complacency had disappeared. Economic and financial bungling had provoked dissatisfaction with the regime, while the decades preceding its final fall were an exceedingly agitated era which also affected the artists. Their lives were occasionally in danger, their existence always beset by difficulties. The xylographers were forced to find new subject matter. The Japanese had always enjoyed traveling through their country. Several beautifully executed guidebooks, the *meisho-zue*, had been in existence at least since the eighteenth century. The slowly developed maturity of landscape painting in Ukiyo-e reached the point where it could be used in this outlet; the influence of European engraving had encouraged this development, as we will see later on. Furthermore, the Fourth Street school brought pic-

tures of flowers, birds, fish, etc., into fashion. Inasmuch
as it was the poor man's art, engravings also used
these subjects. Pictures of the ladies of the Yoshiwara
were not made much after 1830 or 1840. Pictures showing theatrical subjects became the lowest category of
imagery after the last Utagawa. Such was the atmosphere in Japan into which came the two universally
known masters, Hokusai and Hiroshige, who were to
give engraving a new lease on life.

KATSUSHIKA HOKUSAI

Hokusai was raised by the family that made the mirrors
for the shogunal court, and for reasons of which we
are uncertain, was forced to earn a living at a very early
age. He was always a crusty character with a "persecution" complex. Nearing the age of fifteen, he was apprenticed to Katsukawa Shunsho, in whose workshop
he fought with the elder pupils and from which he was
expelled for not attending the Kano workshop. He attached himself to Tawaraya Sori and for some time
signed himself as "Hishikawa Sori." He was then
taken to Nikko by a Kano painter charged with a state
commission, with whom he had a stupid quarrel; and,
to his chagrin, he was sent back. He earned his living
by making illustrations and *surimono* (greeting or
congratulation cards) in the elegant style of the
Katsukawa school. In 1788 he published a "Dutch
Suite" of small views of Edo which lampooned European engravings; the blacks are very somber; there are
clouds in the sky, and the inscriptions are horizontal.
Life became more and more difficult for this artist. In
1790 he was "forbidden to publish useless books"! In
order to eat, he peddled almanacs, pimentos, etc., and
even did engraving for other artists. (All the xylograph
masters began their careers with an apprenticeship in

engraving, although engraving had, for a long time, been a professional occupation in its own right.)

However, the engravings made during the first half of his life were excellent, personal, and without the vulgarity that, one has to admit, was very much present in his later work.

One day, on his way back from burning a candle to Myokenbosatsu (the polar star that had become a Buddhist deity), he saw a bolt of lightning fall close by, which he interpreted as a sign that his prayers had been heard. Deciding to make himself popular with the masses, he set tools up in the street, and began to draw a horse on a piece of paper 656 feet square; he then added a sparrow on each corner of the watermarks. From this time on, he resolutely oriented himself toward popular art, drawing, by preference, the activities of the city, the country and the roadside, and the working classes. Several albums of the Tokaido (the great arterial road of Japan linking Edo with the capital on which no coach could travel) had a certain amount of success. They were not true landscapes; rather, they were sketches of people one might meet at the fifty-three watering places.

In 1819, he began publishing the *oban* entitled "The Thirty-Six Views of Fuji." They were so successful that he added ten more. Several examples exist in two pulls, one highly colored, the other in blue and green with a few warm accents. The Japanese are less enthusiastic about this series than the Europeans who recognize in "The Clearing," "The Storm," and a few other paintings, early, singularly authoritative forerunners of the major discoveries of impressionism, such as the knowledge that color does not exist alone, but as a creation of light. Other prints in the same series which interest us less are also superior to European work: in revealing the beauty of straight lines and, in general, an air of modernity. (The cult of ruins never interested the artists of the Far East.)

The album pulled in black, with two tones of the most refined gray, entitled "The One Hundred Views of Fuji" (1834), is an admirable summary of Hokusai's mature work, demonstrating his ingenious use of the infinitely varied forms in nature, his dynamism, which exaggerates movement, his wry humor, his invention, which never recoils from either improbability or indelicate taste. The mirror maker's son always seems preoccupied with optical phenomena, such as the effect of a dark room, of shadows falling on paper windows, of the reflections—only of Mount Fuji—on a lake, even of sake in a cup; these reflections incidentally were not well observed.

Among the other works of Hokusai's maturity, we will only mention the large color series of the "Hyakunin-isshu" and "The Curious Bridges." (He loved bridges, and amused himself by placing seven of them in a single frame of the "Hundred Views.") Exactly in the same way as in his innumerable illustrations for novels, his fantasy quite naturally takes a decorative turn. This great genius was no realist; he completely reconstructed nature according to his own imagination. Mount Fuji, which he depicted so many times, is much higher and more pointed than the real mountain. In one engraving, he shows it as a mirror base, that is to say, at the moment when the sun is resting on the peak. In the foreground, a fisherman is climbing a culvert, while at the same time, a boatman guides his boat to the foot of the same culvert. The "unreal" quality of so many simultaneous incidents, such as this one, would be intolerable in a realistic landscape. Indeed, this somewhat surrealistic atmosphere is fascinating.

Hokusai was a difficult person to know. He had fre-
quented all the schools and had broken contact with
every one of them. He himself had a large number of
students; we know of at least seventy. An unsociable
person, he was often in debt; even though he earned
a great deal of money during his old age, he spent all
of it at the Yoshiwara and at the shop of a good ca-
terer. It is said that he moved ninety-three times during his long career and changed his name almost as
often. His masterpieces, dated between 1820 and 1840,
are signed "I-itsu, ex Hokusai." Later, he changed his
name to Gwakyo rojin, "the old man with a passion for
drawing," and then to Manji, "of the swastika sign,"
etc. Katsushika is a village near Edo. Allusions to the
polar star are frequently found in his pseudonyms:
Hokusai ("Northern Workshop"), Taito (the "Big
Bear"), etc. He often sold his name to wealthy amateurs.

During the second half of his life, he was obsessed
with the idea of making drawings available to everyone, showing that it is easy to find the simple form
that characterizes a person or an object. In the fifteen
small albums entitled "Mangwa" ("abundant drawings"), one sees clearly that he drew with childlike
freedom anything that came into his head, showing,
for example, detailed figure studies, then a repetition
of the same figures simplified; then they appear for the
third time, the second simplification. Another series is
entitled "Santaigwafu," an album in three parts of images borrowed from the characters, square, bastard,
and cursive. In his last works, he often used a large
format with simple colors. The engravers, colorists, and
printers did him a great disservice, for their work is
visibly negligent.

One or two of his pupils, among them Hokuju, succeeded in adapting the European landscape, which had been a dream of the old master for a long time. The work of other pupils was elegant but superficial; for example, that of Hokutei and Gakutei, who were particularly famous for their sumptuous *surimonos* in embossed gold and silver. However, Hokusai's influence extended further afield than his workshop. One can feel its presence in the work of Keisai Eisen, who would have been one of the best landscape xylographers if he had devoted his energies to *bijin* paintings in the Utamaro style, as did his contemporary, Kikugawa Eizan. Neither of these artists was connected with Eishi's workshop, though they were slightly in touch with the Utagawa.

The Utagawa drawings of theater scenes and women were steadily declining in quality, though not in quantity. Numerous engravings by Toyokuni III and Kunisada and his pupils are to be found in France (because the blocks were still in existence until the beginning of the Meiji period, Japan had to sell anything she could in Europe). We are often forced to describe the scenes as theatrical rather than historical or literary. Between 1830 and 1850, popular taste required that everything be presented in a theatrical manner, in the same way as in Europe today we seem to show little interest in history, science, the novel, or painting unless the subject is presented in cinematographic form. Due to this appetite, the people in these pictures strike poses, making the prescribed facial gestures. The buildings have a functional appearance and the landscapes, particularly the sky, act as backdrops. And yet, the colors, despite there being too many, are still attractive, and the overcharged composition is often divided in a delightful manner. Several of the last of the Utagawa practiced their art in the Kyoto and Osaka regions.

HIROSHIGE

Utagawa Hiroshige, pupil of one of Toyokuni I's brothers, never severed his connection with the workshop. His real family name was Ando, but, as far as we know, he never used it professionally. The son of a fireman, he was himself a member of the brigade until 1823, when he married his first wife. His second wife was a peasant woman. He was a modest, good, simple man. In 1827, he had already published some fairly original, if not sensitive, views of Edo, the first pulling of which was lightly colored. In 1832, a trip to Kyoto resulted in the sudden blossoming of his gifts as a landscape artist. "The Eight Views of the Omi," "Lake Biwa," the "Views of Kyoto," "The Environs of Kyoto," and the first large "Tokaido" (fifty-five plates), a series that appeared during the coming years, are masterpieces.

We rarely come across a realistic landscape in the work of Hokusai. Indeed, we see a somewhat theatrical dream world. Hiroshige, on the other hand, makes us feel the heat of the sun, makes us shiver with people floundering about in snow, and drenches us to the skin with pouring rain. He was very fond of rain, of sudden showers lit up by an oblique sun ("Shono"), of threatening downpours ("Nihonbashi" in the "Totomeisho" series), and of persistent rain falling vertically ("Karasaki"). When working on "Tokaido," Hokusai observed the people rather than the buildings or the landscapes, whereas Hiroshige depicts every detail in a street scene or country field, animating them with figures that are natural and alive. One should take a look at his landscapes while reading the highly amusing *Hizakurige* by Jippensha Ikku (1803). (Incidentally, Hiroshige illustrated this book, though perhaps less successfully than the author himself.) In the *Hizakurige* we can see porters fleecing travelers at river crossings. Having extracted a good tip under the pretext that the river was rising, they go off to find other victims by returning to the other side of the river, 164 feet further down, where the water does not even come up to their knees. Again, at Gyosho, we see the servants at the inn attacking travelers on foot, forcing them to stay at their establishment; then we have pilgrims on their way to Kompira in Kyushu; then we see the procession of a daimyo, obliged to spend six months at Edo. Or again, we can see the boat which plies between Kyoto and Osaka on the river Yodogawa being approached by the restaurant boat. Provincial life in Japan is brought alive in front of our eyes. Hiroshige's color is more intense than natural color, and yet he manages to suggest every detail and nuance of each hour of the day, of every kind of weather.

Hiroshige's talent remained on its high level until he died, as we can see in the five landscape triptychs he executed at the end of his life. Even so, despite himself, he became somewhat commercial. Though not very talented, his pupil, whom we call Hiroshige II, frequently used the ideas of his master. His "Hundred Views of Edo," often with enormous objects in the foreground, are characteristic of his style. Other artists continued to attach the Hiroshige signature to engravings that are fairly faithful copies of the master's style. Some say that his last student died in 1879, others say in 1894, or even 1915!

Europeans immediately understood and appreciated Hiroshige's art because of its connection with the "optical views," for there was no such thing as a low horizon in the Far Eastern tradition. However, his art is quite different from some of the impressionist work of Hokusai and Hokuju. If he taught something to our impressionists, as has been frequently suggested, it was that blacks and neutral tones are not indispensable to the interpretation of nature.

When Hiroshige died in 1858, Japan was concerned about two quite separate questions: first, what attitude should she adopt toward the increasing menace of Europe, and second, the suppression of the shogunal. Nine years later, Emperor Meiji was on the throne, and the increased desire for things European was to all but kill the traditions of national art. The pupils of the last Utagawa made engravings known as the engravings "of Yokohama," which depict in a most naïve and amusing manner the costumes and habits of Europeans visiting this port. These pictures are full of misunderstandings and anachronisms. The very last authentic popular color gravures were published on the occasion of the 1877 campaign against the Kyushu rebels, and even the war against China, which lasted for a year during 1894 and 1895.

The Nagasaki engravings were a local specialty that began to be made during the eighteenth century, reaching the height of its production between 1830 and 1850. They mostly showed the Dutch and their ships, and other foreigners (particularly the Chinese). They were printed in aberrant formats and have nothing in common with the Edo engravings which preceded them. Although they are much like the popular drawings of all nationalities, these are specifically Japanese, due to the happy choice of the expressive element (Fig. 65).

EUROPEAN INFLUENCES BEFORE THE MEIJI

The art schools run by the Jesuits before the end of the sixteenth century had been completely forgotten. It was still permitted to paint (in caricature almost) the "barbarians from the South," but to paint in oils with European techniques was enough to make people

Fig. 65. Porcelain Bottle. A "Dutchman." Tokugawa Period.

suspect you of Catholic tendencies. Almost 150 years went by before Japan rediscovered European art, this time by the introduction of Dutch engravings. The Japanese say that Chinese imagery was copied more than any other, since the same drawing mistakes were made during the nineteenth century when Dutch engravings were very well known. Whatever the truth may be, the Ukiyo-e painters and xylographers saw in our converging perspective a means of interesting and increasing the number of buyers. We have several examples of these Ukiyo-e, or "pictures in relief" as they were called, dating from around 1740. Series of rooms are depicted with the roof going down, retreating toward the vanishing point and meeting the lines of the floor. However, in reality, these parallel lines do not converge on the same point; this, and other similar errors prove that the artists attempted to copy our perspective without knowing its principles.

We have a number of drawings executed during the

second half of the eighteenth century of theater interiors at Edo which have this faulty perspective. Several of them were the work of Utagawa Toyoharu, an artist of considerable taste who also made wooden engravings of views of Venice and other countries. Hirai Gennai, who was a botanist, chemist, and homicidal maniac, is reputed to have played a large role in the dissemination of Dutch techniques. It is quite possible that he had Shiba Kokan as a pupil. In his old age the latter admitted having made Harunobu forgeries around about 1770, probably those which have badly drawn figures placed in front of backgrounds in perspective. In any event, Kokan learned oil painting, engraving, and etching directly from the Dutch. His paintings, which we know only through reproductions, seem to be beautiful. The horizons are placed low on the canvas, the skies are luminous and well painted, and the simplification has a nobility without extravagance. They could be compared to the colonial landscapes of the Dutchman Post, though the latter does not even seem to have visited Nagasaki. However, Kokan's etchings are poor, somewhat muddled, and are hand-colored. Aodo Denzen, his contemporary, was a very fine engraver of etchings and with the burin. He made charming half-Japanese, half-Venetian landscapes. He also used Japanese subjects, notably a beautiful dragon in the clouds, all of which were made to ornament the obi, the wide sashes worn by Japanese women. A famous square-shaped engraving by Harunobu, painted on satin, was made for the same purpose.

We have already mentioned Hokusai's Dutch series (1788). His shadows are, not surprisingly, without hatching. They are simply scratched on one side and neatly incised on the other. The hatch work, equivalent to half-tint, had been used by the anonymous

illustrator of the *Ise Monogatari* in 1608, though only
for the clouds. These were imitated during the seventeenth century, although, after Genroku, they became
thick, meaningless, black lines. In his black-ink illustrations, Hokusai quite often used dotted lines which gave
a thick warmth to his compositions. The same technique was used by his pupil in landscapes. Hokuju was
not afraid to try, with traditional methods, such difficult phenomena as the reflections of the sun on a flowing river, of the shadows of boats on the water, and of
completely clouded skies. Despite their simple quality,
these engravings exude a lively understanding of nature. Utagawa Kuniyoshi used all sorts of subjects. His
excellent landscapes seem to owe more to Hokusai than
to Hiroshige, and the European influence is quite apparent. We believe that Hiroshige was the first Japanese
artist to see the sky at night as a dark blue rather than
black.

THE SUBJECT MATTER OF PRINTS

As we have already mentioned, the theaters and pleasure houses in the early days were the main source of
inspiration for xylographers. H. Amon has listed the
commissions given to the artists by their models (actors and courtesans). This work was paid for twice—
the first payment by the actors and courtesans for the
publicity, the second payment by the purchasers of
the engravings. However, this essentially popular art
was, first and foremost, dominated by the special
flavor of Edo, a rough-and-tumble society that scoffed
at the establishment. The word *ukiyo* is in itself an example. We must also realize that the elite had always
parodied sacred subjects. For instance, the "Three Doctrines," which unites Lao-tzu with Confucius and Sakyamuni, or the "Three Vinegar Tasters," in which we
see Su T'ung-p'o (Confucianist) and his two friends,

one a Taoist, the other a Buddhist, tasting a delicious beverage made of "sinful flowers," were depicted as a group of three people from low life: a courtesan, a madam and an effeminate young man; or three women famous for their seductive prowess: Yang K'uei-fei, Komachi, and Sotoorihime. In some prints, Daruma is gallantly offering a young courtesan shelter under his umbrella. Sometimes the parody is purely verbal, and contained in the inscription. For example, Utamaro writes *Rokkassen*, "The Six Magicians of Poetry" (the six famous Heian poets), by using homophonous characters meaning "one choice in the six houses of pleasure." Again, he writes *Omi Hakkei*, "The Eight Views of Biwa," by using characters that mean "the eight intimate positions of happy lovers." The *Chikurin Shichiken*, the "Seven Sages of the Bamboo Bush" famous during the period of the Three Dynasties, is often written as the "Seven Beauties," and a third character, *ken*, evokes the Seven Houses, *shichi-ken*, which were well known to the gilded youth of Osaka.

In order to increase the number of sales, it was not long before xylographers used the numbering familiar to the Chinese and Japanese, such as the Three Cities (Kyoto, Edo, and Osaka), the Three Duties of Women, the Four Seasons, the Four Pastimes, the Five Confucian Virtues, the Six Great Poets, the Six Tamagawara, the Seven Komachi, the Eight Views, the Twelve Hours, the Twelve Months, etc. Of course, everything was translated into feminine terms: the Three Cities become the Three Courtesans, Tamagawa meant River of Pearls, and many rivers had the same name. (Also, Japanese rivers change names every few miles.) Classical poetry praises six rivers, each characterized by some plant or other, by a historical incident, or by the occupations of the river folk. A horse drinking at a brook and a *yamabuki* bush symbolize the

Tamagawa at Yamashiro; women beat clothes on the *kinuta*, another Tamagawa in Settsu, etc. A small secondary subject often graces a corner of the engraving, instantly recognizable as a landscape. As for the seven episodes in the life of Komachi, it was sufficient to personify the great lady and distinguished poetess of the eleventh century as a Yoshiwara beauty. Harunobu parodied this subject in a much more amusing manner. Komachi, who was accused of having plagiarized his competition's poem for the Manyoshu, destroyed the evidence by throwing the manuscript into the river. Harunobu shows us a little boy who had made ink marks on a letter of which his grandmother was inordinately fond. She is making him remove them! These more-or-less burlesqued adaptations of serious subjects, known as *mitate*, "comparison" or "selection," gave rise to a series of duos. The xylographers even managed to combine the two in numbered series.

Another source of subject matter was the transposing of a theatrical scene into real life. In this series the women do not wear the large ribbon that the actors had to wear in their wigs when playing female roles. However, in the corner of the engraving the *mon* of the actor recalls one of his successes. Actors often changed their names, adopting the *mon* of their illustrious predecessor. Thus, since the seventeenth century we have had nine Ichikawa Danjuros, fifteen Morita Kanyas, etc.

From generation to generation, the Danjuros had eighteen "great roles" in their repertoire. The public never allowed themselves to applaud these performances. The xylographers drew them often, especially in the play called *Shirabaku*, "One Moment," in which the judge very slowly walks along the balustrade above the parterre; enormous, tall, as powerful as a mountain, wearing a dark striped coat stiffened with whalebone,

and an immense saber hanging from his belt, he saves
the life of an innocent person about to be executed.
Another role was Yanone Goro, in which one of the
Soga brothers, preparing his vengeance, sharpens an
enormous pike in a savage passion. The subjects borrowed by engravers from the theater are obviously
much more varied than those they could borrow from
the Yoshiwara. Many of Utamaro's engravings seem,
according to their titles, to have belonged to a series
about which we know nothing. In any event, it was
remarkably successful. Hokusai was able to make the
"Thirty-Six Views of Fuji" and "Fifty-Three Posting-
Houses of Tokaido"; these series were repeated long
after his death by Hiroshige I and Hiroshige II, including "Sixty Views of Various Provinces" and the "Hundred Views of Edo," etc.

THE MINOR ARTS OF RECENT CENTURIES

All sorts of Japanese *bibelots* are, for obvious reasons,
better represented in European public and private collections than are the major art forms. These *objets*,
which were bought indiscriminately and inexpensively
between 1870 and 1895, meant less to the collectors of
the following generation and contributed to the unfair
criticism that asserted that Japanese art was successful
only when it was involved in minuscule *objets d'art*.
They will seem more interesting when we have placed
them properly in the vast ensemble which we are attempting to summarize so briefly.

CERAMICS

Even if we were to ignore the explicit forgeries of Chinese ceramics made since the nineteenth century, the
varieties of Japanese ceramics would still be numerous.
We can only give the reader a brief summary that will
act as a guide to specific works of art. To attempt to

work out a nomenclature is a disheartening task, because we find ourselves confronted with the names of regions, places, workshops, potters, garrisons, aesthetes, etc., all of which are arranged in a confusing order.

To begin with, remains of ceramics dating to the late Middle Ages are rare. One must remember that they were in less common use than in any other civilized country because they were replaced by utensils made of either natural or lacquered wood, bamboo, gourds, etc. The potteries were established, for the most part, in the provinces. The oldest centers were at Sue in Bizen, then at Seto in Owari, followed by those at Karatsu in Hizen (Kyushu). These centers gave the pottery its name, such as *suemono, setomono,* etc. The ancient Seto tiles that have been discovered (Fujiwara and Kamakura periods) do not seem to differ much from the sandstone work still being made in France toward the end of the nineteenth century. It is thought that the Nara potters taught the Chinese the secret of several simple glazes, one of which, the "yellow Seto," the color of oil, was used for a long time. But they would have been forgotten toward the end of the fifteenth century if the admirers of *chanoyu* had not encouraged and guided the artisans, thus transforming what was popular artisan work into an art for aesthetes. Legend has it that the Buddhist monk Dogen, a member of the Zen sect, had taken a Seto potter, Kato Toshiro, to China so that he might learn the secret of brown and black Fuien enamel work. As far as we know, he returned in 1228 and produced tea utensils, notably the exquisite little diamond-shaped beakers (*natsume*) so seductive to touch and see. However, as the tea ceremony had not yet been elaborated by the thirteenth century, it is probable that the great advance in the technique took place, in fact, somewhat later.

Protected by the monks and the nobility, the Seto potters created new centers in several central provinces, namely one near the capital (Kyo-seto), one at Kuriji in the county of Mino, one at "Setomura" in the county of Etchu, etc. During the Momoyama period, the famous *chajin* Furuta Oribe no Kami announced his preference for the pale enamels; the *so-oribe* is greenish.

The Bizen workshops (midwest of the larger island, north of the sound, Sue, Imbe, etc.) were certified from the third century A.D. onward. They were also rediscovered by the aesthetes during the fifteenth century. Their specialty was a very hard sandstone which took twenty days to bake. The paste is of a reddish-brown hue; although often varnished with a mottle brown, black and greenish-gray were sometimes used. In addition to the tea utensils, *bibelots*, incense burners, chandeliers, statuettes, etc., were made at an early date. They were to become the specialty of modern Bizen which so enchanted our first Nippophiles, but whose unrestrained baroque is considered in poor taste today.

Kyushu ceramics

After the disastrous, abortive expeditions to Korea, led by Hideyoshi in 1592 and 1597, we have a new phase developing in the history of Japanese ceramics. The provincial nobility, devoted to *chanoyu*, wanted to create new industries in their fiefdoms, whose products would serve as exchange goods. A number of Korean potters returned with them to Japan. As we have already seen, the Koreans were much more knowledgeable than the potters of the archipelago. The initiative seems to have come mainly from the lords of Kyushu. The main center was moved from Arita in Hizen to Karatsu. The products of this region situated behind

Nagasaki all went to the little port of Imari. The ceramics made in this area were technically far in advance of the ceramics from other areas in Kyushu Province, due to the fortunate discovery of kaolin, quartz, and trachyte deposits in 1605. Each pottery began by making expensive stoneware with gray, brown, or white enameled *chajin*, stemming from the Sung tradition, the *Lakeme* having combed designs in liquid slip. The *koyomide* "calender style" or *mishimade* (Mishima was a center specializing in the casting of calenders) was a design with slight encrusted ornamentation in black or white on a gray background which resembled lines of writing. They were soon to make *akae*, which were more or less copies from the blues, or blues and reds, of the Ming period, followed by *sometsuke* painted in *"petit feu."* During the mid-seventeenth century, Sakaida Kakiemon, with the assistance of the Koreans, managed to make a genuine porcelain which, naturally enough, was mainly inspired by the early Ch'ing period. These highly distinctive specimens have a fine appearance, though they are somewhat stiff. (For example, the border was composed of small rectilinear patterns.) Between 1730 and 1750, Lord Nabeshima, governor of the Okawachi kilns, had made a very fine porcelain vessel for the exclusive use of the shogunal court. Its decor is even more natural and fresh than the Ch'ien-lung style and the bold colors are extraordinarily pure.

Further south, at Satsuma, the Shimazu and the Osumi also manufactured a genuine porcelain, though the glowing black, gray, or green enamel work was to remain the specialty of the region. In the *kinrande*, exceedingly fine designs executed in gold or black were superimposed upon the crackle. These ancient objects are distinctive and original, though the fake Meiji Sat-

suma, commercially manufactured for export, is not
nearly as fine as the real Satsuma ceramics.

In addition to the Hizen and Satsuma works, five
other Kyushu provinces also had kilns whose infinitely
varied production would be impossible to summarize
in so short a space. The only centers of Korean potters
on the main island were at Hagi in Nagato (western
shore).

Kyoto ceramics

We can group together the skillful ceramic work made
during the Tokugawa period around Kyoto and that
made in several provincial areas in the midlands. Kyoto
experienced two periods of prosperity, one during the
first sixty years of the seventeenth century, the other
from the nineteenth century until the early Meiji
period.

The celebrated Kobori Enshu, a contemporary of
Oribe, was the supreme master craftsman of *chanoyu*
pottery. Seven ancient types were his special favorites.
They were Totomi's *shitoro*, Omi's *zeze*, Yamashiro's
asahi, Yamato's *akagawa*, Settsu's *kosobe*, Buzen's
agano, and Chikuzen's *takatori*. (The two last provinces are in southern Kyushu.)

Awat (the name of a boulevard in Kyoto) was the
"Seto of the capital," revived by the Seto potter Owari
in 1624. The *Raku* owed its origin to a certain Chojiro,
son of either a Chinese or a Korean craftsman employed by Hideyoshi. The dictator rewarded him with
a gold seal bearing the word *raku*, which served as
trademark for his long line of successors.

Nonomura Ninsei, first apprenticed to a Korean established in Tosa (Shikoku), spent his youth studying
all the ceramic techniques known in Japan at the time,
and spent the rest of his life developing his art. He
founded a large number of workshops and put new

blood into several which were already in existence. The original materials used seem to have been his idea. However, his technical genius has often been coupled with his artistic talent, which is not impressive. His *chatsubo*, those large globular vases decorated with wisteria, cherry tree, red plum, etc., have often been reproduced in soft and too realistic colors. It is possible that these designs were furnished by contemporary Kano painters. He made porcelain incense burners which were imitations of large shells. He also made *kugikakushi*, concealed hinges for buildings. The story goes that a *chajin* of the period, Kanamori Sowa, was fond of this decadent style of ceramics. The experiments of Ninsei, similar to those of his contemporary, Kakiemon, were responsible for the perfection of the techniques of making Japanese porcelain. From an aesthetic point of view, Japanese porcelain was put back on the path toward perfection during the eighteenth century by such great artists as Korin's brother, Ogata Kenzan, as well as by professional ceramists, who, during the course of their copyings from the Sung, Ming, and delft, were able to demonstrate their taste and originality. Among them were Okuda Eisen and his pupil, Kasuke. At the beginning of the nineteenth century, the convolvulus (morning-glory) was the favorite flower in Kamigata Province, and handsome pots so decorated were commissioned for presentation at court. Hozan, the ninth master of the Awata workshops, was much admired as an artist. His pupil, Mokubei, enjoyed tremendous prestige, which we find hard to understand today, and was a great friend of the *bunjin* group of gentlemen painters.

Eiraku Hozen, his son Wazen, and Ninami Dohachi II were much admired for their copies of ancient ceramics. The Banko workshop at Ise, founded by an amateur toward the year 1740, drew its inspiration for its *oranda*, "Holland ware," from Delft. Though possibly more Louis Philippe than Japanese, they are nevertheless charming creations. Many amateurs at the time were passionate about ceramics and instituted new styles which are little known outside Japan.

A familiar name to European collectors is Kutani in Kaga. In the early days of this workshop, the master potters of this region wanted to learn the Chinese methods. The *bakafu* were against any such idea. The story goes that Kusumi Morikage, a pupil of Tanyu, made designs for them. But old Kutani ware is very rare. Among the more recent genres, the one most often found in our collections is characterized by intense colors of green, purple, and particularly violet, with backgrounds of golden brown.

METALLURGY

Toward the end of the Ashikaga period, the popularity of the ceremony inspired not only the potters but also the metallurgists. The superbly shaped metal hot-water bottles with discrete designs are attributed to the Ashiya workshop at Chikuzen, whereas the perforated lanterns are attributed to the Tempyo workshop of Sano at Shimotsuke.

For luxurious buildings of the Momoyama period (1570–1602), and for seventeenth-century Tokugawa mausoleums, the artisans working in gilt bronze made groups of beautifully designed and executed metal objects. They also made *fusuma* shells and fish for Momoyama's castle in gold and silver, studded with enamel. The famous saber scabbards (*tsuba*) were already decorated with infinite care during the prehistoric era, with the same predilection for silver chasing which we find in contemporaneous Merovingian equipment. Apparently it would seem that there is no example dating back to the late Middle Ages. We can

find them in the fifteenth century, the most beautiful
ancient *tsuba* being attributed to the famous Goto
family, whose fifth paterfamilias died an octogenarian
in 1631. Another engraver, Umetata Ninju, used different alloys in the making of *tsuba,* the new color values
of which were much admired by the Chinese. Among
the armorers of the period, the most famous were the
Myochin and the Saotomo.

It is hard to date the unsigned scabbards. Usually,
the most beautiful are those made for armed combat.
They are made entirely of iron, relatively simple in design, each different and in perfect taste. The craftsmen
aimed at making vivid surfaces by hammering or incis-
ing, although we are not sure of the method used.
Throughout the Tokugawa period the samurai carried
sabers—sometimes two: one small, one large. During
the nineteenth century, those who had adopted peaceful professions often wore wooden sabers. They had
no reason to fight, save in situations when their honor
was at stake. One is very much aware of this change
of occupation, since the *tsuba* were transformed into
exceedingly rich and picturesque jewels, illustrating poems, telling whole legends that ran from one side of
the *tsuba* to the other. It was said that the saber was
for the samurai what the mirror was for the woman.
They were the most precious of the samurai's possessions, one half of his soul, hence the reason for the
decoration, if not of the *tsuba* at least of the *menuki,*
(the fastener) or the *kashira* (pummel) and other sections of the saber and its sheath, which became so complex and detailed that one needs a powerful magnify-
ing glass to see them properly. The samurai would
spend hours examining his sword. When it was forbidden to wear them during the early Meiji period, the
warriors sold the *tsuba* for very little money and kept

the blades, which they considered infinitely more precious.

Bronze mirrors must have disappeared with the advent of glass, for from this time onward, few found their way to Europe. Ornamented with fairly stereotyped, symbolic subjects, such as symbols of longevity, island of happiness, etc., they were of less artistic value than the *tsuba*. During the five-hundred-year supremacy of the warriors (thirteenth to seventeenth centuries), women played a minor role in Japanese society.

THE LACQUERS

The art of lacquer work made great progress during the Ashikaga period, while remaining, at the same time, strictly decorative and subordinate to the utilitarian purposes of the object. The craftsmen now knew how to give certain parts of the design a slight relief by using flat and brilliant golds. They invented the idea of placing floral patterns over geometrical trelliswork, which had the fortunate effect of bringing the whole design into one plane. Using only gold and black lacquer, the artist managed to depict an infinite variety of nature's gifts: trees, rocks, houses, grasses, sand, water, mists, and skies. The landscapes which decorated seventeenth- and eighteenth-century writing desks, and even those of the most recent epochs, have an emotional depth often more moving than those found in landscape painting. We have already mentioned the close alliance between the graphic arts and literature. Lacquer work became the graphic equivalent of poetry. We also have to admire the artisan's confidence in his taste and skill in developing a theme which first appears in the focal point on the lid of a box, for example, and is then repeated on the sides, under the lid, and inside the compartments, all without destroying the

unity and never becoming monotonous. They sometimes used variations over a whole series of objects, as
did Koami Nagashige in 1639 for the daughter of the
third shogun Iemitsu. The theme is the song of the
nightingale, in the *Genji Monogatari*.

Until now, we have been talking about the classical
tradition. We have already mentioned the revolutionary innovations of Koetsu which were developed by
Korin. However, the two aesthetics sometimes were
fused into the more restrained genre of *inro*.

The Japanese have always been somewhat hypo-
chondrial, and were fond of taking pills and cure-all
remedies. City people acquired the habit of wearing
inro (literally, pillboxes) on their belts, in the shape
of flattened cylinders, with several compartments (usually five), each fitting into the other and strung together with a piece of cord. These small portable medicine cabinets were decorated by the lacquer workers
with an infinite variety of subjects using various methods and materials: black and gold lacquer, colored lacquer, mother of pearl, metals, ivory, etc. The decoration usually covered the whole surface of the *inro*. The
workmanship is so precise that the joints of the compartments are barely visible. The cord holding the compartments together was held tight by a little ivory or
wooden ball known as the *ojime*, and ended in a third
object, the *netsuke*, which prevented the *inro* from
sliding along the belt. The *netsuke* was also used to
hold other objects, such as a snuffbox, a pipe case,
and a writing case containing a brush and some India
ink in a sponge.

Netsuke means literally an "affixed root." They
were first carved out of bamboo root, then out of hard
wood such as wild cherry, palm tree, ebony, and box-
wood. Later on, an assortment of other materials was
used, such as amber, coral, tortoise shell, rock crystal,

metals, ceramic enameling, wild boar tooth, buffalo horn, and deerhorn. Elephant ivory was not imported in great quantity until the eighteenth century. It was used to make samisen plectra, and it is thought that the pyramidical form of many ivory *netsuke* was due to the use of waste material. *Netsuke* were used from the beginning of the second quarter of the seventeenth century until the fall of the Tokugawa. However, from 1800 onward, even in Japan, they tended to become collectors' items. Their subject matter is even more varied than the *tsuba*'s, for all kinds of humor was permitted. One might say that embodied in these objects is everything that was close to the heart of the Edo middle classes. The absence of any real religious motif is significant. The arhats are often depicted, though in the mocking spirit of the era. Even Daruma, the great Zen patriarch, became such a popular fetish that the courtesans always carried numerous figurines of him (in the slang of the period, *daruma* meant woman of pleasure). Even more frequently seen, needless to say, are the seven happiness gods whom popular superstition had borrowed from the Chinese, and who were treated without any respect at all. They were Fukurokuju, "Luck, Gain, and Longevity"; Daikoku, god of riches; Ebisu, god of profit; Hotei, god of happiness; Bishamon (the Buddhist Kuvera), another god of riches; Jurojin, sometimes replaced by Kichijoten (Lakshmi). Also included was Benten (Sarasvati), the goddess of the arts and exquisite language. All the mythical beings, the tengu, the long-legged, long-necked phantoms, wolves, and badgers playing wicked tricks on human beings are represented, as well as all the professions and all stages of life. Female nudes are rarely found, though one sometimes comes across veiled, licentious allusions. All the animals, insects, plants, all household appliances are depicted. Ikkwan

excelled at sculpting rats, Tomotada at buffalo, Tametaka at wild boar, Tadatoshi at reptiles, Kokei at tigers,
Tomokazu and Noriyuki at monkeys and octopuses,
Masanao at toads, and Ishishusai at wasps. One senses
the influence of the Fourth Street school, which was
fond of realistic animals. Toward the end of the eighteenth century, Deme Uman, one of the long line of
mask sculptors, made *netsuke* which were small no
masks. The no characters are vaguely related to this
genre, along with the "famous poets." The *netsuke*
were made for a much more discriminating audience
than the engravings were. Catalogs of large collections
reveal a multitude of signatures which can rarely be
dated. Many *netsuke* were certainly carved by amateurs
for their own amusement and for their friends'. In
1951, Tikotin, a famous connoisseur of Japanese art,
organized an exhibition of *netsuke* in Brussels with
photographic enlargements accompanying each piece,
often revealing remarkable sculptural qualities. *Netsuke* art, so appreciated by our grandfathers, is still
just as fine as it always was. They were made to be
handled with love, not to be imprisoned behind the
glass of museum cases.

THE NO MASKS

Although the no have been played continuously since
their creation during the beginning of the Ashikaga
period, it is actually a dead dramatic and literary form,
since its repertoire has not evolved and hence has not
been enriched. The no and the *kyogen* (buffoon)
masks are frequently seen in our collections and are
copies of much more ancient examples. However, they
are just as beautiful as their fifteenth-century prototypes. Even a casual observer may see at a glance that
there were few types, while the specialist recognizes a
large number of sub-variations. One can say that all

these masks are admirable, due to the lively and inventive modeling. Certain feminine masks are, in addition, extraordinarily pathetic, rarely attempted by the sculptors of other countries and never successfully. One character in the play wore a mask. During the first act, he played an ordinary man or woman. In the second he came on stage as a genie, or demon, or sinner, etc. Therefore, two masks were usually needed for each play. The secular theater (kabuki) did not use masks, the actors making highly contorted grimaces. The finish and delicate coloring of Japanese masks was obtained by a coating of color with a base of extremely soluble glue. One must not attempt to wash them in water.

THE POPULAR OR FOLK ARTS

Before leaving a Japan that, prior to 1868, had not been Europeanized, we should pay brief homage to her really autochthonous popular arts. We find them even more valuable than everything else they copied from the Chinese. Few collectors were advised to buy and preserve the splendid inexpensive wickerwork, bamboowork, etc., that Japan was still sending to Europe in 1890. Even rarer are the travelers who looked for the old ex-votos (e-ma), the ships' chests with beautiful metalwork, the wooden potholders carved like fishes (shown to us by Leroi-Gourhan). This is not counting the unpretentious pottery, the saucers that were placed under oil ewers, the faïence droppers which everyone needed for the dilution of ink, the peasant's straw coats or mino, with their beautifully decorated V-shaped yokes, exquisitely colored, provincial fabrics, and the magnificent papers which were the specialty of certain regions, some thick, infinitely more supple and solid than our own, others transparent; all of them were precious, subtle materials. Then there were the toys, made with the simplest materials such as two pillars of bamboo, a fir cone or clam shells; the ingenious little folding theaters made of printed paper with a few strings and wooden pulleys that changed the decor and animated the actors; and again, the infinite variety of objects which the artistic genius of the country made spontaneously. They all form part of the whole, along with the old Shinto temples, the ancient Yamato-e, chanoyu pottery, anonymous Momoyama paintings, and even the metalwork of the *tsuba*. It would be an effrontery to write a history of Japanese art without mentioning its Chinese derivation. Despite the definite successes of the Japanese with religious sculpture, wash painting, porcelain, and twenty other genres borrowed from the continent, were we to remain silent on the debt owed by the Japanese to the Chinese, Japanese art would appear far more powerful.

JAPANESE ART SINCE THE MEIJI

The Meiji reform had serious effects on the artistic world. From one day to the next, the traditional arts saw their *raison d'être* vanish. Open to any sort of novelty, the Japanese once again gorged themselves on European civilization, though this time it was quite a different story from what it had been in the sixteenth century. The young artists went to Europe to study oil painting. This art has nothing but an introspective melancholy interest, for it is really mediocre—not irrelevant is the fact that many painters succumbed to consumption. Italian artists were summoned to Tokyo to teach painting, sculpting, and graphic arts at a school of fine arts. In addition, the teaching of traditional painting was resumed. Finally, the salons were opened and there were museum group shows. Still, the two traditions remained irreconcilable.

Engraving disappeared due to the change in mores, coupled with the development of photomechanical devices. Early in his career, Kobayashi Kiyochika still engraved realistically-colored engravings, but he had started out as an apprentice photographer, and this influence can be felt in his last plates. Toward 1900, engraving found a new lease on life, as it did in Europe, using the grandiloquent title of "works of art." One should remember that in book illustration the Japanese used etching instead of wood engravings, as was done throughout Europe. In this process they imitated, with a certain amount of transmutation, the engravings found in our publications. These illustrations, which no one seems to have noticed, are often absolutely exquisite. Lithography was only used for industrial purposes in the Meiji era.

Painters and sculptors followed European artistic fashions, and the Kano, Nangwa, Fourth Street, and Tosa schools could find nothing further to do. Only between the two wars did they begin to show signs of a new art, of a revival. We shall not mention the Japanese artists who resided in Paris for so long. The paintings they exhibited in the French salons were always noted for their native qualities of delicacy and sensitive choice of subject matter. Some of them appeared to be on the verge of a synthesis of the traditions. In Japan, oil painting sometimes managed to evoke a strong sense of terror. One thinks, for example, of Makino Torao's "Moisson," exhibited in Paris in 1922. However, more important, perhaps, is the depth achieved by the Tosa school; yet it is difficult to explain what this evolution really consists of, since it resembles no painting familiar to Europe, and is antipodal to European experiments. Vermeer, in some of his paintings—for instance, "The Painter and His Model"

—is the only name that comes to mind. By this I mean that the detailed realism suddenly is transformed and causes the material world to disappear in order to express life itself. At least, this is the feeling we have when standing in front of "Ohara in Winter," the screens made by Tsutaya Ryuko, in which there are no figures. Kawamura Manshu, who was connected with the Tosa school, but had continued in the style of Korin, painted "Mount Hei" in a fluid wash with a few colors. His marvelous triptych, now hanging in the Tokyo Museum, is more than a landscape. It seems to embody the full spirituality of Japan throughout the centuries of its existence.

We have yet to see recently-made original works of art. No one can say what the consequences will be from the American occupation shock, for the condition of the world today has given Japan an air of gravity which it never had in any previous period of its history.

ART OF THE RYUKYU ISLANDS

The Loochoo archipelago, spread over 620 miles between Kyushu and Formosa, has a curious hybrid culture, whose prehistoric origins are very much like those of Japan. At the same time, on account of its diminutive size and the isolation of the islands, archaic characteristics were preserved for a long time, and the Japanese find in them the key and explanation for ethnographic phenomena, both religious and linguistic. Since the Nara epoch, imperial sovereignty extended at least over the islands nearest the mainland, and during the following centuries, the influence of Japanese civilization was late in reaching them. The Shingon and Zen sects prospered while they were still powerful in Japan. However, during the period of an-

archy of the Ashikaga regime, the minor kingdoms of
Okinawa (the largest island, some sixty-two miles
long) ignored their allegiance to Japan and declared
themselves vassals of the Ming. The Loochooans were
hardy sailors and active merchants. From the fifteenth
to the eighteenth century, their junks visited Korea,
Japan, South China, Formosa, the Philippines, Borneo, the coast of Vietnam, Burma, and the islands of
Sunda. They brought spices and drugs to China, and
also resin, ivory, mother of pearl, and other materials
used in the arts. In addition, they brought copper in
bullion form. They exported Japanese swords (much
sought after throughout Oriental Asia), screens, lacquers, and precious metals. When Japan's internal
struggles became less pressing, she once more showed
an interest in the little archipelago. After many vain
attempts to exact tribute, the Shimazu expedition of
1609 once again established a nominal Japanese suzerainty. Under the rule of Ieyasu, the smaller archipelago was not ruled by a Japanese colonial policy, but
by the new merchant nobility. They eliminated, to the
profit of Satsuma Province, all competition with the
port of Hakata in Chikuzen.

ARCHITECTURE

Whatever the business relations might have been, they
were singularly strained; these, with the established independence of the archipelago and the racial mixture
living side by side in a majority of paleo-Japanese and
numerous Chinese and Malays, determined the facets
so typical of Ryukyu art. Ito Chuta, the celebrated
Japanese architectural historian, says that all the Loochoo buildings gave the appearance of being small.
Due to the frequency of typhoons, the roofs were solid,
the tiles thick and bound together by a kind of cement,

whereas the pillars and all vertical elements were notably graceful. Great simplicity and a sound sense of taste
in the proportions prove that the radical tradition was
stronger than the Cantonese influence. Also, Zen Buddhism seems to have had even more control over secular architecture than it did in Japan. At Shuri, near
Naha, the main center on Okinawa, there are still
standing some fine buildings dating back to the end of
the fifteenth century. The islands are rocky, and carved
stone was used soberly and with intelligence. At the
temple of Enkakuji, on a stretch of water in the shape
of the character meaning "heart," there stands a Chinese stone bridge. The panels of the balustrade are
sculpted in the Indian manner, more *Sanchi,* so to
speak, than they really were in China. A palace, which
toward 1730 became the principal *jinja* (Shinto temple), is still a noble structure, despite economical restoration. It rises from a terrace to which one gains
access by a flight of some ten steps. A sort of terrace
protruding over the façade is crowned with a majestic
karahafu. Wooden piles ending in *shishi* heads (dragons rather than lions) rise on both sides of the flight of
steps. There are powerfully modeled acroteria made of
baked clay standing on the roofs. Even more curious
is the Gongendo of Ishigakijima in the southern group
of Yaeyama Islands. The rafters are visible in layers of
three, separated by horizontal planks which form a sort
of "bee's nest" cornice. Seen in profile, the flight of
steps and its sculptured balustrade are S-shaped. Metal
appliqué in the form of dragonflies hold the woodwork
together. The lintel over the porch ends with two
handsome elephant heads.

In Ryukyu sculpture, one can find traces of funerary
rites dating back to prehistoric times. Many of the grottoes were frequently used. During the period of Chi-

nese influence, tombs were built into the hillsides and surrounded by rectangular or horseshoe-shaped low walls. Oval in shape with convex roofs, they represented the maternal uterus where the human being could find a new shelter. Other tombs were shaped like cottages.

PAINTING AND THE MINOR ARTS

Apart from architectural sculpture, there does not seem to have been any statuary. Painting, on the other hand, is most interesting. They are all rather naïve, precise and inscribed. The descendants of the ancient kings of the Sho dynasty (Shang in Chinese) had many ancestral portraits dating back to the mid-fifteenth century. The most ancient in the series are more often than not seventeenth-century copies made from murals. Under a palanquin, between the open curtains, the sovereign is shown seated on his throne in a full-face pose. Seven or eight people, in a much smaller scale, stand on either side, including two fan-holders. Toward the beginning of the nineteenth century the painters of the Yaeyama archipelago made large landscapes or screens showing local life. They are primitive and stiff, though composed with considerable taste. A faint Tosa influence is sometimes discernible. Other artists copied Kano pictures, and even made skillful copies of seventeenth-century Chinese painting. The specific gifts of this small nation were nearly always the ability to create their special flavor of elegance and strength.

The brocades show, for the most part, a strong Chinese and Japanese influence, though sometimes the Chinese motifs are ranged in repetitive friezes with a purely Malay rhythm. Large wall hangings were hand-painted in a precise and thin manner which is not without decorative charm. Their lacquer work has forms which are neither Chinese nor Japanese but suggest a Siamese influence. The ordinary Ryukyu fabrics were much appreciated by the Japanese. Their design is thin, the color little varied. These consist of yellows, reds, and greens, all of which have a gay and sharp air to them. From the Momoyama period onward, Japan adopted Ryukyu musical instruments, notably the many varieties of samisen, which were to have a long life as musical accompaniment in the marionette and legitimate theaters, and in the making of light music for the geisha girls.

CHINESE ART

1. SHANG DYNASTY. Tripod Vessel. *Ting,* 1400-100 B.C. 9½"
high. Art Institute of Chicago.

2. NEOLITHIC PERIOD. Tripod Vessel. *Li.* From Ssu-wa, Kansu.
c. 1500-1000 B.C. 3¾" high. Ostasiatiska Museum, Stockholm.

3. HAN DYNASTY. Bronze Mirror Back. Second Century B.C.
7¼″ diam. Freer Gallery of Art, Washington, D.C.

4. SHANG DYNASTY. Ceremonial Bowl (Chien). Bronze. 11" diam. Freer Gallery of Art, Washington, D.C.

5. BUDDHIST ART OF CENTRAL ASIA. Goddess and Celestial
Musician. Wall Painting. 53″ wide. Kizil. A.D. 600-650.
Indische Kunstabteilung, Staatliche Museum, Berlin.

6. BUDDHIST ART OF CENTRAL ASIA. Amitabha
Paradise. Cave 139A, Tun-Huang. Ninth Century A.D. Musée Guimet, Paris.

7. SIX DYNASTIES AND THE WEI DYNASTY. Colossal Buddha.
Yun Kang, Shansi. Second Half Fifth Century A.D. 32' high.

8. SIX DYNASTIES AND THE WEI DYNASTY. Sakyamuni and Prabhutaratna. Gilt Bronze. 10¼″ high. A.D. 518. Musée Guimet, Paris.

9. NORTHERN WEI DYNASTY. The Empress as Donor. From Pin Yang Cave, Lung-Men. c. A.D. 522. Nelson Gallery of Art, Kansas City, Missouri.

10. T'ANG DYNASTY. Colossal Vairocana Buddha. Lung-Men, Honan. A.D. 672-676. Stone. 85' high.

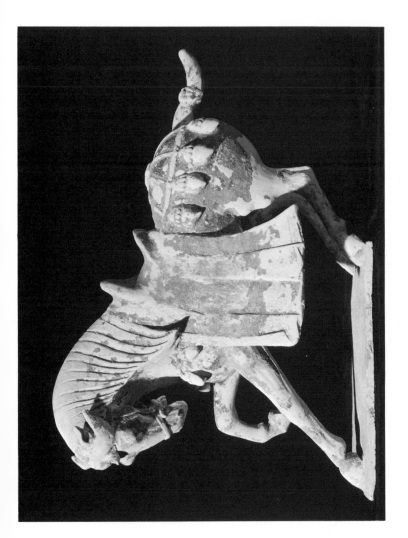

11. T'ANG DYNASTY. Prancing Horse. Clay. 15" high. A.D. 618-906. Fogg Art Museum, Cambridge, Massachusetts.

12. Six Dynasties or T'ang Dynasty. Bronze Mirror, Grape
Design. Courtesy, Museum of Fine Arts, Boston.

13. Pagoda of *Ta-yen-t'a* of *Tz'u-en-ssu*, Hsia-an-fu. Mid Seventh and Early Eighth Centuries. Shensi.

14. SUNG DYNASTY. Attributed to Yen-Li-Pen (d. 673). Portraits of Thirteen Emperors from the Han to the Sui Dynasty (detail). Courtesy, Museum of Fine Arts, Boston. Ross Collection.

15. T'ANG DYNASTY. Attributed to Han Kan (active 742-756). Mongols Bringing Tribute Horses. Freer Gallery of Art, Washington, D.C.

16. FIVE DYNASTIES. Tung Yuan (907-960). The Sky Clearing over the Valley. Scroll. Courtesy, Museum of Fine Arts, Boston.

17. SUNG DYNASTY. Mi Fei (1051-1107). Grassy Hills and
Leafy Trees in Mist. Freer Gallery of Art, Washington, D.C.

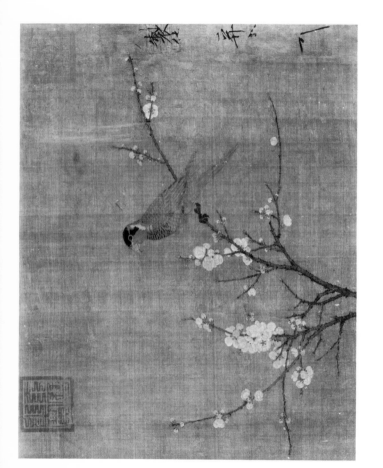

18. Sung Dynasty. Hui-Tsung (1082-1135). A Five-Colored Parakeet on the Branch of a Blossoming Apricot Tree. Courtesy, Museum of Fine Arts, Boston. Maria Antoinette Evans Fund.

19. Sung Dynasty. Kuo-Hsi (Active 1060-1075). Winter Landscape. Toledo Museum of Art, Ohio.

20. SUNG DYNASTY. Ma Fen (Active Late Twelfth Century). The Hundred Wild Geese (detail). Honolulu Academy of Arts, Honolulu, Hawaii.

21. SOUTHERN SUNG DYNASTY. Ma Yuan (Active 1190-1224). The Four Sages of Shang-San (detail). Cincinnati Art Museum. Anonymous Gift.

22. SOUTHERN SUNG DYNASTY. Ma Lin (Active c. 1215-
1225). The Lady Ling-chao Standing in the Snow. Courtesy,
Museum of Fine Arts, Boston.

23. SOUTHERN SUNG DYNASTY. Liang K'ai
(Active Thirteenth Century). Sakyamuni
Leaving His Mountain Retreat. Formerly
Count Saki Collection.

24. SOUTHERN SUNG DYNASTY. Mu Ch'i (Active Thirteenth Century). Eight Views of Hsiao-Hsiang—Returning Sails off a Distant Coast (detail). Count Matsudaira Collection, Tokyo.

25. MING DYNASTY. Tai Chin (Active 1430-1450). Autumn River Landscape with Many Fishing Boats. Freer Gallery of Art, Washington, D.C.

26. MING DYNASTY. T'ang Yin (1470-1523). Drinking Tea under Wu-t'ung Trees. 1509. The Art Institute of Chicago.

27. CH'ING DYNASTY. Yun-Shou-p'ing (1633-1690). Peonies by a Rockery, after a Sung Master. Freer Gallery of Art, Washintgon, D.C.

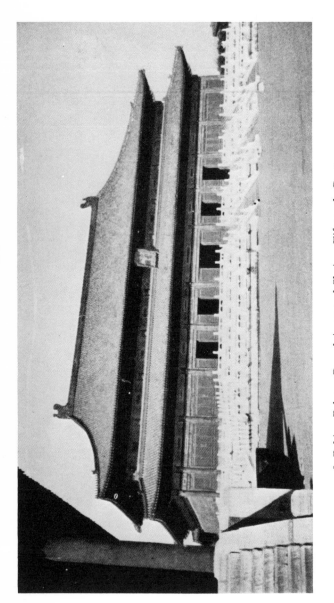

28. Peking Palace, Grand Ancestral Shrine. Fifteenth Century.

KOREAN ART

29. GREAT SILLA DYNASTY. Pulguksa, North Kyongsang Province. Eighth Century.

30. OLD SILLA (SHIRAGI) DYNASTY. Maitreya. Sixth-Seventh
Centuries. Gilt-Bronze. 30″ high. National Museum of
Korea, Seoul.

31. KORYO DYNASTY. Bowl. Celadon Glaze. Inlaid Decoration. Mid Twelfth Century. National Museum of Korea, Seoul.

JAPANESE ART

32. ASUKA PERIOD. Tori Busshi. Shaka Triad. A.D. 623.
Bronze. Great Hall, Horyuji.

33. Asuka Period. "Kudara" Kwannon. Wood. Seventh
Century A.D. Horyuji Temple.

34. ASUKA PERIOD. Tori Busshi. Yakushi. A.D. 607.
Bronze Golden Hall, Horyuji Temple.

35. Asuka Period. Doors of Tamamushi Shrine. Bodhisattvas. Seventh Century. Lacquer. Golden Hall, Horyuji Temple.

36. NARA PERIOD. Sutra of Causes and Effects (detail). 710-794. Imperial School of Art, Tokyo.

37.Fujiwara Period. Attributed to Jocho (d. 1057). Amida
of Hoodo. Wood. Byodoin Temple, Uji, Kyoto Prefecture.

38. Fujiwara Period. Phoenix Hall. 1053. Byodoin Temple, Uji, Kyoto Prefecture.

39. KAMAKURA PERIOD. Unkei. Dainichi. Wood. c. 1176.
Enjoji Temple. Nara Prefecture.

40. ASHIKAGA PERIOD. Sesshu (1420-1506). Winter Landscape. Imperial Household Museum, Tokyo.

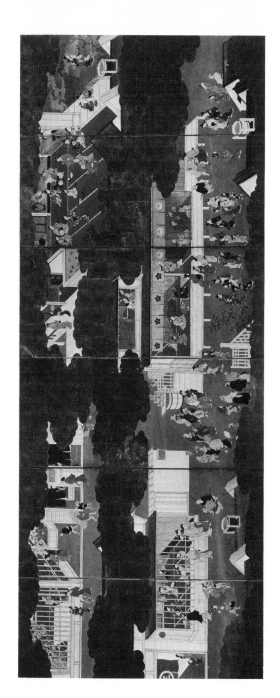

41. TOKUGAWA PERIOD. Hishikawa Moronobu. Gay Life in Early Edo. Courtesy, Museum of Fine Arts, Boston. Gift of Oliver Peabody.

42. TOKUGAWA PERIOD. Torii Kiyomasu (1694-1716). The
Actor Matsumoto Hyozo as a Woman. c. 1715. Courtesy,
Museum of Fine Arts, Boston.

43. TOKUGAWA PERIOD. Kitagawa Uttamaro (1753-1806).
Geisha Girls. c. 1793. Courtesy of the Art Institute of
Chicago.

44. TOKUGAWA PERIOD. Toshusai Sharaku (Active 1794-1795). Ichikawa Ebizo IV as Washizuka Kwanda Yu (?). c. 1794. The Metropolitan Museum of Art, New York. The Howard Mansfield Collection, Rogers Fund, 1936.

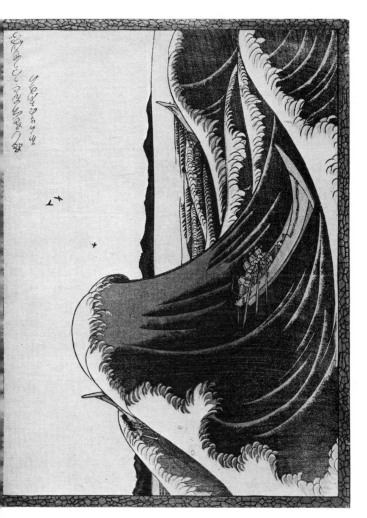

45. TOKUGAWA PERIOD. Katsushika Hokusai. (1760-1849). Boat Being Carried by a Great Wave. Courtesy, Museum of Fine Arts, Boston. William S. and John T. Spaulding Collection.

46. TOKUGAWA PERIOD. Ando Hiroshige (1797-1858). Travellers at Shono in Heavy Rain. Courtesy, Museum of Fine Arts, Boston. Gift of William Sturgis Bigelow.

TONKINESE AND ANNAMESE ART

The culture of the country formerly known as Indo-China has always been a hybrid between that of India and that of China. For a long period of time, most of the Indochinese peninsula was an offshoot of Indian civilization, except for Tonkin, whose history begins at precisely the time when the Han era became a Chinese outpost. Only toward the end of the fifteenth century and during the sixteenth century were the ancient Champa, and then the Indochinese, because of the Annamite expansion, conquered by China. Hence only a few pages need be devoted to the many art works of these countries, whose artistic contribution can unfortunately be reduced to a minimum, since wars, man's carelessness, and the destructive forces of nature—notably termites—have almost completely destroyed all the monuments of the past. In recent centuries, a tyrannical regime, particularly in Annam, prevented gifted artisans from raising themselves to the rank of artists.

DONG-SON ART

The most original Annam culture is at the same time the oldest, namely that which the Chinese expansionists encountered on their southern frontier during the late Han era. It is known as the Dong-Son culture after the site at Dong-Son.

This culture probably sprang from a race that appears to have been driven off the Chinese mainland. Some scholars believe that this civilization owed its bronze work to the Chinese. It seems to us, however, that it is more likely that China once again borrowed a fairly large number of motifs from her barbarian neighbor. Indeed, this Annam culture has magic,

barrel-shaped drums in the shape of a circular stool
that were quite different from Chinese drums. Furthermore, their decor cannot be compared to anything
in prehistoric Chinese art. We call these drums "rain
drums" because they have small sculptured frogs
around the edges of the disks. The rest of the decoration is in very flat relief, laid out in concentric areas
around a large star. This traditional form was retained
for a considerable period of time after the Chinese
conquest (it is believed until the fifteenth century).
However the ornamentation soon ceased to be figurative and became more and more schematized and
geometrical. The Chinese seem to have appreciated
these barbaric drums, and perhaps to have added
"faith" to their magic properties, for they transported
specimens over very large distances from their country
of origin. One of the oldest and most beautiful was
discovered in 1903 in the province of Ha-Nam. The
figurations are clearly visible, and Victor Goloubew has
compared them to the motifs and rites still in use
among the Dyaks of Borneo. He picked out the "death
ship," a theme often to be found on Javanese fabrics.
In Japan, these ships are part of the annual rite during
the feast day of the dead when small boats are
launched downstream. One is surprised to find them
depicted again in Scandinavian petroglyphs with details astonishingly similar to those in Javanese pictures
(Willekes Macdonald).

HAN AND SUNG ART AT TONKIN

In their chronological order, we find purely Chinese
antiquities at Tonkin, consisting of tombs of Chinese
officials, or of colonists of the late Han period. In 1932,
Olov Janse conducted a thorough excavation. To this
day, we know hardly enough about Chinese archaeology proper to be able to confirm that the peculiarities

of these antiquities are purely regional. The plan of Nghi-ve's tomb, for example, which is highly complex, resembles a lock with several bolts and two catches. It contains no less than twelve narrow cradle-vaulted chambers, each two grouped around an axis. The bricks in the arches are shaped like keystones. Delicate pottery, of elegant and extremely simple appearance, typically Han, was covered with a yellowish or cream-colored slip, which had not yet been discovered in China itself. A bronze figurine, supporting a chandelier, very baroque and extremely ugly, looked at first sight as if it were an equal mixture of colonial and barbaric art, although one comes across equally disconcerting objects in China itself during the periods of the Three Kingdoms and the Six Dynasties. The tombs also contained Chinese money, mirrors of the late Han period, models of houses, granaries, and even a small citadel (*Bac-ninh*), all made out of baked clay. There were no funerary statuettes, except for one ram and two pigs.

In the meantime, Chinese civilization hardly prospered in Tonkin as it did later in Korea and then in Japan. Goloubew tells the story of a Chinese traveler who, in 990, visited Hoa-lu, the capital of the Le dynasty, and considered the city rustic. Ch'an Buddhism, born in China toward the beginning of the sixth century, flowered in Tonkin from the T'ang epoch onward. We have writings of this period, which have been translated, but nothing of any particular artistic merit. Perhaps the constant infiltration of earlier ethnic elements, coming from mountain communities, accounts for the slow Sinification of this region, and for the slow spread of religious ideology.

During the late Ly dynasty (1009–1225)—synonymous with the mid-Sung period in China—the palace situated near Dai-la had four stories, a feature rarely found in China. Nothing remains of this capital but flagstones of baked clay, bricks, and tiles that were occasionally varnished. There were certainly substantial numbers of colonists. They brought with them from their fatherland ceramics typical of the Sung epoch, a number of celadons and large oval urns enameled in browns and whites, decorated with peonies, etc.

In China, the most durable Buddhist buildings have been the pagodas built of stone or brick. A few such buildings were also erected at Tonkin. During the eleventh century, a tower was built at Phat-tich measuring some 27 feet in diameter at the base and 138 feet in height. None of these buildings stands today except the commemorative pagoda of Binh-so'n near Vu-hi.

Throughout the Middle Ages, Tonkin was at war with her southern neighbor, Champa, who, as we have mentioned, had become Hindu and, as a result, was unwilling to concede to Chinese influence. However, a famous Cham monument still stands—Thapman's *chevet*—whose *makara* has been replaced by a dragon which is Chinese rather than Hindu and exceedingly ugly. Little study has been made of the antiquities of southern China, which would be the foundation for all rational studies of Tonkin art. The Nara temples contain two or three bronze gongs, which undoubtedly come from the extreme south of China. They are extraordinary, technically speaking, but have a frantic baroque quality to them that is difficult to admire. The Cham were gradually driven toward the south, particularly in 982, and were finally totally annihilated in 1471. From that moment on, Chinese influence spread throughout the eastern coast of the peninsula. Let us remember that the Tran dynasty, which reigned over Tonkin during the thirteenth century, succeeded in repulsing the Mongols who conquered the whole of China. At the end of the eighteenth century, in 1773, the Annamites, who retained nothing of the Hindu culture of their predecessors, the Chams, seized the southern part of Cochin China, from Tonkin to the north. A party of Japanese who were shipwrecked off the coast around the year 1794 have told the story of what they saw (*Nampyoki*, translated by Mrs. Muramatsu-Gaspardone, *B.E.F.E.O.*, XXXIII, 35). They were able to communicate with the inhabitants via Chinese characters. It is obvious that they looked upon the country as civilized, but very provincial, lacking in buildings and even an industry that warranted mention. They were astonished at the small number of metal or wooden utensils. All the dishes were pottery. They found no lacquer *objets*. In 1801, the French missionary Pigneau de Behaine persuaded the Emperor of Annam, Gia-long, to bring in French officers to help him in the construction of fortresses to be built in the Vauban style. They are still standing today.

The wooden buildings are never very old, although it is claimed that many temples were built during the twelfth or thirteenth century. These dilapidated old buildings have a picturesque quality, but from a purely architectural point of view it is hard to see them as anything but provincial Chinese art. The charm of their squat structure is descended from lay buildings, like the famous covered market at Yen-phu. The covered bridges in certain districts have the same rustic flavor. The ground plan of Buddhist sanctuaries is often an inverse T shape, or a horizontal H. It is curious to find that the same schema influenced the Japanese Shinto sanctuaries during the Ashikaga period. The Van Mieu (in Chinese, Wen Miao), the temple of Confucius at Hanoi, is a particularly well-known building. It is a smaller version of the one at K'iu-fou, the birthplace of the philosopher. The temple at Van Mieu appears to be strictly un-iconographic, the opposite of a Japanese Confucianist temple of the Ashikaga period, containing statues of the master and of his chief disciples.

The Buddhist temples are not lacking in statues, but French writers mention very few that deserve to be called works of art. In Bezacier's schematic plan, we see on the left and right sides of the main chamber the Ten Kings of Hell. In the entrance to the enclosed area, the two Dvarapala and eighteen arhats are ranged along the lateral walls. In the middle of the chamber stand the offering tables and the four Lokapala (these were called the four Bodhisattvas); behind these were the Buddha nascent, then Brahma and Indra. At the end of the largest room stood the Parinirvana, that is to say, Buddha on his deathbed, and behind him, in the median axis, four triads, one behind the other. Also, Buddha as future Maitreya stands between Manjucri and Samantabhadra, Sakyamuni between Kashyapa and Ananda, and once again, Sakyamuni, Maitreya, and Kshitigarbha. Finally, there are four other statues, Avalokiteshvara and Kshitigarbha to the right, and Ananda and Bodhidharma.

The wooden statue of the seventeenth-century monk Minh Hanh is often reproduced, and the head at least is very fine. He was Chinese, and the sculptor perhaps a compatriot. Certainly the artisans of the period were incapable of doing anything so fine, although they do not seem to have been accustomed to sculpting portraits.

Annam was a great center for expert bronze casting, and it is unfortunate that it did not have artists of the same quality as its technicians. The bells, ritual vases, dynastic urns, even cannons are successful in their own way, but of no artistic interest.

The history of regional ceramic art is even more obscure. Chinese ware is to be found intermingled in all periods. In the meantime, one has considerable admiration for the work executed at Bat-trang, situated on the Red River, the oldest piece of which is dated 1575. They made a fine faïence there during the seventeenth and eighteenth centuries. Georges Maspero mentions a variety with "fragile enamel leaves behind patches of delicate tones of cream and pale celadon." The Chinese and Japanese gave the name of Kiao-tche, Koshi (the ancient name for the Hanoi area), to the brown earthenware analogous to the boccaro that Europe was importing from Canton. We also have "Hué White," which in fact, according to Goloubew, comes from Kingtehchen (now called Fowliang) or from Fukien.

The Hué monuments, even the oldest, the nineteenth-century tombs of the emperors of Gia-long at Tu-duc, impress travelers with their deep poetic feeling, so well described by Georges Maspero: "In the calm and majesty of these locales, nature and the climate have undoubtedly made a distinct contribution toward the genius of man."

BIBLIOGRAPHY

CHINA

General Works

BUHOT, J. *Arts de la Chine.* Paris, 1951.

DAVID, M. *Arts et styles de la Chine.* Paris, 1953.

ELISSEEV, S. *Art chinois,* Volume IV of *Histoire universelle des arts.* Paris, 1939.

GOLDSCHMIDT, D. *L'Art chinois.* Paris, 1931.

GROUSSET, R. *La Chine et son art.* Paris, 1951.

SIRÉN, O. *Histoire des arts anciens de la Chine.* 4 vols. Paris, 1929–1930.

Prehistory

ANDERSSON, J. G. "Preliminary Report on Archeological Research in Kansu," *Memoirs of the Chinese Geological Survey* (Series A), V, 1, Peiping, 1925.

———. "The Prehistory of the Chinese," *Bulletin of the Museum of Far Eastern Antiquities* [B.M.F.E.A.], No. 15, Stockholm, 1943.

———. *Researches in the Prehistory of the Chinese,* B.M.F.E.A., 15, 7, Stockholm, 1943.

———. *Prehistoric Sites in Honan,* B.M.F.E.A., 19, 1, Stockholm, 1947.

WU GIN-DING. *Prehistoric Pottery in China.* London, 1938.

Shang Period

CREEL, H. G. *Studies in Early Chinese Culture.* Baltimore, 1937.

———. *Naissance de la Chine.* Paris, 1939.

PELLIOT, P. *The Royal Tombs at Anyang.* London, 1936.

UMEHARA, SUEJI. "Antiquities Exhumed from the Yin Tombs outside Chang-te fu," *Artibus Asiae,* XIII, 3, Ascona, 1950.

Bronzes and Jades

ACKERMAN, PH. *Ritual Bronzes of Ancient China.* New York, 1945.

ANDERSSON, J. G. "The Goldsmiths in Ancient China," *B.M.F.E.A.,* No. 8, Stockholm, 1936.

HANSFORD, H. *Chinese Jade Carving.* London, 1950.

JENYNS, S. *Chinese Archaic Jades in the British Museum.* London, 1951.

KARLGREN, B. "Yin and Chou Researches," *B.M.F.E.A.,* No. 8, Stockholm, 1936.

———. "New Studies in Chinese Bronzes," *B.M.F.E.A.,* No. 9, Stockholm, 1937.

———. "Huai and Han," *B.M.F.E.A.,* No. 13, Stockholm, 1941.

———. "Weapons and Tools of the Yin Dynasty," *B.M.F.E.A.,* No. 17, Stockholm, 1945.

LAUFER, B. *Jade.* Chicago, 1912.

LEMAITRE, S. *Les Agrafes chinoises jusqu'à la fin de l'époque Han.* Paris, 1939.

LOEHR, M. "Beitraege zur Chronologie der alteren chinesischen Bronzen," *O.Z.N.F.,* XII, Nos. 1 and 2, Berlin and Leipzig, 1936.

PALMGREN, N. *The Collection of H.R.H. the Crown Prince of Sweden.* Stockholm, 1948.

PELLIOT, P. *Jades archaiques de la Chine.* Paris, 1925.

SALLES, G. "Les Bronzes de Li-yu," *Revue des Arts asiatiques,* Vol. VIII, No. 3, Paris, 1934.

SALMONY, A. *Carved Jade of Ancient China,* I. Berkeley, Calif., 1938.

STEIN, R. Compte rendu de Jong Keng: "The Bronzes of Shang and Chou," *Bulletin de l'École française d'extrême Orient,* pp. 394–406, Hanoi, 1941.

TEILHARD DE CHARDIN, P., and PHEI, W. C. *Le Neolithique de la Chine.* Peiping, 1944.

WATERBURY, F. *Early Chinese Symbols and Literature.* New York, 1942.

WHITE, C. *The Tombs of Old Lo-yang.* Shanghai, 1934.

YETTS, W. P. *The George Eumorfopoulos Collection.* London, 1929.

——. *The Cull Chinese Bronzes.* London, 1939.

Nomadic, Korean, Mongolian, Indo-Chinese, and American Art

BOROVKA, G. *Scythian Art.* New York, 1928.

GHIRSHMANN, R. Review of S. V. Kisseliev: "Histoire de la Siberie du Sud," A.A., Vol. XIV, No. 1, Paris, 1951.

GROUSSET, R. "Nouvelles vues sur L'art des steppes," *Revue des Arts,* No. 2, Paris, 1951.

HAGUENAUER, CH. "La Tombe du panier peint," *Revue des Arts Asiatiques,* Vol. X, No. 7, Paris, 1936.

HARADA, J. *The Tomb of the Painted Basket of Lo-lang.* Keijo (Seoul), 1934.

——. *The Tomb of Wang Kuang of Lo-lang.* Keijo (Seoul), 1935.

HENTZE, C. *Mythes et symboles lunaires, objets rituels, croyances et dieux de la Chine antique et de l'Amérique.* Anvers, 1932.

JANSE, O. *Archeological Researches in Indo-China.* Cambridge, Mass.: Harvard University Press, 1947–1951.

ROSTOVTZEFF, M. I. *Animal Style in South Russia and China.* Princeton, N.J.: Princeton University Press, 1929.

UMEHARA, SUEJI. "Nouvelles découvertes archéologiques en Corée," R.A.A., Vol. III, No. 2, Paris, 1928.

Architecture

BOERSCHMANN, E. *La Chine pittoresque.* Paris, n.d.

——. *Chinesische Architektur.* Berlin, 1926.

——. *Chinesische Pagoden.* Berlin and Leipzig, 1931.

ECKE, G., and DEMIEVILLE, P. *The Twin Pagodas of Zaytun.* Cambridge, Mass.: Harvard Yenching Institute, 1933.

ERDBERG, E. VON, *Chinese Influence on European Gardens.* Cambridge, Mass.: Harvard University Press, 1933.

SIRÉN, O. *Histoire des arts anciens de la Chine; Architecture,* Vol. IV. Paris, 1930.

———. *Les Palais imperiaux de Pekin.* 3 vol. Paris, 1926.

STEIN, R. "Jardins en miniature d'Extrême Orient," *B.E.F.E.O.,* Vol. XLII, Hanoi, 1943.

Sculpture

CHAVANNES, E. *Mission archéologique en Chine septentrionale: I, La sculpture sur pierre à l'époque Han; II, La sculpture bouddhique.* Paris, 1913 and 1915.

CHENG TE-K'UN. "The Royal Tomb of Wang Chien," *Sinologica,* II, Bale, 1949.

MIZUNO, S. *Chinese Stone Sculpture.* Tokyo, 1950.

SEGALEN, V., VOISINS, G., and DE LARTIGUE J. *L'Art funeraire à l'époque des Han.* Paris, 1935.

SIRÉN, O. "Chinese Marble Sculpture of the Transition Period," *B.M.F.E.A.,* No. 10, Stockholm, 1940.

———. "Chinese Sculpture of Song, Liao and Chin Dynasties," *B.M.F.E.A.,* No. 14, Stockholm, 1942.

———. *Histoire de la sculpture chinoise.* 4 vols. Paris, 1925–1926.

TOKIWA, D., and SEKINO, T. *Buddhist Monuments in China.* 6 albums and 6 vols., with English text. Tokyo, 1926.

Painting

AUBOYER, J. *Les Influences et les reminiscences étrangères au Kondo du Koryuji.* Paris, 1941.

CHIANG YEE. *The Chinese Eye.* London, 1935.

COHN, W., and DAVID, M. *Peinture chinoise.* Paris, 1948.

DUBOSC, J. P. *Exhibition of Chinese Painters of Ming and Ch'ing Dynasties.* New York, March–April, 1949.

———. "A New Approach to Chinese Painting," *Oriental Art,* III, London, 1950.

ELISSEEV, S. *Notes sur le portrait en Extrême Orient, dans Mélanges Linossier,* Vol. I, Paris, 1932.

FISCHER, O. "La Peinture chinoise au temps des Han," *Gazette des beaux-art,* July, 1932.

———. *Chinesische Landschaftsmalerei.* Munich, 1921.

GROSSE, E. *Le Lavis en Extrême Orient.* Paris, n.d.

HACKIN, J. *Guide-catalogue du musée Guimet,* Buddhist Collections. Paris, 1923.

PELLIOT, P. *Les Grottes de Touen-houang.* 6 vols. Paris, 1920–1924.

———. "La Peinture et la gravure européennes en Chine au temps de Mathieu Ricci," *T'oung Pao,* Vol. I, No. 20, Leiden, 1921.

———. *Les Influences européennes sur l'art chinois au XVIIᵉ et au XVIIIᵉ siècle.* Paris, 1948.

PETRUCCI, R. *Encyclopédie de la peinture chinoise.* Paris, 1918.

SIRÉN, O. *The Chinese on the Art of Painting.* Peking, 1936.

———. *Histoire de la peinture chinoise.* 2 vols. Paris, 1934–1935.

———. *History of Later Chinese Painting.* London, 1938.

———. *Chinese Painting, Leading Masters and Principles.* 3 vols. London, 1956.

STEIN, SIR AUREL, and BINYON, L. *The Thousand Buddhas; Ancient Buddhist Paintings from the Cave-Temple of Tunhuang on the Western Frontier of China, Recovered and Described* (2 vols. of plates). London, 1923.

WALEY, A. *An Introduction to the Study of Chinese Painting.* London, 1923.

WHITE, W. C. *Chinese Temple Frescoes.* Toronto, 1940.

WRIGHT, H. K. "The Thousand Buddhas of the Tunhuang Caves," *New China Review,* IV, 401, Shanghai, 1922.

CENTRAL ASIA

HACKIN, J. *L'Art indien et l'art iranien en Asie centrale,* Bk. IV, Vol. IV of *Histoire universelle des arts.* Paris, 1938.

Lacquers

JENYNS, S. "Chinese Lacquers," *Transactions of Oriental Ceramic Society,* London, 1939–1940.

LOW-BEER, F. "Zum-Dekor der Han Lacke," *Wiener Beiträge zur Kunst und Kulturgeschichte Asiens,* XI, Vienna, 1937.

———. *An Exhibition of Chinese Antiquities from Ch'ang-*

sha. New Haven, Conn. Gallery of Fine Arts, Yale University, 1939.

MANCHEN-HELFEN, O. "Zur Geschichte der Lackunst in China, "*Wiener Beiträge zur Kunst und Kulturgeschicte Asiens*, XI, Vienna, 1937.

Materials

CAMMAN, S. "Notes on the Origin of Chinese K'o-sseu Tapestry," *Artibus Asiae.*, Vol. XI, Nos. 1, 2, Ascona, 1948.

DUBOSC, J. P. *Contribution á l'étude des tapisseries d'époque Song*, R.A.A., Vol. XI, Nos. 1, 2, Ascona, 1948.

SYLWAN, V. "Investigations of Silks from Edsen-gol and Lopmor," *Report from the Scientific Expedition to the North-Western Provinces of China under the Leadership of Dr. Sven Hedin*, Vol. VII, No. 6, Stockholm, 1949.

Ceramics

BRANKSTON, A. D. *Early Ming Wares of Chingtechen*. Peking, 1938.

DAVID, M., and LION-GOLDSCHMIDT, D. *Ceramique chinoise*, Guide du musée Guimet, Vol. III. Paris, 1950.

HETHERINGTON, A. L. *Early Ceramic Wares of China*. London, 1924.

HOBSON, R. L. *Catalogue of the Collection of Sir Percival David*. London, 1934.

———. *Handbook of the Pottery and Porcelain of the Far East*. London: British Museum, 1937.

HONEY, W. B. *The Ceramic Art of China and Other Countries of the Far East*. London, 1945.

KOYAMA, F. *The Story of Old Chinese Ceramic*. Tokyo, 1950.

Minor Arts

BUSHELL, S. W. *Chinese Art*. London: Victoria and Albert Museum Handbook, 1914.

CHAVANNES, E. "De l'Interpretation des voeux dans l'art chinois," *Journal Asiatique*, pp. 193–235, Paris, 1922.

ECKE, G. *Chinese Domestic Furniture.* Peking, 1944.

HARADA, J. *The Shosoin.* Tokyo, 1950.

MASPERO, H., GROUSSET, R., and LION, L. *Les Ivoires réligieux et médicaux chinois.* Paris, 1939.

TÔEISHUKO. *Selection of Objets d'Art from Shosoin.* 6 vols. Tokyo, 1926.

WANG, Y. C. *Early Chinese Coinage.* New York, 1951.

Printing

DENSMORE, M. "Essai pour servir à l'étude de l'estampe chinoise," *R.A.A.,* Vol. XI, No. 1, Paris, 1937.

DUBOSC, J. P. "Images imprimées," in *Grosse Chinesische Maler und Chinesische Volkkunst.* Zurich, 1950.

KURTH, J. *Der Chinesische Farbendruck.* Plauen im Vogtland, 1922.

VANDIER-NICOLAS, N. "L'Estampe chinoise," in the *Catalogue for the Exhibition of Ancient Chinese Art, Orangerie.* Paris, 1937.

CHINA AND EUROPE

BELEVITCH-STANKEVITCH. *Le Goût chinois en France au temps de Louis XIV.* Paris, 1910.

CORDIER, H. *La Chine en France au XVIIIᵉ siècle.* Paris, 1910.

ERDBERG, E. VON, *Chinese Influence on European Garden Structures.* Cambridge, Mass.: Harvard University Press, 1936.

REICHWEIN, A. *China and Europe.* London, 1925.

KOREA

DAVID, M. *Quelques notes sur l'histoire et l'art de la Corée,* exhibition of Korean Art at the Musée Cernuschi. Paris, 1946.

ECKARDT, A. *History of Corean Art.* London, 1929.

JAPAN

AUBOYER, J. *Les Influences et les reminiscences étrangères au Kondo du Horyuji.* Paris, 1941.

BUHOT, J. *Histoire des arts du Japon, des origines à 1350.* Paris, 1949.

BINYON, L., and O'BRIEN, J. J. SEXTON. *Japanese Colour Prints.* London, 1923.

ELISSEEV, S. "L'art japonais," in *Histoire universelle des Arts.* Paris, 1939.

———. *La Peinture japonaise contemporaine.* Paris, 1923.

HARADA, J. *Treasures in the Imperial Repository.* Tokyo, 1932.

MINAMOTO, H. *History of Japanese Art.* Kyoto, 1935.

SOPER, A. C. *The Evolution of Buddhist Architecture in Japan.* Princeton, N.J.: Princeton University Press, 1942.

TAKI, S. *Japanese Fine Art.* Tokyo, 1931.

TAZAWA and OMOOKA. *Zuzetsu Nihon Bijutsushi* (300 plates). Iwanami, 1933.

TODA, K. *Japanese Scroll Painting.* Chicago, 1935.

TSUDA, N. *Handbook of Japanese Art.* Sanseido, 1936.

VIGNIER and HINADA. *Estampes japonaises* (6 portfolios). Paris, 1910–1934.

WARNER, L. *Japanese Sculpture of the Suiko Period;* and *Pageant of Japanese Art,* Vols. I and II, Paintings; Vol. III, Sculpture; Vol. IV, Ceramics and Metalwork; Vol. V, Textiles and Lacquers; Vol. VI, Architecture and Gardens. Edited by the Staff Members of the Tokyo National Museum. Tokyo, 1952–1953.

Seikai bijatsu zenshu. A general history of art of which Vols. IX, XV, XXI, and XXV are devoted to Japan. Tokyo, 1950–1954.

Toeishuki. Selection of Objets d'Art from Shosoin. 6 vols. Tokyo, 1928.

VIETNAM

ANONYMOUS. "Art annamite," *B.E.F.E.O.,* XXI, 161–164, Hanoi, 1921.

BEZACIER, L. "Essai sur l'art annamite," *I.D.E.O.,* Hanoi, 1944.

———. *L'Art vietnamien.* Paris, 1954. (With detailed bibliography.)

CLAEYS, J. Y. "Introduction á l'étude de l'Annam et du Champaf," *Bulletin des Amis du Vieux Hue*, Hué, 1944.

GOLOUBEW, V. "L'Age du bronze au Tonkin et dans le Nord-Annam," *B.E.F.E.O.*, XXIX, 1–56, Hanoi, 1929.

JANSE, O. *Archeological Research in Indochina*. Monograph series, Vols. VII and X. Cambridge, Mass.: Harvard Yenching Institute, 1947 and 1951.

PARMENTIER, H. "Anciens tombeaux au Tonkin," *B.E.F.E.O.*, Vol. XVII, No. 1, Hanoi, 1917.

———. "Le Tombeau de Nghi-ve," *B.E.F.E.O.*, Vol. XVIII, Hanoi, 1918.

CHRONOLOGICAL TABLE

CENTRAL ASIA	CHINA, TONKIN AND ANNAM	KOREA	JAPAN
Painted pottery of Anau (Central Asia).			
3000 B.C.	Neolithic — Gray pottery, Red pottery, Black pottery	Neolithic Korean-Manchu.	Neolithic: Jomon culture of hunters-fishermen. Pottery with cord impressions.
Neolithic forester of Baikal.			
2500 Serovo (Baikal) culture. Neolithic culture of Kelteminar (Central Asia). Neolithic culture of Afanasievo (Ienissei).	Painted pottery (Yang-shao). Hia.		

2000 Kitoi (Baikal) culture. Bronze of Andronovo (Ienissei). Bronze of Glaskovo (Baikal). Tazabagiab (Central Asia) culture.	
1500	Shang Bronze Age.
1400	Anyang, last capital Shang. Divinatory inscriptions.
1300	Bronze and jade rituals; bronze arms. Ancestral cult.
Bronzes of Cliweisk (Baikal).	
1200 Bronzes of Qarasuk (Siberia). Bronzes of Aminabad.	

CENTRAL ASIA	CHINA, TONKIN AND ANNAM	KOREA	JAPAN
12th–8th cent. Sumerian culture (Black Sea).			
	1028–256 Chou dynasty.		
	1027–771 West Chou. Capital: Hao, near Chang-an in Shensi.		
	Beginning of Chinese colonization toward the south.		
	770–256 East Chou. Capital: Loyang (Honan).		

1000

900

800

700
Construction of large systems of irrigation in Central Asia.
Tagar (Siberian) culture.
Beginning of the Iron Age among the Scythians.

600

500

772–484
Annals of Spring and of Autumn.

Iron Age.

551–479
Confucius.

481
Period of fighting kingdoms.
Acceleration of Chinese colonization.
Development of Taoism.
Mirrors
Fastenings } in bronze.
Encrusted bronzes.
Glass.

Beginning of Chinese influences in North Korea: metal.

CENTRAL ASIA	CHINA, TONKIN AND ANNAM	KOREA	JAPAN
400 Hunno-Sarmatian culture in Siberia.			
300 Treasures of Oxus. Kurganes of Pasyryk (Altaï).			
4th–1st cent. Greco-Bactrian culture.	256 Downfall of the Chou who passed under the domination of the dukes of Ch'in (Shen-si).		
	221 The duke of Ch'in, having unified China, takes the title of first August Emperor (Ch'in Shi Huang-ti).		
210–174 Hunnic confederation of Mao-touen	209 Downfall of the Ch'in. 206 B.C.–220 A.D. Han dynasty.		

206 B.C.–209 A.D.
Earlier Han.
Capital: Chang-an.

200
About 160 Migration of the Yueh-chih of Kansu toward the Bactrian.

Mission of the Chinese general, Chang Ch'ien, to Ferghana, occupied by the Yueh-chih.

140–86
Wu-ti.
Expansion toward the Tarim basin in Korea, Tonkin, and Annam.

117
Tomb of Hou K'iu-ping.
Development of funerary ritual; *ming-ch'i*.

108
Creation in North Korea of four Chinese commands of which the principal is Lolang.

Central Asia	China, Tonkin and Annam	Korea	Japan
100 Tashtyk (Siberian) culture. Sepulchral mound of Chibe (Altai).	Chiseled bas-reliefs of the little funerary rooms of Shantung and Honan.	In the South, the three Han who accept, with some delay, the influence of Chinese civilization.	
59 Chinese protectorate over Serind. Struggles for independence of the Indo-European kingdoms of Serind.			
Christian era.	9 A.D. Usurpation of Wang Mang.		
1st–3rd cent. Kushan culture in Central Asia.			

Introduction of Buddhism.

100 A.D.

130
Chinese hegemony in the Tarim basin.
Proto-Mongol empire of the Hsien-pei extends from Manchuria to Russian Turkestan.
Frequent invasions of the Hsien-pei in China.

25 A.D.–220 A.D.
Eastern Han.
Capital: Loyang (Honan).
Development of minor arts: imperial manufacture of lacquers at Szechwan.
Development of funerary sculpture at Szechwan.
Beginning of Chinese culture at Than-hoa (Annam).

65?
First Buddhist community.

75–93
Pan Ch'ao conquers the Indo-Iranian kingdoms of Tarim.

Period of Yayoi at Kyushu and of Hondo in the south: introduction of agriculture and the use of metal.

CENTRAL ASIA	CHINA, TONKIN AND ANNAM	KOREA	JAPAN
200			
216–276 Mani. Manichaeism at Merv.			
	220 Downfall of the Han. Epoch of the Three Kingdoms:		
	220–265 Wei (Loyang, North China),		
	221–263 Han (Szechwan),		
	221–280 Wu (Nanking). Development of Taoism.		
260 Installation of the barbaric T'o-pa in Shanshi. Chinese garrison in Lob Nor to watch over the approach of Serind.			

	China	Korea	Japan
265	Epoch of the Six Dynasties.	Appearance of the Koguryo on the bank of the Yalu.	Beginning of the period of the large tombs.
265–316	First: West Chin (capital: Loyang).		
300			
315		Downfall of Lolang; establishment of the Koguryo on the banks of the Ta-t'sung River.	
316	Division of North and South: North: Six kingdoms of the Five Barbarians. Anarchy. South: 317–420 Second: East Chin (capital Nanking). Development of calligraphy; Wang Hsi-chih; of poetry; of painting.		
330	Nestorian Episcopate at Merv.		Use of the potter's wheel. Goldsmiths.
344–406	Ku K'ai-chih.	Great painted tombs.	
366	Grottoes of Tunhuang.		*Haniwa:* funerary figurines. Emergence of the clan of Yamato.

CENTRAL ASIA	CHINA, TONKIN AND ANNAM	KOREA	JAPAN
386 Kumarajiva in China.			
399–414 Voyage of the pilgrim Fa-Hsien.	398–534 Foundation of the Wei dynasty of the North by the T'o-pa (capital: Tai-tsung).		
400 Beginning of Buddhist works at Kucha-Karashar (Turfan).		In the south two kingdoms form: Paekche in the West, Silla in the East. In the far south, Japanese establishment. Period of the Three Kingdoms which converted to Buddhism and entered into rivalry.	
402 Empire of the Barbarians (or Avars), Jouan-Jouan, from Korea to Irtysh.			
About 410 Kingdom of the Hephtalites from Altai to Iran.			
	420–479 Third: Sung.		

450–650
Buddhist frescoes of Kizil, of Indian influence.

Ca. 450–460
Buddhism, state religion.

460–494
Foundation of the rock sanctuary of Yün-kang.

479–501
Fourth: Ch'i.

494
Transfer of the capital to Loyang.

Rock sanctuary of Lung-men.

500

520?
The Indian monk Bodhidharma introduced Ch'an Buddhism.

530
Nestorian Episcopate at Samarkand.

Central Asia	China, Tonkin and Annam	Korea	Japan
	534. Division of the North Wei: East Wei (Honan, 534–550) West Wei (Shensi, 534–557).		540–572? Reign of Kimmei Tenno.
	550–577 Pei Ch'i (Honan). Sanctuary of T'ien-lung-shan.		
552 Turk hegemony of the Tou-k'iue.		The sovereign of Paekche sends some sutras and a Buddhist statue to the sovereign of Yamato.	
553 Kingdom of East Turks, and Kingdom of West Turks.	557–581 Pei Chou (Shensi).		

557–588
Sixth: Ch'en.
Maintenance of Chinese culture.
Great funerary sculptures.
Development of Buddhism.

593–629
Asuka epoch.
Reign of Suiko; regency of Shotoku Taishi.

589
Unification of China by the Sui dynasty.

604
Edict founding Buddhism.
Foundation of Horyuji.

618–906
Dynasty of the T'ang.

622
Triad in gilded bronze by Tori.

600

CENTRAL ASIA	CHINA, TONKIN AND ANNAM	KOREA	JAPAN
Introduction of Buddhism at Tibet.		624 Pagoda of Punhwangsa at Kyongju.	
	626 Li Yuan (T'ai Tsu) emperor.		
		668 Unification of Korea by Silla.	
630 T'ai-tsu destroys Khanate of the East Turks. Voyage of Hsuan-tsang in Central Asia and in India from where he brings back some Buddhist texts and some Gupta statues.	638 Construction of a Nestorian church at Chang-an.		
7th–10th cent. Rock paintings of Tunhuang.	641 Tibet vassal of China.		

641–648
Chinese suzerainty over the oases of the Silk Route.

Up to ca. 650
The Buddhist frescoes of Kizil.

649
Sassanid embassy near T'ai-tsung.
Bas-reliefs of the tomb of T'ai-tsung.

650
Kao-tsung emperor.
The painter Li Ssu-hsün.

Ca. 650–750
Frescoes of Kizil, second style, of Sassanid influence.

652
Foundation of *Ta-yen-t'a* (reconstructed in 701).

660–668
Conquest by China.

668–936
Hegemony of Silla (Shiragi).

670–692
The Tibetans occupy the Tarim Basin.

Central Asia	China, Tonkin and Annam	Korea	Japan
	672 Large Rock Buddha of Lung-men.		673–686 Hakuho epoch.
	673 Death of Yen Li-pên, painter of the court of T'ai-tsung and of Kao-tsung.		
		677–744 Koryo dynasty.	
682 Reinstatement of the Turkish Khanat of Mongolia.			
692–694 Reconquest of Tarim by the Chinese.			
700	700–740 Great Buddha of T'ien-lung-shan. The poet Li T'ai-po (died 762).		

8th–9th cent.
Paintings of Dandan-Oiluq.

712
Hsüan-tsung, Emperor and Maecenas, founds the Han-lin Academy. The poet Tu Fu (died 770). The painter and poet Wang Wei.

747   Chinese expedition against the Tibetans.

751
Chinese defeat of Talas: Central Asia, zone of expansion of Islamism.

The *Pulguksa*, temple-monasteries.

710–784
Nara epoch.

712
The *Kojiki*.

754
Ganjin at Japan.

756
Emperor Shomu Tenno bequeaths his collections to Todaiji.

Central Asia	China, Tonkin and Annam	Korea	Japan
			760? The *Manyoshu*.
			794 Beginning of Heian epoch.
	Dai-la period in Vietnam.		797 The *Shoku-Nihonji*.
800			
	804–805 Sancho in China. The Jen-che Tchouan.		806 Return from China of Kobo Daishi, founder of the Shingon sect.
	837 Stone engraving of Confucian writings.		

840
The Kirghiz hunt the Turkish Uigurs of Mongolia.

844–1184
Fujiwara epoch.

845
Beginning of persecutions against Buddhism.

868
The *Sutra of the Diamond*, first known printed text.

894
Disgrace of Michizane. The embassy from China is suppressed.

The *Ise Monogatari*. Substitution of Japanese writing for Chinese writing.

900

907
Beginning of the period of the Five Dynasties in the North; breaking up of the South.

Ca. 922–929
The *Kokinshu*.

Central Asia	China, Tonkin and Annam	Korea	Japan
924 Invasion of Mongolia by the Khitans.	Blossoming of pictorial art, influenced by Ch'an Buddhism; renewing of style and techniques. Ceramic art: Celadons of Yue.		
		926 The Khitans destroy North Korea.	
		936–1392 Korye Epoch.	
	939 Constitution of the Annam empire. Temples of Angkor, Koh-Ker, Banteay Srei.		
947 Khitan Leao dynasty.			
			959 The Nembutsu-in is added to the Todaiji.

960
Sung Dynasty; reunification of the North.

The Korean dynasty recognizes the suzerainty of the Sung emperors: influence of Chinese art and culture.

981
Le Dynasty at Dai Viet.

1004
The Genji Monogatari of Murasaki Shikibu.

1004
The Khitan reign at Peking.

1009
Dynasty of the Ly at Dai Viet.

1014
Attacks of the Khitans who find themselves in conflict with the Jurchen.

1015
Restoration of the statues of the grottoes of Lung-men.

1000

CENTRAL ASIA	CHINA, TONKIN AND ANNAM	KOREA	JAPAN
Tomb of king Khitan Chen-tsung (died 1031) at War Man-ha (Inner Mongolia).	1036–1101 The poet Su Tung-p'o. Extension of Khmer domination toward Siam and the north of Laos under the reign of Suryavarman I (1002–1049).		Construction of the Hoodo.
	1040–1106 The painter Li Kung-lin.		
	1050? Invention of movable characters of printing.		
	1082 Hui-tsung, emperor, philosopher, and aesthete.		

1100

11th–12th cent.
Importance of the quality
and production of
ceramics.

1107
Death of the painter Mi
Fei.

Suryavarman II (1113–
1150) builds Angkor-
Vat.

1114–1125
Conquest of the Khitan
kingdom by the Jurchen.

1123
Kin Dynasty among the
Jurchen.

1125
The Jurchen masters of
North China.

1127
Dynasty of the Sung of
the South.
Celadons of Lung-shan.

1153
Peking, capital of the Kin.

CENTRAL ASIA	CHINA, TONKIN AND ANNAM	KOREA	JAPAN
1167 Birth of Genghis Khan.	1177 Sacking of Angkor, burnt by the Chams.		
			1181–1185 Struggle between the Minamoto and the Taira.
			1185–1333 Kamakura epoch.
			1185 Shogunate of Minamoto Yoritomo who established the *bakufu* at Kamakura. Resumption of relations with China through some Buddhist monks.
	1190–1224 The painter Ma Yüan.		1190 Reconstruction of Todaiji. Founding of Zen.

1200
Reconstruction of Angkor by Jayavarman VII (Bayon).

Ca. 1200
The sculptor Unkei.

12th–13th cent.
Scrolls of narrative paintings yamato-e: Ban Dainagon, Shigizan engi, *Heiji monogatari.*

1203
Beginning of the campaigns of Genghis Khan.

Mu-ch'i, Ch'an monk and painter.

1215
Taking of Peking by the Mongols.

1219
Conquest of Korea by the Mongols.

1226
The Fujiwara replace the Minamoto as shogunate. Power of the Hōjō.

1227
Death of Genghis Khan.

1229
Accession of Ogadai Khan.

1232
Law Code Joei Shikimoku.

CENTRAL ASIA	CHINA, TONKIN AND ANNAM	KOREA	JAPAN
	1234 Beginning of the conquest of the Sung Empire by the Mongols.		
1246 John of Plancarpin, legate of Innocent IV, near the Mongolian Khans of Karakorum.			1253 The Buddha of Kamakura.
	1260 Mongol dynasty of the Yüan. Khubilai, emperor. The painter Chao Mêng-fu (1254–1322).		
	1271–1292 Voyage of Marco Polo.		1274–1281 Fruitless attempts of invasion by the Mongols. Decadence of the Hojo.

1285 Check of Mongol invasion at Tonkin.

1298
John of Montecorvino at
    Peking.

1300

1306
The Annamites take the
    Hué religion from the
    Chams.

1330?
The Novel of the Three
    Kingdoms.
The landscape painters of
    the Southern provinces:
Huang Kung-wang (died
    1354)
Wu Chen (died 1354)
Ni Tsan (died 1374)
Wang Meng (died 1385)

1333
Downfall of the Kamakura
    regime.
Northern court and
    Southern court.

CENTRAL ASIA	CHINA, TONKIN AND ANNAM	KOREA	JAPAN
			1338 Second *bakafu:* Ashikaga epoch.
			1340 *Tsurezuregusa*, of Kenko.
	1352 Beginning of revolts in southern China.		
			1367 Yoshimitsu, shogun. Golden Age of the no.
	1368 Taking of Peking.		
	1368–1644 Ming Dynasty. Restoration of the Great Wall.		
1370 Tamerlane, king of Transoxiana.			
1372	Chinese colony up to Tula.		

1373
Ming Code.

1381–1382
Annexation of Yunnan.

1392
Suzerainty of the Ming
over the Li Dynasty
(1392–1910).

1397–1408
Construction of the
Kinkakuji.

1396   Turfan recognizes the suzerainty of China.

1400

1403
Emperor Yung Lo.

1405
Beginning of maritime
expeditions.

1407–1428
Chinese occupation of
Annam and Tonkin.

1405
Death of Tamerlane on
the brink of an expedi-
tion against China.

CENTRAL ASIA	CHINA, TONKIN AND ANNAM	KOREA	JAPAN
	1409 Peking, capital of the Ming. "Purple-violet Forbidden City," at Peking.		
	1416 The Temple of Heaven at Peking.		
	1428 The Loi hunt the Chinese and found the Annamite dynasty of the Le (Hanoi).		
1434 Domination of Mongolia by the Oirat (West Mongols).	15th–16th cent. Literary painters of the Wu school opposed to the professional painters of the Che school.		
			1449–1474 Yoshimasa shogun. The painter Sesshu (1420–1506).

1467–1477
Onin War.

1488
Revolt of Ikko sect.
Beginnings of the Kano
school: Kano Masanobu
(1453?–1530).
Kano Motonobu (1476–
1559).

1453
Peace between China and
the Oirat.

1471
Tonkin eliminates
Champa; taking of
Vijaya.

1505–1521
Wu Tsung, emperor.

1512
Revolt at Szechwan.

1500

CENTRAL ASIA	CHINA, TONKIN AND ANNAM	KOREA	JAPAN
	1517 The Portuguese Fathers of Andrade at Canton.		
1529 Beginning of Altan inroads at Shensi and Hopei.			
	1540 Portuguese commerce with Cochin China.		
			1542–1543 Arrival of the Portuguese.
			1549 Arrival of Francis Xavier.
1550 The Mongols (eastern) of Altan advance to Peking.			
1552 The East Mongols dominate the Oirat.			
	1555 Some Japanese pirates pillage Nanking.		

1557
Portuguese countinghouse at Macao.

End of Altan inroads.

1570

1573–1619
Wan Li, emperor.
Ceramics of Bat-trang in Annam.

1582
Arrival of the Jesuit Matteo Ricci.

1568
Nobunaga, shogun *de facto.*

1570–1610
Momoyama epoch.

1571
Struggle of Nobunaga against the Buddhist church.

1582–1598
Shogunate of Hideyoshi.

1587
Persecution of the Christians; regulation of sea transport.
Conquest of Kyushu.

Central Asia	China, Tonkin and Annam	Korea	Japan
		1588–1589 Japanese invasion.	1590 Founding of Edo.
		1592 Expedition of Hideyoshi.	
		1593 The Japanese evacuate Korea.	1593 Printing of first book. The Franciscans in Japan.
	1596 Sino-Japanese peace.	1597 New Japanese expedition.	
		1598 The Japanese evacuate Korea.	1598 Ieyasu, shogun.
	1601 Father Ricci at Peking.		1602–ca. 1740 First Tokugawa period: Tokugawa Ieyasu founds the third bakufu at Edo.
1600			

1608
Illustrated edition of *Ise
Monogatari.*

1609
Second suzerainty of Japan
over the Ryukyu.

1615
Ieyasu, supreme chief of
Japan.
"Laws of the Military
Houses."

1617
Persecution of the
Christians.

1622
Great persecution of
Nagasaki.

1619
Korea backs up the Ming
against the Man-
churians.

1607
Sino-Japanese peace.

1622
Arrival of the Jesuit Adam
Schall von Bell.

1607
Founding of historic
Manchu Kingdom
(Jurchen).

Central Asia	China, Tonkin and Annam	Korea	Japan
	Publication of the method of painting: *The Studio of Ten Bamboos*.		
1624 Nourha-tchi extends the Manchurian domination over the Khortchin Mongols.			1624 Expulsion of the Spanish.
1627 Abahay succeeds Nourha-tchi.		1627 Invasion by a Manchurian army.	
	1636 Adam Schall von Bell equips a foundry of cannons for the emperor.		1635 Mausoleum of Ieyasu at Nikko.
			1638 Expulsion of the Portuguese.

1639
Closing of Japan to foreigners.

1641
The Dutch confined to Deshima.

1639
Recognition of Manchurian suzerainty.

1644
Taking of Peking by the Manchurians.

1644–1911
Dynasty of the Ch'ing.

1645
The Manchurians take Nanking; unification of the North and South.

1649
All inner Mongolia in the hands of the Manchurians.

Rise of painting in the provinces of the South: the four Wang, including Wang Hui (1632–1717).

CENTRAL ASIA	CHINA, TONKIN AND ANNAM	KOREA	JAPAN
	1657 Alexander VII admits "the rites."		1657 Great fire of Edo.
	1661–1722 Reign of K'ang-hsi.		
	1665 Proscription of Christianity.		
	1669 Condemnation of the rites by Clement IX.		
		1673 Tumulus of Li Hiao-tsung at Shiragi.	
	From 1679 Mustard Seed Garden (method of painting, with engravings in colors).		
1676 Galdan, chief of the Jungar.			

1685
The Chinese raze Albazin.

1685?
Impression at Su-chou of "Kaempfer" prints.

1686
The Russians reconstruct Albazin; siege by the Chinese.

1688–1689
Jungar Galdan subdues Mongolia and the Khalkha.

1688–1704
Genroku era.

1689
Treaty of Nertchinsk.

1690
K'ang-hsi victorious over Galdan.

1692
Edict of tolerance in favor of Christianity.

1695
Galdan in Upper Mongolia.

The Tosa school, which from the sixteenth century tried out new techniques, finds itself at its zenith with Korin (1665–1716).

CENTRAL ASIA	CHINA, TONKIN AND ANNAM	KOREA	JAPAN
1696 Victory of the Chinese over the Jungar; protectorate over the Khalkha and the Ordos.			
1700			
1715–1720 Chinese occupation of Turfan.	1715–1764 Father Castiglione, Jesuit and painter, at Peking.		1716 Yoshimura, shogun. Rise of xylography; Torii studios, Kaigetsudo, Okumura.
1720 The Chinese at Lhasa.	1723–1735 Reign of Yung-Cheng.		
	1724 Expulsion of the missionaries (those of the court excepted).		

1727
Russo-Chinese Treaty.

1731
Expedition against the Jungars; defeat of the Chinese; new evacuation of Turfan.

1735–1796
Ch'ien Lung emperor.

1736–1743
Ceramics of the imperial factory of King-to-tchen attain point of perfection.

1740–1800
Middle period Tokugawa.

1750
Revolt at Tibet.

1759
The Chinese take Kashgaria and Yarkand, and create Sinkiang.

1764
Last reconstruction of the Great Temple of Izumo.

CENTRAL ASIA	CHINA, TONKIN AND ANNAM	KOREA	JAPAN
	1767 Campaign in Burma; Chinese suzerainty.		Harunobu and Koryusai, masters of the print in colors. Buson, poet and painter of Chinese inspiration (1716–1783).
1771 Destruction of the Jungar kingdom by the Chinese.	1773 The Annamites take possession of Cochin China and Tonkin.		1787 Reforms of Matsura Sadanobu. 1788 Beginning of the career of Hokusai.

1788
The *Chosen Insects* of
Kitagawa Utamaro
(beginning of his
career).

1797
The American ship *Eliza*
at Nagasaki.

1794
Beginning of evangeliza-
tion of Korea (from
China).

1793–1802
Revolt of the White
Lotus.

1798
French company at
Canton.

1801
Taking of Hué by Nguyen
Anh, Emperor of
Annam.

1800

CENTRAL ASIA	CHINA, TONKIN AND ANNAM	KOREA	JAPAN
	1802 Gia-long (Nguyen Anh) takes Hanoi and founds the Nguyen dynasty (1802–1945).		
	1804 Empire of Vietnam unified (by Gia-long).		
		1831 Apostolic vicariate of Korea.	
	1842 Opium War; Nanking treaty.		
	1844 Treaties of Wanghsia and Whampoa.		
			1849 Death of Hokusai.

1858
Death of Hiroshige.

1867
Accession of Meiji.
End of the shogunate.

1868–1912
Meiji era.
Civil war; charter of Five
Articles.

1851–1866
Revolt of the T'ai P'ing.

1858
Treaty of Tientsin.

1860
Franco-British expedition;
taking of Peking; Peking
treaty; Russo-Chinese
treaty.

1861–1875,
T'ung Chih, emperor;
Coregency of Empress
Tzu Hsi.

1862
Concession to France of
eastern Cochin China.

1867
Annexation by France of
the western Cochin
Chinese provinces.

CENTRAL ASIA	CHINA, TONKIN AND ANNAM	KOREA	JAPAN
			1871 Suppression of the feudal system.
			1873 Beginning of exhibitions of the treasure of Shosoin.
			1874 Revolt of the samurai.
	1875–1908 Reign of Kuang Hsü		1875 South of Sakhalin surrendered to the Russians.
	1876	Dispute with Japan over Korea. Nippo-Korean treaty.	The last prints of Yokohama.
	1887 Creation by France of the Indochinese Union.		

1900

The painter Kawamura Monshu.

1910

Annexation of Korea by Japan.

Oct. 10, 1911.
Revolution.

1913
Autonomy of Outer Mongolia.

1922

Treaties of Washington (treaties of Nine Powers).

ANALYTICAL TABLE

CHINESE ART

PROTOHISTORIC EPOCH: Difficulties in history of Chinese art.

THE BEGINNINGS: Peoples. Geography.

THE THREE DYNASTIES: Antiquity of objects found.

THE EXCAVATIONS OF ANYANG: The "inscribed bones." Sculptures. Statues. Civilization.

RITUAL VASES: Shapes of the vases. Inscriptions. Process of fabrication.

STYLES OF THE SHANG PERIOD: Author's theories, theories of Karlgren and Max Loehr on the styles of the bronzes. Problem of priority of one in relation to others. The *t'ao t'ieh* motif, its components. An allusive fauna. Order of motifs.

ZOOMORPHIC VASES: The vase in the shape of a crouching tiger in the Cernuschi Museum (Paris). Different types of zoomorphic vases. Other Shang objects. The animal style in China and in Siberia: Kisseliev's theory.

NEOLITHIC AND PREHISTORIC POTTERY: Gray pottery; red pottery: Andersson's discovery; its expansion, its resemblance to that of Bessarabia; its spiral decorations; value of the red pigment, symbolism of the cowrie shell; Grecian decoration; tall urns; decadence of this pottery. Black pottery. White ceramics: form and decoration.

THE CHOU PERIOD: Divisions of this period.

THE YIN-CHOU PERIOD: Evolution of religious thought. New types of bronzes: their decoration.

THE MID-CHOU ERA: Decadence of the bronzes: forms and decorations. Achaeminian influence. New forms.

RITUAL JADES: Symbolism of jade objects: official seals. Funerary jades.

ANALOGIES WITH AMERICAN-INDIAN FOLK ART: Work of Hentze. Affinities with Siberia and America.

THE ERA OF THE WARRING STATES: Historic context. Impetus of curved lines. *P'an long* decoration. THE LI-YU STYLE: The round and oblong *ting*. The *yi*. Decorations. Evolution of the *Hu*. The bell in the Stoclet Collection. MIRRORS PRIOR TO THE HAN DYNASTY: Craze for these mirrors. Decoration of the backs, evolution of the mirrors. The central rondelle. Evolution of the decoration. EURASIAN ANIMAL ART: Diffusion of this art. Its peculiarities. Principal types. Dating them. The Sarmatians. The creative centers. Evolution of this art: appearance of the human figure. Ordos country. THE INFLUENCES OF ANIMAL ART ON CHINESE ART: Influence under the Chou. Apparition of horseback riding and its consequences: the clasp. Types of clasps. Natural forms and the freedom with which they are handled. Inhibitions in representation of man.

THE HAN EPOCH: History. Contacts with Central Asia and Iran, and through the Parthians with Rome; with Tonkin (Indo-China): through the Koreans with Japan. An art based on joy of living. VASES AND SMALL BRONZES: Ordinary types of vases. Niello incrustations or Limoges-type enameled vases. Abstract decoration comparable to that on silk fabrics of Leou-lan. Evolution that brings the decorative motifs closer to those of protohistoric vases. FUNERARY ART: Figurines in terra cotta. Tumuli and exterior statues. Korean tombs and objects in lacquer. Modest tombs. CARVED STONES: Little houses for offerings and their decorated flagstones. Description of the stones of the Wu tomb. The metal stampings. THE HAN MIRRORS: Decoration with magic symbols. Beginning of vegetable design in Chinese art. Borrowing of motifs from barbarians of Kwangsi and from Tonkin (Indo-China), and from Near East.

GENERAL CHARACTERISTICS OF HAN ART: An art without exterior finality. Exterior influences on decorations. Paintings. Sculptured lions.

SECULAR ART OF THE THREE KINGDOMS (THIRD CENTURY) AND OF THE SIX DYNASTIES (FOURTH, FIFTH, SIXTH CENTURIES): Division of China. Funerary art. Monuments around Nanking.

BUDDHIST ART IN CENTRAL ASIA: Lacunae in the history of Central Asia. The two routes of north and south. Culture at a crossroads.

THE KIZIL GROUP: The region of Kizil. Iranian and Persian influences. Paintings: figures, the War of the Relics; narrative painting, mural painting. Clay modeling.

THE TURFAN REGION: Mixture of populations. Turkish influence. Devotional and hieratic painting. Coexistence of Buddhist, Nestorian, Manichaean religions and their respective paintings. Representation of nature; the mountains. Pictorial material. The stupas.

THE SOUTHERN ROUTE: Mediterranean influence, with clumsy interpenetration. Description of a fragment of a successful work.

TUNHUANG: A revolving plaque. Discoveries. List. Dating. Evolution of Buddhism. The Buddhist paradise and representation of its deities. Narrative paintings. Hieratic images. Full-face and profile painting. A painting full of movement. Key to Buddhist art.

THE BEGINNINGS OF CHINESE BUDDHIST ART AND THE WEI AND SUI EPOCHS (FOURTH TO SIXTH CENTURIES): Beginning of Buddhism in China. First statuettes. Study voyages of monks: Fa-Hsien. Votive steles in the shape of a pointed leaf.

YÜN-KANG: The T'o-pa kingdom. Increase in figures. Niches. The Maitreya. Scenes from the life of Buddha. Indian influence. Rendering of clothing. Expression of spirituality.

THE SMALL BRONZES AND STELES: The gilded bronze in the

Guimet Museum (Paris) 518 A.D. Commemorative and votive steles.

LUNG-MEN: Dating. Plan of the ensemble. Evolution toward realism. Pin-yang cave.

THE SUI ERA AND THE T'IEN-LUNG-SHAN GROTTOES: The Sui. Bas-relief decorations. Position of the statues. Clumsiness of this art. A Taoist stele.

THE T'ANG EPOCH: Historic facts. Conquest of Central Asia, voyages, T'ang decadence after Hsüan Tsung, and falling-back of China.

BUDDHIST SCULPTURE: Religious art at an impasse. The attitude of Buddha, the conventional. Bas-reliefs and small bronzes.

FUNERARY ART: The horses of T'ang T'ai-tsung by Yen Li-pên. Funerary statues of Kao-tsung. Statuettes and evolution of feminine styles. Animal art.

T'ANG CERAMICS: Blurring of colors. Iranian influence. Porcelainized ceramics.

THE MIRRORS: Decorations of mirrors and Iranian influences. Multifoil forms. Collections of Shosoin.

MARQUETRY, STRINGED INSTRUMENTS, LACQUERS, AND FABRICS: Instruments (musical) of Shosoin. Their decoration. Plaques protecting the sounding-boards of lutes. Complex influences on these objects. The two games of the salon of the Shosoin. Glass. Fabrics. Sassanid and Chinese ewers. Plates of lacquered wood.

BUDDHIST ARCHITECTURE: Religious influence. Belvederes and watchtowers, Chinese stupas. From the Indian stupa to the Chinese pagoda. Pagoda of Sung-shan (Sung-yüeh-ssu). Pagodas around Chang-an. The first curving roofs preserved at Horyuji.

THE SUNG AND YÜAN EPOCHS (TENTH TO FOURTEENTH CENTURIES): The Five Dynasties. The Ch'an sect. Evolution of Taoism. The Sungs of the north. The Jurchen invasion and the Chin kingdom. The Sungs of the south. Maritime connections. Mongol invasion and the Yüan dynasty. Relations with the Near East.

BUDDHIST SCULPTURE: Sculpture too much influenced by

painting. New themes. Cast statues. Influence of Ch'an. Taoist sanctuaries. Reliefs of Shansi. Funerary art; evolution of rites.

SUNG CERAMICS: Technical progress. Form more important than ornament. Colors used. Centers of fabrication of the Northern Sung. Those of the southeast. Forms and colors. Large decorative vases.

THE BRONZES AND JADES: Imitation of Shang and Chou bronzes. Traces of great epochs in jades also.

PAINTING FROM ITS BEGINNINGS TO THE NORTHERN SUNG DYNASTY: FROM THE BEGINNINGS TO THE T'ANG ERA: Polychrome walls of Anyang. Engraved stones only evidence of Han painting. Painting and religion. Painting of Ku K'ai-chih in British Museum. Principles of Hsieh Ho. Explanation. Religious painting, contrary to that of Western painting, springing from secular painting. Pre-eminence of the human figure.

THE T'ANG MASTERS: Reconstitution through ancient copies. Yen Li-pên. Wu Tao-tzu.

ANIMAL PAINTING: Han Kan. Types of subjects. Symbolism of birds and flowers. Their character.

LANDSCAPE ART: Sudden mastery of the landscape. Li Ssu-hsün and Li Chao-tao. Wang Wei.

PAINTING IN THE ERA OF THE FIVE DYNASTIES AND THE NORTHERN SUNG DYNASTIES: Difficulty of grasping the concepts of Chinese aesthetics. Description of a painting in Peking Museum. A poetic mountain, parallel to Renaissance painting.

PAINTED SCROLLS: A type of painting that unrolls in time. Landscapes seen from above and very far away. Importance of mountains. Painting, intellectual expression. Painters. Ideas of Kuo Hsi presented by Kuo Jo-ssu. Those of the pseudo Wang Wei. Mi Fei. Collection of Huei-tsung. Painters. Painting of bamboos. Li Kung-lin.

SOUTHERN SUNG AND YÜAN PAINTING: Influence of Ch'an. Ma K'uei and Ma Yüan. Ma Lin. Hsia Kuei. Liang K'ai. Mu-Ch'i. The traditionalists.

KOREAN ART

STUDIES OF KOREAN ART. Civilization (neolithic, similar to that of Japan). Chinese colonization.

THE KOGURYO MONUMENTS: Tombs: the Tomb of the General; dolmens covered by tumuli: "Indian ceilings" (corbeled); mural paintings.

SHIRAGI ART: The three Han. The royal crowns. Art of the silver- and goldsmiths. Influence of Central Asia. Ceramics.

BUDDHIST BUILDINGS: Granite temples. Observatory in Kyonju.

THE PULGUKSA: Description of the temple. Seated Buddha in nearby grotto.

SMALL SCULPTURE: Beginning with seventh century. The bell at Shiragi. Ceramics.

NORTHEAST KOREA DURING THE ELEVENTH CENTURY: The Maitreya of Kwanshokuji. Art of gold- and silversmiths.

THE TOMBS OF THE SHIRAGI KINGS: Tumulus of Seitoku. The Li tombs. Pagodas after the fourteenth century. Chinese influence in architecture; buildings and bridges. Ceramics. Painting.

JAPANESE ART

THE ORIGINS

THE NEOLITHIC PERIOD: The Ainu. Common culture of the north Pacific. Pottery. Anthropomorphic figures. Kamegaoka pottery.

THE APPEARANCE OF THE JAPANESE RACE: Immigrations. Archaeology and historical tradition.

KOREAN-JAPANESE NEOLITHIC CULTURE: Yayoi pottery. Bronze objects: mirrors, *dotaku*. The *kitsune no kuwa*, the *magatama*.

THE PROTOHISTORIC PERIOD:

THE GREAT SEPULCHERS: Form of the tombs. Exterior decoration. Interior aspect. Objects found within them. The "mirrors of imitation."

SCULPTURE: Evolution toward the baroque. Fixation of the Buddha type.
RELIGIOUS PAINTING: Hieratic paintings enriched with gold leaf.
THE TOJI SCREEN. Representations of the death of Buddha. "Amida and his Bodhisattva" of Genshin.
EARLY YAMATO-E: The Taira in power. Decorated frontispieces of sutras. Illustrations for *Genji Monogatari* by Fujiwara no Takayoshi: the Kasuga style. Tosa style. Satirical paintings.
FUJIWARA ARCHITECTURE: The Hoodo of Byodoin of Uji and the paintings that ornament it.

THE KAMAKURA ERA (1185–1333): The shogun Yoritomo. Results of renewal of relations with China.
THE YAMATO-E IN THE KAMAKURA ERA: Illustrations of popular books. Illustrations of the *Heiji Monogatari* and Buddhist legends. The "Ban Dainagon." Portraits.
RELIGIOUS PAINTING: Subjects and technique.
THE SCULPTOR UNKEI AND HIS SCHOOL: His statues. His studio. The colossal Buddha of Kamakura.
ARCHITECTURE AND THE MINOR ARTS: The Wayo tradition. *Tahoto*. Masks, bronzes, and lacquers. Success of the traditional *maki-e* process for masks.

THE ASHIKAGA AND MOMOYAMA PERIODS (FOURTEENTH, FIFTEENTH, SIXTEENTH CENTURIES): The Ashikaga in power. Zen. Influence of Chinese painting. Ashikaga wash painting: Principal artists: Sesshu, Sesson; Tosa style.
THE FOUNDING OF THE KANO SCHOOL: Kano Masanobu and Kano Motonobu. Anonymous works.
THE MOMOYAMA PERIOD (*ca.* 1570–1610): Nobunaga, Hideyoshi, and Tokugawa Ieyasu. Interest in art of a new social class. Kano school of painting. Portuguese screens. Paintings of theatrical people.
THE ARCHITECTURE OF RECENT CENTURIES: Shinto buildings. Zen temples. Villas of retired emperors.
NIKKO AND OTHER SHOGUN MAUSOLEUMS: The mausoleums

of Nikko. The Yomeimon portal at Nikko. Decoration of the rooms. The last *otamaya*.
SECULAR ARCHITECTURE: Pavilions for the tea ceremony and gardens.
MILITARY ARCHITECTURE: Description of fortified castles. Bridges.

TOKUGAWA EPOCH: FIRST PERIOD (*ca.* 1602–1740): Economic direction of the Tokugawa. Edo.
BIRTH OF THE UKIYO-E: Meaning of the word. The founder of this type of art.
THE TOSA SCHOOLS OF THE TOKUGAWA EPOCH: The two Tosa schools. Renewal of interest in the nineteenth century.
THE DECORATORS: Koetsu and Sotatsu. Korin. Kenzan. Haritsu.
THE UKIYO-E AND THE FIRST PRINTS: The Ukiyo-e paintings. Prints. Moronobu. Other artists. The Torii, Kaigetsudo, Masanobu. Improvement of the color print.

TOKUGAWA EPOCH: MIDDLE PERIOD (*ca.* 1740–1800): Japan and its relations with other countries. Role of the theater.
THE SINOMANIA OF THE ELITE AND THE BUNJINGWA: Revelation of *wu-jen-hua* and Sinomania. Buson and Ikeno Taiga. Buncho and other artists of the *Bunjingwa* tradition.
SHÊN NAN-P'IN: Subjects and technique of. Influence upon Ito Jakuchu. Insipid Confucian painting.
THE MARUYAMA AND SHIJO SCHOOLS: Okyo; the Fourth Street School: eclectic painting. Sosen. Hoitsu renews the style of Korin.
THE PRINT AT THE END OF THE EIGHTEENTH CENTURY: The engravers. Harunobu and Koryusai. Shunsho and his pupils. Shunman, Kiyonaga, Ippitussai Buncho. Utamaro: subjects, technique. Successors. Toshusai Sharaku. Less important eclectic artists. Parallel between French engravers and Japanese engravers of the eighteenth century.

THE END OF THE TOKUGAWA EPOCH (1800–1860): Conditions of the artists' lives.
KATSUSHIKA HOKUSAI: Artistic formation of. Works after 1819. The album "One Hundred Views of Fuji," done in

PAINTING AND THE MINOR ARTS: Royal portraits and landscapes. Fabrics. Musical instruments.

TONKINESE AND ANNAMESE ART

EXPANSION OF CHINESE ART: Rarity of artistic remains.
DONG-SON ART: Rain drums. Motifs. Other objects.
HAN AND SUNG ART IN TONKIN: Tombs. Rejection of influences. The capital of the later Ly. Pagodas. Extension to the south. Sculpture. Bronze objects. Ceramics. Imperial tombs at Hué.

INDEX

The Wade System for the Pronunciation of Romanized Chinese Words

ai = *y* as in *why*; ao = *ow* as in *how*; an = long *a*; ang = very long *a*, *ong* in many words; ch = initial *j* as in *jam*; ch' = an emphatic initial *ch* as in *church*; ê, ên, êng = nearly *er*, or short *u* as in *flung*; en = as in *ten*; ei = *ey* as in *Weybridge*; eh = French *é*; i = *ee* as in *see*; o = nearly *or*; ou = o as in *Joseph*; u = *oo* as in *too*; ü = French *u*; ung = *oong*; hs = emphatic initial *sh* (*s* in the South); hua, huo = *hwa, hwo*; hui = *whey*; j = between an initial *r* and *z*; k = initial *g*; k' = emphatic initial *k* aspirated; p = initial *b*; p' = emphatic initial *p*; ssŭ = *sir* with hissing *s*; t = initial *d*; t' = emphatic initial *t*; ts = *ds*; ts' = emphatic *ts*; tz = *dz*; tz' = emphatic *tz*. The two very common words "tzŭ" and "wang" are pronounced *dzer* and *wong* respectively.

The Pronunciation of Japanese Words

Japanese is pronounced as spelled, with, in general, no accent.

[Courtesy Harry N. Abrams, Inc., Publisher]

Vases (cont'd)
lain, 43; ritual, 9–11, 24–25,
32, 34–35; Shang, 26; Sung,
109; T'ang, 94; T'ao t'ieh,
23, 25–26, 48; Tchertomlyk
(Greek), 41; ting, 32, 34,
36, 110, Fig. 1, 10; tripod
(chüeh), 17–18; wooden,
12; yi, 34; Yin-chou, 27; zoomorphic, 16–19, 25
Venice, 299
Vermeer, 317
Vietnam, 198, 319; architecture, 160
Vignier Collection, 27
Vikings, 39
Votive pictures, 70
Votive steles, 77, 82, 83

Waldschmidt, E., 61
Waley, Arthur, 121
Wang Chien, 152
Wang Chih-ch'eng, 154
Wang Ch'uan, 120
Wang Hiuan-tso, 88
Wang Hui, 152
Wang Mang, 46
Wang Meng, 144, 151
Wang Shih-min, 152
Wang Wei, 120–21, 125, 127,
129–30, 133
Wang Yüan-ch'i, 152
"War of the Relics," 64
Warring States. See Era of the
Warring States
Warriors. See Samurai
Wash painting, 151, 247–50
Water colors, 236, 239
Wei epoch, 58, 74–77, 78, 83,
85, 101, 184, 395–96; sculp-
ture, 86, 214
Wei River, 5
Wên-jên hua, 148
Wên T'ung, 132

West, the: Chinese six princi-
ples, 114–16; Korean art,
171; originality, demand for,
132. See also Europe
Women: Chinese art, 92,
153, Fig. 25, 93; drawings,
285–86; Fujiwara, 232; Ja-
pan, 230, 272, 281, 284,
301–2, 311; masks, 314–15;
obi, 299; Ukiyo-e, 269
Woodblocks, 70
Woodcuts, 152, 157
Wooden carvings, 14
Wooden sculptures, 65
Wooden structure, 223
Wou family, 54, 58
Wrestlers, 284
Writers, 178, 232
Writing (chou), 120
Wu Chen, 142
Wu Hou, 89
Wu-jen-hua (lettered paint-
ings), 276
Wu Kingdom, 58
Wu Li, 151–52. See Father
d'Acunha
Wu Pan, General, 89
Wu school, 147–48, 152, 154
Wu Tao-tzu, 117, 133, 148,
157, 177, 251

Xylography, 70, 154, 270–71,
272, 281, 283, 287, 288,
289; China, 157; Japan,
301–2; masters, 290–91;
subject matter, 300

Yaeyama Islands, 320
Yakushiji, 218–19
Yalu River, 174
Yamamoto Collection, 156
Yamato-e, 234–38, 247, 260,
281, 282; Kamakura, 240–
43